Contrasts

and

The True Principles of Pointed or Christian Architecture

THE PUGIN SOCIETY EDITION

Contrasts

and

The True Principles of Pointed or Christian Architecture

A. W. N. Pugin

WITH INTRODUCTIONS BY
TIMOTHY BRITTAIN-CATLIN

 Spire Books Ltd
in association with the
Pugin Society

Published by
Spire Books Ltd
PO Box 2336
Reading RG4 5WJ

CIP data:
A catalogue record for this book is available from the
British Library
ISBN 0 9543615 4 7

Designed by John Elliott
Thanks to Catriona Blaker, Nick Dermott, Mrs David Houle and
Alexandra Wedgwood for their assistance
Text set in Adobe Bembo

Printed by Alden Group Ltd
Osney Mead
Oxford OX2 0EF

Contrasts: or, A Parallel between the Noble Edifices of the Fourteenth and Fifteenth Centuries, and Corresponding Buildings of the Present Day; shewing the Present Decay of Taste

Introduction

Timothy Brittain-Catlin

There are very few books by architects that have changed architecture altogether. Architects are not great philosophers or theoreticians on paper. The first canonical written work of Western architecture, the *Ten Books on Architecture* by Vitruvius, is in effect a technical manual, and it is more remarkable for its being a record of a way of building, and a definition of the scope of the architectural profession, than for any originality or foresight on the part of its author. The Renaissance texts that followed – the treatises of Alberti, Serlio, and Palladio – owe their form to Vitruvius' original; and whilst it is true that the theoretical publications of the seventeenth, eighteenth, and early-nineteenth centuries – the works of the followers of Lodolí, of Laugier, of Quatremère de Quincy in Europe, and the writings of Chambers, and the lectures of Cockerell and Soane in Britain – caused an occasional storm amongst academic practitioners, they all were firmly set within the tradition of classical architecture, and none of them sought to bring about a fundamental change in the way in which buildings were designed. *Contrasts: or, A Parallel between the Noble Edifices of the Fourteenth and Fifteenth Centuries, and Corresponding Buildings of the Present Day; shewing the Present Decay of Taste* was different. It aimed to overthrow every aspect of modern design; and in England, its influence has been prolonged and fundamental.

Augustus Welby Northmore Pugin (1812-1852) had only completed one building by the time he first put his *Contrasts* before the public in 1836: his small house at Alderbury, just outside the city of Salisbury. The house fitted into no distinct category: although irregular in outline it was certainly not a *cottage orné*, not 'Picturesque', because its blocky red-brick silhouette stuck out bluntly against the meadows on the banks of the River Avon. Its planning was eccentric; built without hall or corridors, it required its residents to walk through each room to reach the next, in a manner that recalls Amy Robsart's chambers at Cumnor Place, in Walter Scott's *Kenilworth*.

The architect himself might often have been seen admiring and sketching the remaining Gothic masonry of Salisbury's cathedral and churches. What he saw there caused him great distress. In common with many other of the churches of England, its cathedral had been mutilated during the seventeenth and eighteenth centuries, often in the name of transient fashion; in Salisbury's case, James Wyatt, the leading architect of his day, had razed chapels, tidied monuments into neat rows, and introduced a great deal of second-rate modern work in the form of funereal statuary of dubious taste and gimcrack building works, all in an era which saw the organic and sprawling nature of Gothic art as 'curious' and primitive, and any symbolic interpretation of its forms as 'papist' and, by extension, suggestive of a foreign threat to England's Protestant establishment. It was thus in the shadow of decaying splendour, of which Salisbury cathedral was a painful example, that Pugin converted to Catholicism in June 1835, in a humble chapel in the city.

Pugin was aged 23 when he first moved to his new home on its completion in September 1835; he came from a background steeped in antiquarianism. His father and immediate circle had been in the vanguard of the movement to restore the prestige of Gothic architecture as England's national style. Augustus Charles Pugin (*c*.1769-1832) had become a draughtsman for John Nash, amongst others, following his immigration from France some time after the French Revolution. His style of exact architectural drawing, applied to Gothic architecture both ancient and modern, was a novelty at a time when the mediaeval method of setting up a pointed arch was still unknown to modern designers. The older Pugin had illustrated the great buildings of London for Rudolph Ackermann's *Microcosm of London* of 1808-11, in conjunction with the artist Thomas Rowlandson (who supplied the human figures that populate the scenes); and in the 1820s he collaborated with the publisher and writer John Britton to produce some of the finest examples of contemporary measured draughtsmanship, eschewing the conventional practice of drawing mediaeval remains as romantic scenes of decay and instead producing accurate reconstructions of the sections and elevations of Gothic cathedrals and churches, which were translated into engravings of unprecedented clarity by innovating engravers such as Henry and John Le Keux.

By the time that A.C. Pugin set off, accompanied by his young son, to draw the monuments of Normandy for John Britton in the mid-1820s, a new and distinct characteristic of contemporary literature had begun to make itself felt in the work of those people that the Pugins knew and worked with: the comparison between the old and the new. In 1820, the French writer Charles Nodier, with his colleagues Isidore Taylor and Alphonse de Cailleur, published the first volume of studies from a 'romantic and picturesque tour' of France: the ruins of cathedrals and monasteries evoked in them the contrast between the splendours of mediaeval life and the despoliations of modern times, most particularly of the 1789 revolution. Some English visitors to Normandy, the region of France that Nodier had chosen for his first two volumes, were struck by a similar feeling, although in reverse: John Sell Cotman and Dawson

Turner's *Architectural Antiquities of Normandy* compared the 'indecent and scandalous scenes' recalled by the remains of the pre-revolutionary churches unfavourably with modern times. Britton, who saw his life's work as the representation of mediaeval architecture in a 'scientific' light that would enable it stand every comparison with classical paradigms, was likewise disgusted by 'silly superstitious stories' of the past.

But now these rationalists were confronted by a popular taste for mediaevalism, fed by tales of the romance and splendour of mediaeval and Tudor life. Walter Scott, a celebrated writer by the 1820s, devised tales written in archaising language that were widely popularised by stage versions and other adaptations. More elevated writers took up the theme. In 1831, the poet Robert Southey published his *Sir Thomas More*, which took the form of a series of debates between More's shade and a figure called Montesinos, who appears to represent the writer himself. More disputes the achievements of the Reformation – 'it has done them no good', he says, referring to the food, clothes and habits of Englishmen; to his interlocutor he pronounces that 'the spirit which built and endowed the monasteries is gone. Are you one of those people who think it has been superseded for the better by that which erects steam-engines and cotton-mills?' A few years later, Dawson Turner's son-in-law, Francis Palgrave, published his *Truths and Fictions of the Middle Ages: The Merchant and the Friar*, which afforded another historical figure, in this case Roger Bacon, an opportunity to comment on the future that is the present day. In describing the superiority of the Norman feudal system to modern society, Palgrave was probably consciously reflecting something of the political and religious discussion that preceded Catholic emancipation: the view he was putting forward was derived from St Robert Bellarmine, whose doctrine of 'popular sovereignty' provided Cisalpine Catholics with a historical and moral basis for their desire to be integrated into English society. The message of *Truths and Fictions* is that a comparison between the England of Bacon and that of the present reveals the poor state of the latter.

The young Pugin's idea of presenting his manifesto in the form of a series of contrasts between old and new comprised therefore not only the romantic appeal of a Nodier, a Walter Scott, a Southey or a Palgrave, but also (from his father and his father's friends and colleagues) the proud boast that England's Gothic architecture was historically, structurally, academically and decoratively able to stand comparison with the desiccated canon of classical architecture. In February 1836, perhaps elated by the realisation of his first ideal home and by the announcement only a month beforehand that Charles Barry's scheme (that he had draughted) had won the prestigious competition for the new Houses of Parliament,

Pugin recorded in his diary that he had finally settled down to write his 'work of contrasts'. It took him until early May to finish etching the plates; but the letterpress was completed before the end of the same month. He published the book himself on 4 August, and sent out copies to acquaintances, including the Earl of Shrewsbury's chaplain Daniel Rock, in September. Pugin always sent his publications to influential people.

The first edition of *Contrasts* consisted of five concise chapters and a short conclusion describing the despoliations of English churches by Henry VIII and the Reformation, and attributing the demise of England's Gothic architecture to the rise of Protestantism. The text was followed by a series of etchings contrasting modern scenes with ones drawn from mediaeval times, in places caricaturing the work of distinguished living architects including Sir John Soane's house in Lincoln's Inn Fields, and All Souls church, Langham Place, by his father's patron Nash, mixed without comment with third-rate work by third-rate architects. In depicting this modern architecture Pugin used a stiff, sketchy style which exaggerated the meanness and the flatness of the elevations; by contrast, the Gothic work he presented was more heavily drawn, emphasising the perspectival depth of buildings such as St Mary Redcliffe church in Bristol as much as the richness of their detail; comic human scenes of mild depravity on the one hand, and of splendour and devotion on the other, enhanced these effects. The book caused a stir amongst the inhabitants of Salisbury; more significant, however, was the notice that *Contrasts* received in the national and professional press during the course of 1837.

The reactions that Pugin's new book aroused testify to the prevailing preoccupations of contemporary critics. John Loudon's *Architectural Magazine*, which stood for practical and efficient planning in architecture, declared that the Gothic had nothing to offer the modern dwelling. W. H. Leeds, in *Fraser's Magazine*, suspected that Pugin's Catholicism itself flowed from his love of Gothic; whilst the *Gentleman's Magazine*, which was susceptible to romantic aspirations, praised the book's original, bold, spirited manner. In an article in the *Dublin Review* that may have done more than any other to establish Pugin's career within the Catholic Church, Nicholas Wiseman declared that 'Mr Pugin' – in practice, almost untried in his new profession – 'is an architect of acknowledged merit, and of established reputation'.

Contrasts, in its later edition of 1841, has remained a remarkable piece of work. The architectural world had undergone enormous changes in the five years since 1836, and Pugin's revision and additions reflected them. The new British Parliament, designed in its idiosyncratic Tudor style, was now rising from the Thames embankment; the Cambridge Camden

RVE DE L'HORLOGE ROVEN

CONTRASTED
HOVSE & FRONTS

THE PROFESSOR'S OWN HOVSE

SIR I SOANE ARCH

Society had been founded, with the aim of returning the Church of England to the Gothic fold; and Pugin himself was fêted by the Catholic press and had become professor of ecclesiastical antiquities at Oscott College, in the heartlands of the Catholic Revival, and was thus equipped with a platform for his sermons. Charles Dickens had completed *Oliver Twist*, too. Perhaps the most 'architectural' of his novels, it begins in a workhouse and goes on to provide a shocking contrast between the slums and the fashionable residential areas of London's East and West Ends. It was now that Pugin added two of the most famous plates in *Contrasts*: the poor-house, and the town.

A new preface addressed the historical-theological arguments that had originally been raised against him: principally, that he had appeared to blame Protestantism itself for the demise of the Gothic. The fault was now that of 'some other more powerful agency', he claimed. He added a more purely architectural argument about the symbolic power of the pointed arch, and the theological significance of the equilateral triangle. He erased his original short second chapter that had praised the domestic architecture of the Tudor era, and replaced it with a much longer account of the growth of classical, 'Pagan' art, allowing him to emphasise that English Protestantism was itself a side-effect of 'Catholic degeneracy'; and he called upon allies that he had discovered since 1836 – the French cultural critics Rio and Montalembert: a new appendix reproduces the latter's account of 'the destructive and revived Pagan principle in France'. He removed a sentence from his chapter on Henry VIII in which he had referred to the 'intimate connexion' between the decay of architecture and the changes in religion at the time of the Reformation; and he provided a new conclusion in which he appears more hopeful that Gothic architecture can be restored and revived in England than in the churches of Catholic countries devastated by 'Paganism'. And whilst he added five new plates, he withdrew the contrast between Soane's house and the timber architecture of Rouen, possibly out for respect for the now-dead Soane, but probably also because continental, late-Gothic architecture, such as he had illustrated, was no longer consistent with his message: that omitted plate is presented here as an illustration to this introduction. In every respect, the second edition aimed to make Pugin's faith in Gothic appear less partisan and certainly less 'Roman'. Yet throughout there is still a sense of the personal turmoil of an architect who adored the great Gothic monuments of England, but had consigned himself to worshipping in the tawdry chapels of the early days of Catholic emancipation, and also the desperate but optimistic urgency of a young man who had already begun to feel the whole weight of the Gothic revival on his shoulders.

Pugin etched most of the plates himself, although his friend Talbot

Bury etched (from Pugin's drawings) the title page and possibly others. They illustrate the humiliation of modern architects, great and small; the silliness and nastiness of modern design; the grand vision of starting the profession all over again so that architecture could become once more the supreme art form, the mother of all the arts. And it is here that *Contrasts* has achieved its lasting fame. Perhaps contemporary critics recognised that Pugin's text reflected the various voices of his generation; but the architect reader will have understood perhaps at once from these illustrations that there was here something entirely new: a link between an architectural style and a moral obligation. Pugin was appealing above the heads of modern architects and modern clerics to a vision of England where architecture was not so much representative of faith, as part of the faith itself in every one of its details. It would not be enough to copy ancient details: the builder must share 'the ancient feelings and sentiments' of the Gothic builders. Good building was the product of a good society; and it is perhaps through good building that society can be redeemed. It is this revolutionary combination that has proved stronger than the aesthetic appeal of Pugin's own work to other architects, and has lain in the background of much of the history of architecture as far as the late-twentieth century, when an architect's education and professional practice required him or her to express a political view or a social commitment through the medium of the very buildings that they designed; and when the adoption of a single, truthful, 'modern', style was considered indispensable by critics. It is in these pages that Pugin set out an entirely new way of approaching the practice of architectural design; and it is thanks to the painful truth and clarity of these illustrations that his message achieved the success that it did.

This second edition of the book of 1841 was republished in Edinburgh in 1898, just as the late-Victorian admiration for Pugin was at its height; it was reproduced again in 1969, when the work of Nikolaus Pevsner and Phoebe Stanton had brought him to the fore of the contemporary debate about functionalism and Modernism. The year before, Stanton had contributed a valuable chapter on 'The sources of Pugin's *Contrasts*' to John Summerson's *Concerning Architecture*, citing as influences authors from Pugin's extensive library of historians and antiquarians and also contemporary writers, such as William Cobbett and Kenelm Digby. The present new edition of *Contrasts* is combined with Pugin's other great work of 1841, his *True Principles*, both presented as authentic facsimiles, allowing the reader an unprecedented opportunity to enjoy the writings of an architect in the full flower of his creativity within a single volume.

CONTRASTS DRAWN & ETCHED BY. A.W. PVGIN

SELECTIONS FROM THE WORKS OF VARIOVS CELEBRATED BRITISH
ARCHITECTS

Contrasts

or a parallel between the architecture of the 15th & 19th centuries

by

A W Pugin

CONTRASTS:

OR,

A Parallel

BETWEEN THE

NOBLE EDIFICES OF THE MIDDLE AGES,

AND

CORRESPONDING BUILDINGS OF THE PRESENT DAY;

SHEWING

THE PRESENT DECAY OF TASTE.

Accompanied by appropriate Text.

———

By A. WELBY PUGIN, Architect.

———

LONDON:

CHARLES DOLMAN, 61, NEW BOND STREET.

———

M.DCCC.XLI.

PREFACE TO THE SECOND EDITION.

THE author gladly avails himself of the opportunity afforded him by the publication of this edition, to enlarge the text, and correct some important errors which appeared in the original publication. When this work was first brought out, the very name of Christian art was almost unknown, nor had the admirable works of Montalembert and Rio appeared on the subject. It is not by any means surprising that the author, standing almost alone in the principles he was advocating, should have adopted some incorrect views, in the investigation of a subject involved in so many perplexing difficulties: the theory he adopted was right in the main point, but indistinctly developed. He was perfectly correct in the abstract facts, that *pointed architecture was produced by the Catholic faith*, and that it was destroyed in England by the ascendency of Protestantism; but he was wrong in treating Protestantism as a *primary cause*, instead of being the *effect* of some other more powerful agency, and in ascribing the highest state of architectural excellence to the ecclesiastical buildings erected immediately previous to the change of religion; as, although immeasurably excelling the debased productions of the Elizabethan period, they still exhibited various symptoms of the decay of the true Christian principle.

The real origin of both the revived Pagan and Protestant principles is to be traced to the decayed state of faith throughout Europe in the fifteenth century, which led men to dislike, and ultimately forsake, the principles and architecture which originated in the *self-denying Catholic principle, and admire and adopt the luxurious styles of ancient Paganism*. Religion must have been in a most diseased state, for those two monsters, revived Paganism and Protestantism, ever

A

to have *obtained a footing*, much less to have overrun the Christian world. We cannot imagine a St. Ambrose or St. Chrysostom setting up Bacchanalian groups and illustrations of Ovid's fables as decorations to their episcopal residences, nor a St. Bede or St. Cuthbert becoming Calvinists. If Henry VIII exceeded Nero himself in tyranny and cruelty, had not the Catholic spirit been at an exceedingly low ebb, the Church of England, instead of succumbing, would have risen in glory and purity, for such has ever been the effect of persecution in the days of lively faith. But when the will of a schismatical king could so prevail with the whole clergy of this country, that they actually erased from their missal and breviaries the most glorious champion and martyr of the Church, St. Thomas of Canterbury, and even put out the commemoration of the holy father himself (only one bishop and a few abbots and priests being found true witnesses of the faith), it is evident that England's Church had miserably degenerated.

The so-called Reformation is now regarded by many men of learning and of unprejudiced minds as a dreadful scourge, permitted by divine Providence in punishment for its decayed faith; and those by whom it was carried on are now considered in the true light of Church plunderers and crafty political intriguers, instead of holy martyrs and modern apostles. It is, indeed, almost impossible for any sincere person to see all episcopal and ecclesiastical power completely controled at the pleasure of a lay tribunal, without condemning the men who originally betrayed the Church, and feeling that in our present divided and distracted state, consequent on the *Reformation,* we are suffering severely for the sins of our fathers. This is the only really consistent view which can be taken of the subject. England's Church was not *attacked by a strange enemy and overthrown,* she was consumed *by internal decay;* her privileges and abbeys were surrendered by dissembling and compromising nominally Catholic ecclesiastics, and her revenues and her glorious ornaments were despoiled and appropriated by so-called Catholic nobles. Both Protestantism and revived Paganism were generated by unworthy men who bore the name of Catholic; the former is, indeed, a consequence of the latter, as will be shown hereafter; and, strange as it may appear, there is a great deal of connexion between the gardens of the Medici, filled with Pagan luxury, and the Independent preaching-houses that now deface the land; for *both are utterly opposed to true Catholic principles, and neither could have existed had not those principles decayed.* When that great champion and martyr for the truth, Savonarola, the Dominican monk, preached his first sermon at Florence, he predicted the desolation about to fall on the Church; and after pourtraying, in the most powerful language, the terrible danger in the then new rage for classic and Pagan styles, that were beginning to usurp the place of Christian art and feeling, he exclaimed, "By your continued study of these things, and your neglect of the sublime truths of the Catholic faith, you will become ashamed of the cross of Christ, and imbibe the proud luxurious spirit and feelings of Paganism; till, weak both in faith and good works, you will fall into heresies, or infidelity itself."

Who cannot see this terrible prediction fulfilled in the desolating religious revolution of the sixteenth century, to which we owe the present divided state of religious parties in this country?

Having explained and rectified the errors into which he had fallen, the author is quite ready to maintain the principle of contrasting Catholic excellence with modern degeneracy; and wherever that degeneracy is observable, be it in Protestant or Catholic countries, it will be found to proceed from the decay of true Catholic principles and practice.

It may be proper to observe, that most of the reviewers of this work have fallen into a great error, by reproaching the author for selecting buildings of the modern style to contrast with the ancient edifices, when so many better buildings had been erected during the last few years in imitation of the pointed style. This objection may be answered in a few words: *revivals of ancient architecture,* although erected *in,* are not buildings *of,* the nineteenth century,—their merit must be referred back to the period from whence they were copied; the architecture of the nineteenth century is that extraordinary conglomeration of classic and modern styles peculiar to the day, and of which we can find no example in any antecedent period.

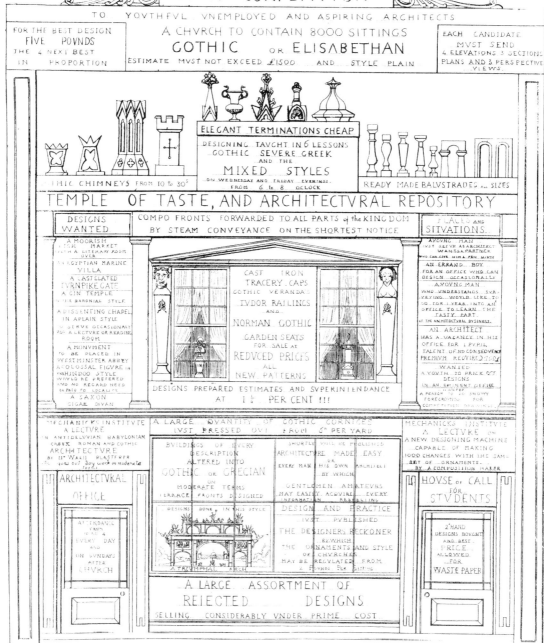

NEW CHVRCH
OPEN COMPETITION

TO YOVTHFVL VNEMPLOYED AND ASPIRING ARCHITECTS

FOR THE BEST DESIGN
FIVE POVNDS
THE 4 NEXT BEST
IN PROPORTION

A CHVRCH TO CONTAIN 8000 SITTINGS
GOTHIC OR **ELISABETHAN**
ESTIMATE MVST NOT EXCEED £1500 AND STYLE PLAIN

EACH CANDIDATE
MVST SEND
4 ELEVATIONS 3 SECTIONS
PLANS AND 3 PERSPECTIVE
VIEWS.

ELEGANT TERMINATIONS CHEAP
DESIGNING TAVGHT IN 6 LESSONS
GOTHIC SEVERE GREEK
AND THE
MIXED STYLES
ON WEDNESDAY AND FRIDAY EVENINGS
FROM 6 to 8 OCLOCK

GOTHIC CHIMNEYS FROM 10 to 30

READY MADE BALVSTRADES ALL SIZES

TEMPLE OF TASTE, AND ARCHITECTVRAL REPOSITORY

DESIGNS WANTED

A MOORISH FISH MARKET WITH A LITERARY ROOM OVER

AN EGYPTIAN MARINE VILLA

A CASTELATED TVRNPIKE GATE

A GIN TEMPLE IN THE BARONIAL STYLE

A DISSENTING CHAPEL IN A PLAIN STYLE TO SERVE OCCASIONALLY FOR A LECTURE OR READING ROOM

A MONVMENT TO BE PLACED IN WESTMINSTER ABBEY A COLOSSAL FIGVRE IN THE HINDOO STYLE WOVLD BE PREFERED AND NO REGARD NEED BE PAID TO LOCALITY

A SAXON CIGAR DIVAN

COMPO FRONTS FORWARDED TO ALL PARTS of the KINGDOM
BY STEAM CONVEYANCE ON THE SHORTEST NOTICE

CAST IRON
TRACERY. CAPS
GOTHIC VERANDAS
TVDOR RAILINGS
AND
NORMAN GOTHIC
GARDEN SEATS
FOR SALE AT
REDVCED PRICES
ALL
NEW PATTERNS

DESIGNS PREPARED ESTIMATES AND SVPERINTENDANCE
AT 1½ PER CENT !!!

PLACES AND SITVATIONS.

A YOVNG MAN JVST SETVP AS ARCHITECT WANTS A PARTNER WHO CAN GIVE HIM A FEW HVNDS

AN ERRAND BOY FOR AN OFFICE WHO CAN DESIGN OCCASIONALLY

A YOVNG MAN WHO VNDERSTANDS SVRVEYING WOVLD LIKE TO GO FOR 1 YEAR INTO AN OFFICE TO LEARN THE TASTY PART OF THE ARCHITECTVRAL BVSINESS.

AN ARCHITECT HAS A VACANCY IN HIS OFFICE FOR 1 PVPIL TALENT OF NO CONSEQVENCE PREMIVM REQVIRED 300£

WANTED A YOVTH TO PRICK OFF DESIGNS IN AN EMINENT OFFICE ALSO A PERSON TO DO SHOWY FORESHORTENING FOR COMPETITION DRAWINGS

MECHANICKS INSTITVTE A LECTURE ON ANTIDELVVIAN BABYLONIAN GREEK ROMAN AND GOTHIC ARCHITECTVRE BY MR WASH PLASTERER

A LARGE QVANTITY OF GOTHIC CORNICES
JVST PRESSED OVT FROM 6d PER YARD

MECHANICKS INSTITVTE A LECTVRE ON A NEW DESIGNING MACHINE CAPABLE OF MAKING 1000 CHANGES WITH THE SAME SORT OF ORNAMENTS BY A COMPOSITION MAKER

!!! ARCHITECTVRAL OFFICE
ATTENDANCE FROM 10 TILL 4 EVERY DAY AND ON SVNDAYS AFTER CHVRCH

BVILDINGS OF EVERY DESCRIPTION ALTERED INTO GOTHIC or GRECIAN ON MODERATE TERMS TERRACE FRONTS DESIGNED

DESIGNS DONE IN THIS STYLE

A TRIVMPHAL ARCH

SHORTLY WILL BE PVBLISHED ARCHITECTVRE MADE EASY OR EVERY MAN HIS OWN ARCHITECT BY WHICH GENTLEMEN AMATEVRS MAY EASILY ACQVIRE EVERY INFORMATION RESPECTING

DESIGN AND PRACTICE JVST PVBLISHED THE DESIGNERS RECKONER BY WHICH THE ORNAMENTS AND STYLE OF CHVRCHES MAY BE REGVLATED FROM 2 POVNDS PER SITTING

HOVSE OF CALL FOR STVDENTS
2ND HAND DESIGNS BOVGHT AND BEST PRICE ALLOWED FOR WASTE PAPER

A LARGE ASSORTMENT OF
REJECTED DESIGNS
SELLING CONSIDERABLY VNDER PRIME COST

THIS ILLVSTRATION
OF THE PRACTISE OF ARCHITECTVRE IN THE 19 CENTVRY ON NEW IMPROVED AND CHEAP PRINCIPLES
IS DEDICATED WITHOVT PERMISSION TO
THE TRADE

CONTRASTS:

OR,

𝔄 Parallel

BETWEEN

THE NOBLE EDIFICES OF THE MIDDLE AGES, AND SIMILAR BUILDINGS OF THE PRESENT DAY,

&c. &c. &c.

CHAPTER I.

ON THE FEELINGS WHICH PRODUCED THE GREAT EDIFICES OF THE MIDDLE AGES.

ON comparing the Architectural Works of the last three Centuries with those of the Middle Ages, the wonderful superiority of the latter must strike every attentive observer; and the mind is naturally led to reflect on the causes which have wrought this mighty change, and to endeavour to trace the fall of Architectural taste, from the period of its first decline to the present day; and this will form the subject of the following pages.

It will be readily admitted, that the great test of Architectural beauty is the fitness of the design to the purpose for which it is intended, and that the style of a building should so correspond with its use that the spectator may at once perceive the purpose for which it was erected.

B

Acting on this principle, different nations have given birth to so many various styles of Architecture, each suited to their climate, customs, and religion; and as it is among edifices of this latter class that we look for the most splendid and lasting monuments, there can be little doubt that the religious ideas and ceremonies of these different people had by far the greatest influence in the formation of their various styles of Architecture.

The more closely we compare the temples of the Pagan nations with their religious rites and mythologies, the more shall we be satisfied with the truth of this assertion.

In them every ornament, every detail had a mystical import. The pyramid and obelisk of Egyptian Architecture, its Lotus capitals, its gigantic sphynxes and multiplied hieroglyphics, were not mere fanciful Architectural combinations and ornaments, but emblems of the philosophy and mythology of that nation.

In classic Architecture again, not only were the forms of the temples dedicated to different deities varied, but certain capitals and orders of Architecture were peculiar to each; and the very foliage ornaments of the friezes were symbolic. The same principle, of Architecture resulting from religious belief, may be traced from the caverns of Elora, to the Druidical remains of Stonehenge and Avebury; and in all these works of Pagan antiquity, we shall invariably find that both the plan and decoration of the building is mystical and emblematic.

And is it to be supposed that Christianity alone, with its sublime truths, with its stupendous mysteries, should be deficient in this respect, and not possess a symbolical architecture for her temples which would embody her doctrines and instruct her children? surely not,—nor is it so: from Christianity has arisen an architecture so glorious, so sublime, so perfect, that all the productions of ancient paganism sink, when compared before it, to a level with the false and corrupt systems from which they originated.

Pointed or Christian Architecture has far higher claims on our admiration than mere beauty or antiquity; the former may be regarded as a matter of opinion,—the latter, in the abstract, is no proof of excellence, but in it alone we find *the faith of Christianity embodied, and its practices illustrated.*

The three great doctrines, of the redemption of man by the sacrifice of our Lord on the cross ; the three equal persons united in one Godhead ; and the resurrection of the dead,—are the foundation of Christian Architecture.

The first—the cross—is not only the very plan and form of a Catholic church, but it terminates each spire and gable, and is imprinted as a seal of faith on the very furniture of the altar.

The second is fully developed in the triangular form and arrangement of arches, tracery, and even subdivisions of the buildings themselves.

The third is beautifully exemplified by great height and vertical lines, which have been considered by the Christians, from the earliest period, as the emblem of the resurrection. According to ancient tradition, the faithful prayed in a standing position, both on Sundays and during the pascal time, in allusion to this great mystery. This is mentioned by Tertullian and by St. Augustine. *Stantes oramus, quod est signum resurrectionis;* and, by the last council of Nice, it was forbidden to kneel on Sundays, or from Easter to Pentecost. The vertical principal being an acknowledged emblem of the resurrection, we may readily account for the adoption of the pointed arch by the Christians, for the purpose of gaining greater height with a given width. I say adoption, because the mere form of the pointed arch is of great antiquity ; and Euclid himself must have been perfectly acquainted with it. But there was nothing to call it into use, till the vertical principle was established. The Christian churches had previously been built with the view to internal height : triforia and clerestories existed in the Saxon churches. But lofty as were these buildings, when compared with the flat and depressed temples of classic antiquity, still the introduction of the pointed arch* enabled the builders to obtain nearly double the elevation with the

---

* We may consider the introduction of the depressed or four-centred arch as the first symptom of the decline of Christian Architecture, the leading character of which was the vertical or pointed principle.

same width, as is clearly seen in the annexed cut. But do not all the features and details of the churches erected during the middle ages, set

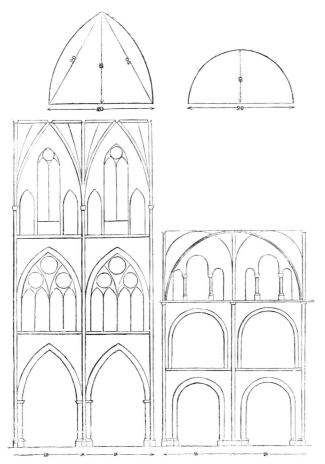

forth their origin, and, at the same time, exhibit the triumphs of Christian truth? Like the religion itself, their foundations are in the cross, and they rise from it in majesty and glory. The lofty nave and choir, with still loftier towers, crowned by clusters of pinnacles and spires, all directed towards heaven, beautiful emblems of the Christian's brightest hope, the shame of the Pagan ; the cross, raised on high in glory,—a token of mercy and forgiveness,— crowning the sacred edifice, and placed between the anger of God and the sins of the city.

The images of holy martyrs, each bearing the instrument of the cruel death by which Pagan foolishness hoped to exterminate, with their lives, the truths they witnessed, fill every niche that line the arched recesses of the doorways. Above them are forms of cherubims and the heavenly host, mingled with patriarchs and prophets. Over the great entrance, is the dome or final judgment, the divine majesty, the joys of the blessed spirits, the despair of the condemned. What subjects for contemplation do not these majestic portals present to the Christian, as he approaches the house of prayer ! and well are they calculated to awaken those senti- ments of reverence and devotion, suited to the holy place. But if the exterior of the temple be so soul-stirring, what a burst of glory meets the eye, on entering a long majestic line of pillars rising into lofty and fretted vaulting! The eye is lost in the intricacies of the aisles and lateral chapels; each window beams with sacred instructions, and sparkles with glowing and sacred tints; the pavement is a rich enamel, interspersed with brass memorials of departed souls. Every capital and base are fashioned to represent some holy mystery; the great rood loft, with its lights and images, through the centre arch of which, in distant perspective, may be seen the high altar blazing with gold and jewels, surmounted by a golden dove, the earthly tabernacle of the Highest; before which, burn three unextinguished lamps. It is, indeed, a sacred place; the modulated light, the gleaming tapers, the tombs of the faithful, the various altars, the venerable images of the just,—all conspire to fill the mind with veneration, and to impress it with the sublimity of Christian worship. And when the deep intonations of the bells from the lofty campaniles, which summon the people to the house of prayer, have ceased, and the solemn chant of the choir swells through the vast edifice, —cold, indeed, must be the heart of that man who does not cry out with the Psalmist, Domine dilexi decorem domus tuae, et locum habitationis gloriae tuae.

Such effects as these can only be produced on the mind by buildings, the composition of which has emanated from men who were thoroughly embued with devotion for, and faith in, the religion for whose worship they were erected.

Their whole energies were directed towards attaining excellence; they were actuated by far nobler motives than the hopes of pecuniary reward, or even the applause and admiration of mankind. They felt they were engaged in one of the most glorious occupations that can fall to the lot of man—that of raising a temple to the worship of the true and living God.

It was this feeling that operated alike on the master-mind that planned the edifice, and on the patient sculptor whose chisel wrought each varied and beautiful detail. It was this feeling that enabled the ancient masons, in spite of labour, danger, and difficulties, to persevere till they had raised their gigantic spires into the very regions of the clouds. It was this feeling that induced the ecclesiastics of old to devote their revenues to this pious purpose, and to labour with their own hands in the accomplishment of the work; and it is a feeling that may be traced throughout the whole of the numerous edifices of the middle ages, and which, amidst the great variety of genius which their varied decorations display, still bespeaks the unity of purpose which influenced their builders and artists.

They borrowed their ideas from no heathen rites, nor sought for decorations from the idolatrous emblems of a strange people. The foundation and progress of the Christian faith, and the sacraments and ceremonies of the church, formed an ample and noble field for the exercise of their talents; and it is an incontrovertible fact, that every class of artists, who flourished during those glorious periods, selected their subjects from this inexhaustible source, and devoted their greatest efforts towards the embellishment of ecclesiastical edifices.

Yes, it was, indeed, the faith, the zeal, and above all, the unity, of our ancestors, that enabled them to conceive and raise those wonderful fabrics that still remain to excite our wonder and admiration. They were erected for the most solemn rites of Christian worship, when the term Christian had but one signification throughout the world; when the glory of the house of God formed an important consideration with mankind, when men were zealous for religion, liberal in their gifts, and devoted to her cause. I am well aware that modern writers have attributed the numerous churches erected during the middle ages to the effect of superstition. But if we believe the great principle of Christian truth, that this life is merely a preparation for a future state, and that the most important occupation of man in this world is to prepare for the next, the multiplicity of religious establishments during the ages of faith, may be accounted for on far nobler motives than have been generally ascribed to them.

It may be objected, and with some apparent reason, that if pointed Architecture had been the result of Christian faith, it would have been introduced earlier. But if we examine the history of the Church, we shall find that the long period which intervened between the establishment of Christianity and the full development of Christian art, can be most satisfactorily accounted for. When the Catholic faith was first preached, *all art was devoted to the service of error and impurity.* Then the great and terrible persecutions of the first centuries, utterly precluded its exercise among the early Christians. The convulsion consequent on the overthrow of the Roman empire, which destroyed, for a time, all the practical resources of art, was a sufficient cause for the barbarous state of Architecture at that period : but when Christianity had over-spread the whole of western Europe, and infused her salutary and en-nobling influence in the hearts of the converted nations, art arose purified and glorious ; and as it had been previously devoted to the gratification of the senses, then it administered to the soul : and exalted by the grandeur of the Christian mysteries, ennobled by its sublime virtues, it reached a point of excellence far beyond any it had previously attained ; and instead of being confined to what was sensual or human, it was devoted to the spiritual and divine. Christian art was the natural result of the progress of Catholic feeling and devotion ; and its decay was consequent on that of the faith itself ; and all revived classic buildings, whether erected in Catholic or Protestant countries, are evidences of a lamentable departure from true Catholic principles and feelings, as will be shown in the ensuing chapter.

CHAPTER II.

ON THE REVIVED PAGAN PRINCIPLE.

" THE ancient Pagans were at least consistent; in their architecture, symbols, and sculpture, they faithfully embodied the errors of their mythology; but modern Catholics have revived these profanities in opposition to reason, and formed the types of their churches, their paintings, their images, from the detestable models of pagan error which had been overthrown by the triumph of Christian truth, raising temples to the crucified Redeemer in imitation of the Parthenon and Pantheon; representing the Eternal Father under the semblance of Jupiter; the blessed Virgin as a draped Venus or Juno; martyrs as gladiators; saints as amorous nymphs; and angels in the form of Cupids."—Translated from *De l'Etat Actuel de l'Art Religieux en France,* par M. le Comte de Montalembert. Paris, 1839.

DID not almost every edifice erected during the last few centuries attest the fact, it would hardly be believed, that after Christianity had utterly overthrown the productions of Paganism, with its false doctrines, and when a new and sublime style of art had been generated by its holy and ennobling influence (in all respects suited to its faith and discipline), its professors in future ages would have abandoned this glorious achievement of their religion, to return to the corrupt ideas of pagan sensuality which their ancestors in the faith had so triumphantly suppressed, and, horrible profanation! turn the most sacred mysteries of Christianity into a mere vehicle for their revival.*   But every church that has been

---

* Almost all the celebrated artists of the last three centuries, instead of producing their works from feelings of devotion and a desire of instructing the faithful, merely sought for a display of their art and the increase of fame; hence they not unfrequently selected the least edifying subjects from sacred writ, such as Lot and his daughters, the chastity of Joseph, Susanna and the elders, and many others of the same description, simply because they afforded a better scope for the introduction of pagan nudities; even St. Sebastian was more frequently depicted from this motive, than from any veneration for the constancy of that holy martyr. And what greater profanation could be conceived, than making the representations of the most holy personages mere vehicles for portraits of often very unworthy living characters, who had the audacity to be depicted as saints, apostles, and even as our blessed Lady and the divine Redeemer himself—a detestable practice, of which we have but too many instances, and which

erected from St. Peter's at Rome* downwards, are so many striking examples of the departure from pure Christian ideas and Architecture; and not only have the modern churchmen adopted the debased style in all their new erections, but they have scarcely left one of the glorious fabrics of antiquity unencumbered by their unsightly and incongruous additions. This mania for paganism is developed in all classes of buildings erected since the fifteenth century,—in palaces, in mansions, in private houses, in public erections, in monuments for the dead; it even extended to furniture and domestic ornaments for the table : and were it not beyond

form strikingly contrasts to the humble piety of the ages of faith, when the donors of sacred pictures were figured kneeling in a corner of the subject in the attitude of prayer, with their patron saints behind them, and not unfrequently labels with pious inscriptions proceeding from their mouths.

* It is surprising how this edifice is popularly regarded as the *ne plus ultra* of a Catholic church, although as a Christian edifice it is by no means comparable to either St. Peter's of York or St. Peter's of Westminster, in both of which churches every original detail and emblem is of the purest Christian design, and *not one arrangement or feature borrowed from pagan antiquity;* and although these glorious piles have been woefully desecrated and shorn of more than half their original beauty, they yet produce stronger feelings of religious awe than their namesake at Rome, still in the zenith of its glory, with all its mosaics, gilding, and marbles. As an English author justly remarks, above thirty millions of Catholic money, gathered for the most part in the *pointed cathedrals of Christendom*, have been lavished in the attempt to adapt classic details to a Christian church, the very idea of which implied a most degenerate spirit. St. Peter's, like other buildings of the same date and style, must convey to every Catholic mind the most melancholy associations,—it marks the fatal period of the great schism, and the outbreak of fearful heresy. England—once the brightest jewel in the crown of the Church— separated from Catholic unity; her most glorious churches dismantled, her religious dispersed, and clergy brought into bondage. France—the kingdom of the saintly Louis—overrun with Calvinists; her cathedrals pillaged, her abbeys given into the hands of lay rapacity, and the first seeds of the terrible revolution disseminated. Germany, Sweden, Holland, and a great part of the Low Countries, the same. For one religious house founded since that fatal period, five hundred have been dismantled and suppressed; for one canonized saint, we find a thousand professed infidels; for one country converted, six lost. These are some of the accompaniments of the grand *renaissance,* or revival of classic art, which moderns so highly extol in preference to the glorious works produced by the faith, zeal, and devotion, of the middle ages; and such have been the results of the revived pagan system, which began with the classicism of the sixteenth century, was fostered in the mythological palaces of the Grand Monarque, and only attained its climax in the great French revolution, when its principles were fully worked out in the massacre of the clergy, the open profession of infidelity, and the exhibition of a prostitute raised over the altar of God.

C

the limits of my subject, I could shew that it has invaded the ordinary forms of speech, and is discernible in modern manners and government.

The most celebrated palaces of Europe are the veriest heathen buildings imaginable; in Versailles, the Tuileries, Louvre, St. Cloud, Fontainebleau, Brussels, Munich, Buckingham Palace, in vain we look for one Christian emblem or ornament. The decoration of garden, terrace, entrance hall, vestibule, gallery, or chamber, ceiling, pannel, wall, window, or pediment, is invariably designed from heathen mythology. Gods and goddesses, demons and nymphs, tritons and cupids, repeated *ad nauseam*, all represented in most complimentary attitudes, with reference to the modern pagan for whom the sycophant artists designed the luxurious residence. In new Buckingham Palace, whose marble gate cost an amount which would have erected a splendid church, there is not even a regular chapel provided for the divine office; so that both in appearance and arrangement it is utterly unsuited for a Christian residence, and forms a most lamentable and degenerate contrast with the ancient Palace of Westminster, of which the present unrivalled Hall was the hospitable refectory, and the exquisitely-beautiful St. Stephen's the domestic chapel.* That was, indeed, a noble structure, worthy of the English monarchs, every chamber of which was adorned with emblems of *their faith and their country.* Conspicuous above the rest were depicted St. George and St. Edward, whose names in moments of desperate peril have oft animated the English in sustaining many an unequal fight

---

* Few persons are aware of the richness of this once glorious chapel, which must have surpassed in splendour any existing monument of pointed art; the whole of the internal architecture was covered with exquisite paintings and diapering. The Society of Antiquaries have engraved portions of them; in Britton's *History of Architecture*, the lower compartments are faithfully figured.

John Carter has etched sections of the chapel in his *Ancient Architecture*, but his restoration of the roof is incorrect, although, in other respects, the plates give a tolerable idea of this wonderful building. Its great beauties, however, found no favour in the eyes of the semi-barbarians of modern times, who fitted it up for the House of Commons in a style not dissimilar to a methodist conventicle. Still fragments of the ancient elaborate enrichments were to be traced behind the unsightly additions till the great fire utterly destroyed them. Britton and Brayley's *Antiquities of the Old Palace at Westminster*, contains many interesting views of this building as it appeared after the conflagration.

with foreign foes. But these saintly names, so famous in our national annals, and the very mention of which wrought such wonders in time of old, have no charm for modern ears. In lieu of their venerable images, we have now a pagan Victory or a Minerva, while the standard of England is hoisted on a scaffold-pole, stuck above a mass of soot-stained marble, miscalled a triumphal arch, and a sorry substitute for the turreted gateways of the ancient palace.

It is very curious to observe the extraordinary change in the decoration of timber houses in the French cities that took place in the short interval between the reigns of Charles VIII and Francis I. Previous to, and during the reign of the former, and even under Louis XII, all the ornaments on private houses were of a devotional and Christian character. The Annunciation of our blessed Lady was frequently carved over entrance doors; saints in canopied niches formed the invariable enrichments of corbels and stauncheons; frequently pious inscriptions were cut on scrolls running on beams and brestsummers, or extended by angels: every detail had a devout and Catholic signification. But no sooner had the principles of modern paganism been introduced, than these holy subjects were discontinued: the fables of Ovid, classic heroes, the twelve Cæsars, and similar representations, were substituted in their place. While Catholic faith and feelings were unimpaired, its results were precisely the same in different countries. There is scarcely any perceptible difference between the sepulchral monuments of the old English ecclesiastics or those of the ancient Roman churchmen ;* we

* It is quite a mistake to suppose that Christian or pointed architecture was not fully developed in Italy, as in other countries, during the ages of faith. Formerly there were most numerous examples to be found; but as it has been the fountain-head of the Pagan revival, few of these monuments of ancient piety have escaped uninjured, while many have been totally destroyed. At Assisium there are several beautiful pointed churches, and one, triply-divided, of unrivalled design and execution, the vaults and walls being covered with frescoes in the finest style of Christian art. The ciboriums or canopies over the high altars of the basilicas, were all in the pointed style. The church ornaments used in the ancient basilica of St. Peter's, of which a few are to be found in the Vatican collection, are exquisitely beautiful, and precisely of the same *form and design* as those which belonged to the old English cathedrals at that period.

Had not the heads of the Catholic Church resided so long at Avignon, Rome would have find precisely the same *ample chasuble*, the same dignified vestments, the same recumbent position, with the hands devoutly joined as in prayer, the same brief and Catholic inscription, the same angelic supporters at the head. But not a trace of one of these beautiful features is to be found in monuments of later times. The inverted torch, the club of Hercules, the owl of Minerva, and the cinerary urn, are carved, in lieu of saints and angels, on the tombs of popes, bishops, kings, ecclesiastics, statesmen, and warriors, frequently accompanied by Pagan divinities, in Pagan nudity; the pious supplication for a prayer for the soul of the deceased, is changed into a long and pompous inscription detailing his virtues and exploits. Although the shameful inconsistency of these monuments may not appear so striking in the modern churches of Italian style, where they are partly in character with the Paganism of the rest of the building, yet when they are intruded beneath the grand vaults of a Westminster or a Cologne, and placed by the side of the ancient memorials of the departed faithful, where every niche and ornament breathes the spirit of Catholic piety, they offer a perfect outrage to Christian feelings.

The furniture executed during and since the reigns of Henry VIII and Francis I, exhibits the same debased and Pagan character of ornament which I have previously remarked about the houses themselves; and this lamentable change of style extended itself to every class of art and manufacture; and when anything Christian or sacred was attempted to be introduced, it was so disguised in classic forms as to be scarcely

possessed a vast number of buildings in the purest Christian style. In the former city are tombs of popes, exquisitely beautiful, and corresponding in style and execution to our finest monuments of the period of Edward III. Italy was the very focus of Christian painting during the middle ages, and produced a most illustrious race of Catholic artists, amongst whom are to be reckoned a Giotto, an Andrea Orgagna, a Fra Angelico, a Perugino, and a Raffaelle. If those students who journey to Italy to study art, would follow in the steps of the great Overbeck, and avoiding equally the contagion of its *ancient and modern Paganism*, confine their researches to *its Christian antiquities*, they would indeed derive inestimable benefit. Italian art of the 13th, 14th, and 15th centuries, is the beau ideal of Christian purity, and its imitation cannot be too strongly inculcated; but when it forsook its pure, mystical, and ancient types, to follow those of sensual Paganism, it sunk to a fearful state of degradation, and for the last three centuries its productions of every class should only be looked upon for the purpose of being avoided.

distinguishable from the Pagan subjects by which it was surrounded. Indeed all idea of the respect due to sacred representations was entirely lost, and the most holy emblems were treated as mere ornament, and placed on a level with the grossest profanities. Not long since I saw a dagger of the sixteenth century, which had been undoubtedly used for assassinations, the blade being *priced for blood* by successive scores, increasing the remuneration in proportion to the depth that the steel was plunged in the body of the victim. Now the handle of this murderous instrument (the very sight of which must fill every Christian mind with horror) was surmounted by an ivory image *of the blessed Virgin with our Lord,* while *Diana and Acteon* were sculptured beneath ! ! And many more instances could I readily adduce to show the utter loss of Catholic art and feelings at this memorable period. The very form of the ecclesiastical seals, which for ages had resembled the Vesica Piscis, or fish, symbolical of the holy name of our Lord, was changed into a circle, in imitation of the classic medals, which were servilely copied even to their very ornaments.

The triumph of these new and degenerate ideas over the ancient and Catholic feelings, is a melancholy evidence of the decay of faith and morals at the period of their introduction, and to which indeed they owe their origin. Protestantism and revived Paganism both date from the same epoch, both spring from the same causes, and neither could possibly have been introduced, had not Catholic feelings fallen to a very low ebb. The ravages of the former were carried on by plunder and violence ; the inroads of the latter by pretended improvement and classic restoration. On the whole, however, it must be admitted, that the axes and hammers of the puritanic factions were far less dangerous or productive of lasting evils than the chisels and brushes of the modern Pagan artists, who, by insinuating their pernicious ideas and emblems into the very externals of true religion, seduced the weak-minded, and gained thousands who would have revolted at the *professed mutilation* of ecclesiastical architecture, to aid in its destruction, under the supposition of replacing it by more ornamental erections. I have here introduced engravings of three sorts of altars to illustrate my position.

In the first (see Plate, No. I)—the true Catholic one—every portion breathes the spirit of purity and reverence; the sacred mysteries are depicted in a mystical and devotional manner; the full, draped, and modest garments of the figures, the devout and placid position of the angels, the curtains, the embroidered frontal, the two candlesticks and cross, are all in strict accordance with Catholic antiquity and feelings.

In the second (see Plate, No. II) an altar used for Catholic purposes, but of a debased and profane style,—we discern the fatal effects of revived Paganism. The loose and indecent costume and postures of the figures intended for saints (but which are all concealed copies of the impure models of Pagan antiquity), the classic details devoid of any appropriate

signification, the paltry and trifling taste of the ornaments, more suited to a fashionable boudoir than an altar for sacrifice, all evince the total absence of true Catholic ideas of art.

In the third (see margin), the effect of the destructive or Protestant principles is depicted. The original imagery and tabernacle work of the altar screen have been mutilated and defaced: the altar itself,—which had served for ages in the most holy mysteries, and was covered with costly ornaments,—has been plundered and demolished, and a cheap ugly table set in its place, on which the book and bason indicate that it occasionally serves for the

No. I.

No. II.

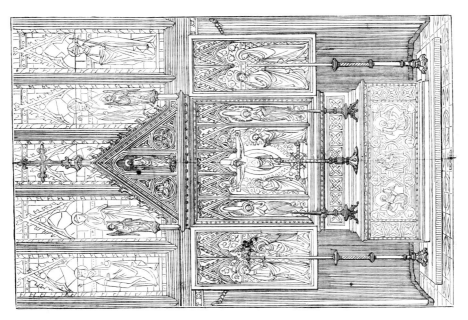

AUTEL PRIVILEGIÉ

Contrasted Altars.

purposes of *baptism*, in lieu of the ancient font, which probably has been removed to serve for some menial purpose. The royal arms, occupying the wonted place of the Redeemer, mark the temporal degradation of the suffering Church, ground down by the civil power. In place of the original rich and splendid window, a few shattered fragments confusedly leaded together, are all that remain, and these will probably be thrown away by the glazier in the next repairs; and the whole exhibits a faithful picture of Protestant desecration and neglect.

In England, as the succeeding pages will shew, the buildings have almost exclusively suffered through the destructive or Protestant principle; but this was not, as I have before remarked, in itself *a cause*, but the effect of Catholic degeneracy, and we must view its ravages as the scourge of the decayed and compromising Church of England. As all the matter of the first edition of this book referred to this country, it is not altogether surprising that I should have overlooked the revival of Paganism, and attributed the loss of Catholic art exclusively to Protestant opinions : I now most readily retract my former error in this respect, and have endeavoured to assign to each principle its real share in the destruction of Christian productions.

I was perfectly right in the abstract fact that *the excellence of art was only to be found in Catholicism*, but I did not draw a sufficient distinction between Catholicism *in its own venerable garb*, or as *disguised in the modern externals of Pagan corruption*.

But however defective my former efforts may have been in principle, their intention, like the present work, is to exhibit in the works and practices of Catholic antiquity—a far higher standard of excellence than any modern productions can possibly afford. If men could only be led to view Catholic truth, not as she appears at the present time, not as she is distorted by popular prejudice, but in her ancient solemn garb, what immense results might we not expect! The ordinary ideas in England of Catholicism (the pure faith of the merciful Redeemer) are associated with faggots, racks, inquisitions, tortures, daggers, poisoning, and all the horrors which wretched crafty politicians have perpetrated in various ages, under the name and cloak of religion; accounts of which, under exaggerated and multiplied forms, are most industriously circulated. On the other hand, the externals and practices of the Church are so decayed at the present time, that it is even difficult to point out to the enquirer after truth any place where he can behold the rites of the Church celebrated with the ancient solemnity.

It is only by communing with the spirit of past ages, as it is developed in the lives of the holy men of old, and in their wonderful monuments and works, that we can arrive at a just appreciation of the glories we have lost, or adopt the necessary means for their recovery.

It is now, indeed, time to break the chains of Paganism which have enslaved the Christians of the last three centuries, and diverted the noblest powers of their minds, from the pursuit of truth to the reproduction of error. Almost all the researches of modern antiquaries, schools of painting, national museums and collections,* have only tended to corrupt taste and poison the intellect, by setting forth classic art as the summit of excellence, and substituting mere natural and sensual productions in the place of the mystical and divine.

Before true taste and Christian feelings can be revived, all the present and popular ideas on the subject must be utterly changed. Men must learn that the period hitherto called dark and ignorant far excelled

---

* Any shapeless fragment, any mean potter's vessel, any illegible inscription, provided it be *but antique,* will be deposited on a pedestal or within a glass case in our national museum. No price can be too great for a cameo or a heathen bust; but every object of Catholic and national art is rigidly excluded from the collection. In the whole of that vast establishment, there is not even one room, one *shelf,* devoted to the exquisite productions of the middle ages. In this we are actually behind every other country in Europe. At Paris, amidst all the Pagan collections of the Louvre, the Christian student will find exquisite specimens of enamels, ivory carvings, jewels, silver work, chasings in metal—all in the first style of Catholic art, and of every date. At Nuremberg, Rouen, and many mere provincial towns, are public galleries of Christian antiquities of the greatest interest. England alone, the country of all others where such a collection could best be formed, is utterly destitute of it. In sepulchral monuments we are rich indeed. If correct casts of all the effigies of royal and ecclesiastical persons, remaining in the cathedral and other churches, were carefully taken, coloured fac-simile from the originals, and arranged in chronological order, what a splendid historical and national series they would form ; and this might easily be done at even a less cost than the transport of a monstrous fragment of an Egyptian god from the banks of the Nile.

our age in wisdom, that art ceased when it is said to have been revived, that superstition was piety, and bigotry faith. The most celebrated names and characters must give place to others at present scarcely known, and the *famous edifices* of modern Europe sink into masses of deformity by the side of the neglected and mouldering piles of Catholic antiquity. If the renunciation of preconceived opinions on these subjects, and the consequent loss of the present enjoyment derived from them, be considered as a great sacrifice, does not the new and glorious field that is opened offer far more than an equivalent? What delight to trace a race of native artists hitherto unknown, in whose despised and neglected productions the most mystical feeling and chaste execution is to be found, and in whose beautiful compositions the originals of many of the most celebrated pictures of more modern schools are to be traced; what exquisite remains of the sculptor's skill* lie buried under the green mounds that mark the site of once noble churches; what originality of conception and masterly execution do not the details of many rural and parochial churches exhibit!† There is no need of visiting the distant shores of Greece and Egypt to make discoveries in art. England alone abounds in hidden and unknown antiquities of surpassing interest.

* During the excavations of St. Mary's abbey at York, exquisite bosses and carved fragments were discovered buried beneath the accumulated rubbish. There can be but little doubt that, by judicious excavations, many interesting monuments and beautiful specimens of ancient skill would be discovered. The excavations at St. Mary's abbey were most laudable, but the discoveries there made hardly compensate for the detestable building, consisting of a Grecian portico and two wings, erected on part of the abbatial site and approach, through a sort of Regent's Park lodge-gate, which is the present entrance to this venerable enclosure. It would have been hardly possible to have erected more offensive objects than these buildings, in the immediate vicinity of one of the purest specimens of Christian architecture in the country.

† There is scarcely an ancient parish church in England which does not present some object of interest. The sculptured details of those churches which were erected about the time of the three first Edwards, are exquisitely beautiful. In accordance with my rule never to pass an ancient church without examining its interior, I entered lately a small church near Stamford of no very promising exterior, where I found a fine family chapel, and in it two canopied niches, surpassing in combination and execution any I had previously seen. Some of the half ruined and almost deserted churches along the Norfolk coast are complete mines of

What madness, then, while neglecting our own religious and national types of architecture and art, to worship at the revived shrines of ancient corruption, and profane the temple of a crucified Redeemer by the architecture and emblems of heathen Gods. The Pagan monster, which has ruled so long, and with such powerful sway over the intellects of mankind, is now tottering to its fall; and although its growth is too strong, and its hold too powerful to be readily overthrown, still its hideous form has been unmasked, and the strength of its assailants daily increases. Already have some desperate wounds been inflicted on the system. The great Overbeck,* that prince of Christian painters, has raised up a school of mystical and religious artists, who are fast putting to utter shame the natural and sensual school of art, in which the modern followers of Paganism have so long degraded the representations of sacred personages and events. In France, M. Le Comte De Montalembert (a man, of whom it may be said as of Savonarola, the Dominican, *sans reproche, et sans peur*), has fully set forth the fatal effects of modern Paganism on Christian feelings and monuments; and already his denunciations of these errors, and his exposition of Catholic art and truth, have produced a great improvement of taste and ideas on these matters; and various publications have already appeared, and many more are preparing, on the excellence of the despised middle ages.

The work of M. Rio on Christian Painting is an admirable production, and must produce many converts to ancient art. In England, much has been done towards restoring Catholic antiquity, and a fine spirit has arisen in the head university itself, where a society of

---

carved and beautiful ornament. How little is really known of old English art. The celebrated cathedral may indeed arrest attention, but few ever penetrate among the many noble churches which lie in unfrequented roads, and where the simplicity of a rural population has proved a far better preservative to the sacred pile than the heavy rates of prosperous and busy towns.

* All those who are interested in the revival of Catholic art should possess engravings from the works of this great artist, the reviver of Christian painting at Rome. He was educated in Lutheran errors, but, a few years since, embraced Catholic truth, with several of his associate artists, who, like himself, have directed their talents to the service of religion, by pourtraying its mysteries in the reverent and devotional form of the ancient days of faith.

learned men has been organised for the study and preservation of Christian architecture. The ecclesiastical antiquities of the country are considered worthy of patient research and elaborate illustration. Innovators are frequently denounced, blocked arches and windows restored, whitewash removed, and stained glass reinserted. All these are good signs, and promise much for the future. It is true that those who are most active in the great revival of Catholic art are as yet but few in number, and, by the multitude, they are yet considered as fanatics, or at best but visionary enthusiasts; but well can they afford to bear any obloquy or ridicule that they may incur in the pursuit of their holy and glorious object. In what, I will ask, on calm dispassionate examination of the opinions, can the fanaticism and extravagance be said to exist? Is it in the assertion that art was carried to far higher degree of perfection by the ennobling and purifying influence of the Christian faith, than under that of Pagan corruption?

In their considering the symbol of our redemption and the images of saintly personages more suitable to the residence of a Christian, than the statue of a lascivious Venus, or the representation of heathen fables?

In their regarding the solemn chaunts composed by St. Gregory himself, and sanctioned by repeated councils, and the universal practice of antiquity, as better suited to divine psalmody, and the offices of the Church, than the extravagant figurings of infidel composers?

In their preferring cloistered, quadrangled, and turreted edifices to long Italian pedimented mansions, for collegiate purposes?

In their following the architecture that emanated from the *faith itself* in the erection of churches, instead of adopting a bastard imitation of Pagan edifices, unworthy and unsuited to so sacred a purpose?

In fine, by their setting forth the self-denying, charitable, devout, and faithful habits of the ages of faith, as far more admirable and exemplary than the luxurious, corrupt, irreverent, and infidel system of the present time?

Surely, if these be fanatical ideas, then must Catholic truth itself be fanaticism, for all these opinions are solidly based on it. And however they may be assailed for a time, they must eventually prevail. A warm temperature is not more necessary for the existence of Eastern exotics, than a Christian atmosphere for the faithful. "Tell me what company you keep and I will tell you what you are," is a homely but true proverb. Hence, when I see a man professedly a Christian, who, neglecting the mysteries of the faith, the saints of the Church, and the glories of religion, surrounds himself with the obscene and impious fables of mythology, and the false divinities of the heathen, I may presume, without violation of charity, that although he is nominally a son of Christian Rome, his heart and affections are devoted to that city in the days of its Paganism.

CHAPTER III.

OF THE PROTESTANT PRINCIPLE AND THE PILLAGE AND DESTRUCTION OF THE CHURCHES UNDER HENRY THE EIGHTH

> I sing the deeds of great King Harry,
> Of Ned his son, and daughter Mary;
> The old religion's alteration,
> And the establishment's first foundation;
> And how the King became its head;
> How Abbeys fell, what blood was shed;
> Of rapne, sacrilege, and theft,
> And Church of gold and land bereft.

THE origin of what is usually termed the Reformation in this country, is too well known to need much dilating upon; but it will be necessary to say a few words on the subject, to explain the rise of the Protestant or destructive principle.

King Henry the Eighth, finding all the hopes he had conceived of the Pontiff's acquiescence in his unlawful divorce totally at an end, determined to free himself from all spiritual restraint of the Apostolic see; and, for that purpose, caused himself to be proclaimed supreme head of the English Church. This arrogant and impious step drew forth the indignation of those who had the constancy and firmness to prefer the interests of religion to the will of a tyrant, and who boldly represented the injustice and impiety of a layman pretending to be the supreme head of a Christian Church.

Their opposition was, however, fruitless, and a bitter persecution was commenced against those who had boldly resisted this dangerous and novel innovation; and amongst the numerous victims who suffered on this occasion, the names of those learned and pious men, Bishop Fisher, Thomas More, and Abbot Whiting, need only be cited to shew the injustice and cruelty of this merciless tyrant.

The king, however, now established in his new dignity, by dint of rewards to those who were base enough to truckle to his will, and axe and halter to any who dared to withstand his usurpations, found it necessary to find some means to replenish his coffers, and to secure the assistance he might require in the furtherance of his sacrilegious projects.

The step he took on this occasion proved the total overthrow of religion, and paved the way for all those disastrous events which so rapidly afterwards succeeded each other.

Ever since the first conversion of this country to the Christian faith, pious and munificent individuals had always been found zealous to establish and endow a vast number of religious houses; to the labours of whose inmates we are indebted not only for the preservation and advancement of literature and science, but even for the conception and partial execution both of the great ecclesiastical buildings themselves, and the exquisite and precious ornaments with which they were filled.

By the unwearied zeal and industry of these men, thus relieved from all worldly cares, and so enabled to devote their lives to the study of all that was sublime and admirable, their churches rose in gigantic splendour; their almeries and sacristies were filled with sacred vessels and sumptuous vestments, the precious materials of which were only exceeded by the exquisite forms into which they had been wrought; while the shelves of their libraries groaned under a host of ponderous volumes, the least of which required years of intense and unceasing application for its production.

It would be an endless theme to dilate on all the advantages accruing from these splendid establishments; suffice it to observe, that it was through their boundless charity and hospitality the poor were entirely maintained.

They formed alike the places for the instruction of youth, and the quiet retreat of a mature age; and the vast results that the monastic bodies have produced, in all classes of art and science, shew the excellent use they made of that time which was not consecrated to devotion and the immediate duties of their orders.

To a monarch, however, who neither respected sanctity nor art, these institutions only offered a lure to his avarice, and the sure means of replenishing his exhausted treasury ; and, regardless of the consequences of so sacrilegious a step, he proceeded to exercise the power of his newly acquired headship, and to devote to his own use and purposes those lands which ancient piety had dedicated to God, and which had been the support of the religious, the learned, and the poor, for so many centuries.

He accomplished this great change in the most artful manner, by instituting commissioners for the pretended reformation of ecclesiastical abuses ; but, in reality, to accomplish the entire overthrow of the religious houses, by forging accusations of irregularity against them,* and by executing those who opposed his intentions, on the score of denying his supremacy.†

By such means, he obtained an act of parliament, for the suppression, to his use, of all those houses whose revenues were 300 marks a-year, and under.

Monstrous as this measure was, by which 376 conventual establishments were dissolved, and an immense number of religious persons scattered abroad, it was only intended as a prelude to one which soon followed, and which was no less than the entire suppression of all the larger abbeys, and a great number of colleges, hospitals, and free chapels : of which Baker, in his " Chronicle," computes the number to have been, of monasteries, 645 ; colleges, 90 ; 100 hospitals for poor men ; and chantries and free chapels, 2374. The whole of the lands belonging to these houses, together with an immense treasure of ecclesiastical ornaments, of every description, were appropriated, by this rapacious and sacrilegious tyrant, to his own use, and the rightful possessors were left utterly destitute.

This measure may be considered as a fatal blow to ecclesiastical Architecture in England ; and, from this period, we have only to trace a melancholy series of destructions and mutilations, by which the most glorious edifices of the Middle Ages have either been entirely demolished, or so shorn of their original beauties, that what remains only serves to awaken our regret at what is for ever lost to us.

* See Appendix, A.   † See Appendix, B.

On the slaughter and dispersion of the religious, all the buildings then in progress were, of course, immediately stopped; a vast number of their former inmates fled, to obtain an asylum in some foreign land, where yet the ancient faith remained inviolate; those who remained, reduced to indigence, became the humble suitors for the charity which they had so often liberally bestowed upon others; and, with bleeding hearts, and bitter lamentations, they beheld those edifices, on which they had bestowed so much labour and consideration, consigned to rapacious court parasites, as the reward of some grovelling submission, or in the chance of play.*

They beheld the lead torn from the roofs and spires of their venerable churches, to satisfy the wasteful extravagance of a profligate court; and those beauteous and precious ornaments, which had enshrined the relics of the departed saints, or served for centuries in the most solemn rites of the church, sink into mere masses of metal, under the fire of the crucible.

Their libraries were pillaged, their archives destroyed; the very remains of their illustrious dead were torn from their tombs, and treated with barbarous indignity.

So suddenly had all this been brought to pass, that many buildings were hurled down, ere the cement, with which they were erected, had hardened with time; and many a mason, by the unwearied strokes of whose chisel some beautiful form had been wrought, lived to see the result of his labours mutilated, by the axes of the destroyer.†

The effect of such scenes as these, on the minds of those clergy who still remained in cathedral and other churches, may easily be conceived. Apprehensive of a similar fate to that which had fallen on their monastic brethren, they remained paralysed; and no further efforts were made at beautifying those edifices, which they so soon expected would be plundered: and they waited, in dreadful suspense, the next step which the sacrilegious tyrant would take, when either his avarice or his necessities should lead him to it.

It is a very common error to suppose that the change of religion, in this country, was the result of popular feeling, but the mass of the

* See Appendix, C.   † See Appendix, D.

people, on the contrary, were warmly attached to the ancient faith : the truth is, that the great fabric of the Church was undermined, by degrees, one step producing another, till, like all revolutions, it far exceeded the intentions of its first advocates ; and I do believe that, had Henry himself foreseen the full extent to which his first impious step would lead, he would have been deterred by the dreadful prospect from proceeding in his career. He was the father of persecution against the tenets of Protestantism in this country.*

By his Six Articles, he confirmed all the leading tenets of the Catholic faith ;† and, indeed, the only alteration he made in the mass itself was, erasing the prayer for the pope, and the name of St. Thomas à Becket, from the missals. In fine, images were retained in churches, the sacrifice of the mass everywhere offered up, in the usual manner, and the rites of the old religion performed, with only this difference, that their splendour was greatly reduced, in consequence of the king having appropriated all the richest ecclesiastical ornaments to his own use.

It is impossible, therefore, that Henry can be, by any means, ranked among the number of what are termed Reformers, except so far as his disposition to plunder and demolition, feelings so congenial to that body, will entitle him to fellowship with them ; for, indeed, in no other respects was he at all similar to those who proceeded afterwards on the foundation he had laid. He had foolishly imagined, he should have been able to seize the Church's wealth and power into his own hands, and preserve the same unity and discipline as those who held it by apostolic right ; but grievously was he disappointed.

The suppression of the religious houses, and the spoliation and desecration of those shrines and places which had so long been considered sacred, had raised doubts and uncertainties among men which were more easily excited than suppressed.

The exercise of private judgment in matters of faith,‡ and various heretical works imported from Germany, had produced feelings of irreverence for the clergy, and contempt for religion, which was increased

* See Appendix, E.   † See Appendix, F.   ‡ See Appendix, G.

E

by the innovations they beheld daily made by those in power, on the rights and property of ecclesiastics; and Henry lived to perceive and deplore, that neither his fagots nor his halters could preserve any thing like unity of creed; but that, the great spell being broken which had so long kept men together, they were as little disposed to be restrained by rules prescribed by him, as he had been by those of the ancient faith from which he had departed.

During his life, however, the cathedral and parochial churches suffered little, except being despoiled of their richest ornaments, all the destruction having fallen on the monastic edifices; nor was it till his infant son, Edward **VI**, ascended the throne, that the real feelings produced by the new opinions were displayed, or the work of robbery and destruction fully commenced.

CHAPTER IV.

ON THE RAVAGES AND DESTRUCTION OF THE CHURCHES UNDER EDWARD VI,
AND AFTER THE FINAL ESTABLISHMENT OF THE NEW OPINIONS
BY ACT OF PARLIAMENT.

> Here altar cloaths lie scattered, and
> There does a broken altar stand ;
> Some steal away the crucifix ;
> And some the silver candlesticks ;
> Rich vestments others do convey,
> And antipendiums bear away ;
> And what they thought not fit to steal,
> They burn as an effect of zeal.
>
> Ward's Reformation.

DISASTROUS as the latter part of Henry's reign proved to religion and ecclesiastical architecture, the succeeding one of Edward VI was doubly so.

The Church in this country had then for its supreme head a boy of nine years of age, incapable, of course, of either thinking or acting for himself, and fit only to be used as a mere machine, by those who actually constituted the government.

These consisted, unhappily, of men who considered Church property in no other light than that of a legitimate source of plunder, and who, fearing that, should the ancient religion be restored, they would not only lose all chance of further enriching themselves, but might even be compelled to restore that which they had so iniquitously obtained, resolved on forming a new system, dependant wholly on the temporal power, under colour of which they might pillage with impunity ; and by abolishing all the grand and noble accompaniments which had, for so many centuries, rendered the sacred rites of religion so solemn and imposing, secure to their own use all those ornaments which served for these purposes, reduce a large number of the clergy, and even demolish vast portions of the fabrics themselves, either to avail themselves of the materials, or benefit by their sale.

In order to accomplish these ends, those of the old bishops who would not consent to the impoverishment of their sees were displaced, and their bishoprics filled by men who were willing to surrender large portions of their temporalities to those in power,* in order to obtain a dignity to which they had no legitimate right, and almost as little reasonable expectation of ever possessing.

The perfidious and dissembling Cranmer, who during the lifetime of Henry had outwardly conformed to the old system, now threw off the mask, declared himself a bitter enemy to what he had professed all his life, and, in order to ingratiate himself with the favourites of the day, was base enough to surrender into their hands half the lands belonging to the See of Canterbury.

All the Church lands were everywhere reduced in a similar manner, and appropriated to the aggrandisement of the nobility's estates; nor were the spoliations by any means confined to landed ecclesiastical property: for the protector, Somerset, having conceived the design of erecting a sumptuous mansion in the Strand, caused the demolition of the magnificent cloisters of St. Paul's, the nave of St. Bartholomew's priory church in Smithfield (which had just been completed), five churches, and three bishops' palaces, for materials—so little veneration for religion or art did these new churchmen profess. Nor, after this, can further proof be wanting to show the total absence of all respect for buildings dedicated to religious worship, when the lord protector, who was nominally the supreme head of the English church, demolishes large portions of the metropolitan cathedral, and a host of ecclesiastical edifices, to gratify a mere vain whim of his own.†

To carry on this work of devastation and robbery, under the cover of restoring primitive simplicity and abolishing superstition, acts were passed for defacing images, pulling down altars, and seizing on all those ecclesiastical ornaments which had escaped the rapacious hands of

* See Appendix, H.   † See Appendix, I.

Henry's commissioners, or which had been suffered to remain as being absolutely necessary to perform the rites in the ancient manner; and so effectually were the churches now cleared out, that only one chalice and paten were suffered to remain in each.* The lay reformers took infinite pains that none of the new rites and ceremonies should either be irksome or expensive, or that they should impede in any way the plunder that was going on by introducing the use of any thing valuable or imposing. In fact, from the moment the new religion was established, all the great Ecclesiastical Edifices ceased to be of any real utility; the new rites could equally well have been performed in a capacious barn, only the policy of these reformers caused them to leave a few of the buildings, and retain some of the old titles, in order to secure the lands and oblations which, without some such show, they thought it would be impossible to retain and collect. It is to this feeling that we are indebted for the preservation of those cathedrals we now see: do not imagine, reader, it was the wonders of their construction or the elegance of their design that operated with these reformers for their preservation. It was not the loftiness of Salisbury's spire, the vastness of Ely's lantern, the lightness of Gloucester's choir, or the solemn grandeur of Wykeham's nave at Winchester, that caused them to be singled out and spared in the general havoc. There are mouldering remains scattered over the face of this country which mark the spots where once, in gigantic splendour, stood churches equally vast, equally fine, with those we now behold. Glastonbury, Crowland, Reading, St. Edmund's, and many others, were not inferior to any in scale or grandeur; they contained tombs of illustrious dead, shrines, chapels, all replete with works of wondrous skill. But they are gone; condemned to ruin and neglect, they perished piecemeal, and all that now remains of their once glorious piles are some unshapen masses of masonry, too firmly cemented to render their demolition lucrative.

And in a similar state should we now behold the cathedrals, had it not been arranged to keep just as much of the old system as would serve for the professors of the new; for these reformers, although they pro-

* See Appendix, J.

fessed to revive the simplicity of the apostles in all such matters, the continuation of which entailed expense or irksome duty on them, were quite unwilling to become imitators of their poverty. No, that was another question ; they did not quarrel with the popish names of dean, canon, or prebend, because good incomes were attached to them, although I never heard of any of these dignitaries being mentioned in Holy Writ, which to persons utterly rejecting the tradition of the Church ought to have proved an insuperable objection. But an altar, which with its daily lighting and decoration entailed a considerable expense, and as its rich appendages formed no inconsiderable plunder, it was condemned to be pulled down, and a common square table set in its place, as being, forsooth, more agreeable to apostolic use.* Why did not these restorers of simplicity fly the churches, and muster in an upper chamber ? because then they must have renounced all pretensions to the lands ; and so they sat down content in the same stalls, and in the same choir as that which had so lately been occupied by their Catholic predecessors.

This is only one among the many inconsistencies that attended the foundation of the Establishment ; and I only mention it to show, to what base and sordid motives we are indebted for the partial preservation of what remains, and how little any feelings, except those of interest and expediency, had any part in it. I have hitherto described the dreadful results which were produced on the buildings by the combined ravages of avarice and fanaticism ; I will now proceed to show how materially they continued to suffer, when the new system was, finally, by law established.

The altars had everywhere been demolished ; the stained windows in many places dashed from the mullions they had so brilliantly filled ; the images of the saints left headless in their mutilated niches, or utterly defaced ; the cross, that great emblem of human redemption, every-where trampled under foot ; the carved work broken down ; the taber-nacles destroyed ; and the fabrics denuded as far as possible, of those

---

* Hooper the puritan was the author of this horrible profanation ; his suggestion, as Heylin says, being eagerly caught up *by those about the court,* who anticipated *no small profit thereby.*

appearances which would announce them as having been devoted to the celebration of the solemn offices of the ancient Church, and left as bare as the strictest disciple of the Genevan Church could desire.

Plunder was likewise nearly over; all that was rich and valuable had long disappeared; even brass was becoming scarce; and the leaden coffins of the dead had been so exhausted, they could but rarely be found to supply the melting-pot.*

Further excesses were forbidden; the buildings were declared to be sufficiently purified of ancient superstition; the axe and the hammer were laid by; and the shattered edifices were ordained to undergo a second ordeal, almost as destructive as the first, in being fitted up for the new form of worship: and, when we reflect on the horrible repairs, alterations, and demolitions, that have taken place in our venerable edifices, —ever directed by a tepid and parsimonious clergy, brutal and jobbing parochial authorities, and ignorant and tasteless operatives,—I do not hesitate to say, that the lover of ancient art has more to regret, during the period that the churches have been used for their present purposes, than even during the fatal period in which they were first desecrated.

The manner of preparing the churches for the exercise of the new liturgy, consisted in blocking up the nave and aisles, with dozing-pens, termed pews;† above this mass of partitions rose a rostrum, for the preacher, reader, and his respondent; whilst a square table, surmounted by the king's arms, which had everywhere replaced the crucified Redeemer, conclude the list of necessary erections,—which, I need hardly say, were as unsightly as the ancient arrangements were appropriate and beautiful.

Had propriety and fitness been considered, instead of economy, the old churches would have been abandoned altogether, and places of worship erected very similar to the dissenting chapels of the present

* See Appendix, K.

† It does not appear, on close investigation, that pews were *generally introduced* as early as Edward VI: they certainly did not attain the *full growth* till the reign of Charles II; nor did the internal fittings of the country parish churches suffer any considerable mutilation till the ascendancy of the puritanic faction under Cromwell, to whose withering influence half the departures from solemnity and ancient observance, which so degrade the present establishment, are to be traced.

day ; for all that was required, and, indeed, what was most appropriate for Protestant service, was a large room, well-aired, well-ventilated ; a pulpit in such a situation that all the congregation might hear and see well ; a communion-table in the middle,* and two or three tiers of galleries ; by means of which a large auditory might be crammed into a small space.†

The old buildings are the very reverse of all this, and totally unfit for any worship but that for which they had been erected ; but there they were, and, fitting or not, they were used for the new service ; hence come all the incongruities we see in all ancient parochial churches. The aisles cut to pieces by galleries of all sizes, and heights ; the nave blocked up with pews ; screens cut away ; stalls removed from their old position in the chancel, and set about in odd places ; chauntry chapels turned into corporation pews ; wooden panelling, of execrable design, smeared over with paint, set up with the Creed and Commandments, entirely covering some fine tabernacle work, the projecting parts of which have been cut away to receive it. Large portions of the church, for which there is no use, walled off, to render the preaching place more snug and comfortable ; porches enclosed and turned into engine-houses,‡ and a host of other wretched mutilations ; and, when all has been done, what are they but inconvenient, inappropriate buildings, for the purpose they are used for ? And, I am grieved to say, these enormities are not confined to obscure villages, or even large parochial churches : abominations equally vile with those I have above stated, and far more reprehensible, as proceeding from men whose name, education, and station, would have led us to hope for better things, are to be found in collegiate and cathedral churches, which are under the control of the highest class, as in those edifices which are confided to the management of the ignorant.   See Appendix, No. II.

* See Appendix, L.

† By the real decrees of the establishment, the churches and chancels were required to remain as in times past : but, notwithstanding, the Genevan doctrines imported with Bucer and Peter Martyr made such rapid progress, that many of the finest churches were soon converted into mere preaching-houses for the propagation of the most pestilential errors, and the sanctity of the chancels shamefully disregarded.   See Appendix, No. I.

‡ The beautiful southern porch of the once magnificent church at Howden, Lincolnshire, has just been converted into a vestry.

I have now, I trust, shown how intimately the fall of ecclesiastical architecture in this country, is connected with the growth of Protestant principles.

I first showed the stop it received through the destructions of the rapacious Henry, and the utter loss of those feelings, by which it had been carried on so successfully, for many centuries.

I then exhibited how avarice and fanaticism, both produced by the new opinions, had instigated the plunder and destruction of all those splendid ornaments which, under the fostering care of the ancient faith, enriched and embellished every sacred pile.

Further, I have shown to what base and sordid motives we are indebted for the preservation of what is now left; and, lastly, I have shown that, in order to render the churches available for the new system, many of their grandest features were destroyed, and their ancient and appropriate arrangement violated.

There is one more result which I have not yet described, but it is one of the most dreadful, the most disastrous, and one which effectually prevents the possibility of achieving great ecclesiastical works : it is the entire loss of religious unity among the people. When the Common Prayer and Articles had been set forth, heavy fines were imposed, and even death was inflicted, on those who did not receive them as the only rule of faith or form of religious worship;* and by such means as these, men had been driven for a short time into an outward show of uniformity. But where was the inward unity of soul—where that faith that had anciently bound men together? Alas! that was utterly fled. Where were the spontaneous offerings, the heartfelt tribute, the liberal endowments, by which the ancient Church had been supported, and the glorious works achieved? The scene was entirely changed, and not only had these feelings ceased, but the commonest and most necessary repairs of those very buildings, which had been raised in splendour by the voluntary offerings of the people, were only effected by rates, wrung by fear of law from the unwilling parishioners, two-thirds of whom, from different motives, equally detested the form that had been forced upon them, and

* See Appendix, M.

F

which they were compelled to support.   No longer were village priests looked on as pastors of the people, or those high in ecclesiastical authority with veneration and respect; the former were considered only as a sort of collectors, placed to receive dues they were compelled to pay, while the latter were eyed with jealousy by the avaricious nobles,* and looked on by the majority of the people as a useless class of state officers. The increase of these feelings within one century of its first establishment caused the overthrow of the new religion, and the entire suspension of its rites, during the rule of the usurper, Cromwell, a period of English history too well known to need dilating on; and which same feelings attended its revival with the restoration of the Stuarts, and even at this present day are openly manifested by a vast body of the people.

It is right to remark, that a great part of the dreadful devastation described in this chapter, was caused by the rapacity of the government or temporal power into whose hands the perfidious Cranmer and his apostate associates had betrayed the clergy of the Church of England, who were compelled in a great measure to be passive spectators of their own ruin.   Even those who framed the new liturgy had no intention of any very wide departure from ancient Catholic practices; but having been once drawn into the vortex of innovation, they were forced on by the Calvinistic faction, who profiting by the confusion, stript the defenceless Church of its solemn rites, the better to plunder its revenues.   Many holy and venerable customs were weakly surrendered, in the vain hope of inducing these pestilent heretics to conform, but, as might have been expected, with miserable success; for at this very day the dissenters clamour as loudly in opposition to the poor shadow of ancient discipline that has been preserved, as they did against the solemnities of the Church in all her ancient glory.

* See Appendix, N.

CHAPTER V.

𝕿𝔥𝔢 𝔰𝔭𝔬𝔱 𝔱𝔥𝔞𝔱 𝔞𝔫𝔤𝔢𝔩𝔰 𝔡𝔢𝔦𝔤𝔫𝔢𝔡 𝔱𝔬 𝔤𝔯𝔞𝔠𝔢,
𝕴𝔰 𝔟𝔩𝔢𝔰𝔰𝔢𝔡 𝔱𝔥𝔬𝔲𝔤𝔥 𝔯𝔬𝔟𝔟𝔢𝔯𝔰 𝔥𝔞𝔲𝔫𝔱 𝔱𝔥𝔢 𝔭𝔩𝔞𝔠𝔢.

I WILL now proceed to examine the present state of ancient Ecclesiastical buildings, after three centuries of mingled devastation, neglect, and vile repair, have passed over them.

In the first place, I will commence with the cathedrals, the most splendid monuments of past days which remain, and, therefore, the most deserving of first consideration.

No person thoroughly acquainted with ecclesiastical antiquities, and who has travelled over this country for the purpose of attentively examining those wonderful edifices, which, though shorn of more than half their beauties, still proudly stand pre-eminent over all other structures that the puny hand of modern times has raised beside them, but must have felt the emotions of astonishment and admiration, that their first view has raised within him, rapidly give place to regret and disgust at the vast portion of them that has been wantonly defaced, and for the miserable unfitness of the present tenants for the vast and noble edifices they occupy.

When these gigantic churches were erected, each portion of them was destined for a particular use, to which their arrangement and decoration perfectly corresponded. Thus the choir was appropriated solely to the ecclesiastics, who each filled their respective stalls; the nave was calculated for the immense congregation of the people, who, without reference to rank or wealth, were promiscuously mixed in the public worship of God; while the aisles afforded ample space for the solemn processions of the clergy.

The various chapels, each with its altar, were served by different priests, who at successive hours of the morning, commencing at six, said masses, that all classes and occupations might be enabled to devote some portion of the day to religious duties. The cloisters formed a quiet and sheltered deambulatory for the meditation of the ecclesiastics; and the chapter-house was a noble chamber, where they frequently met and settled on spiritual and temporal affairs relating to their office.

These churches were closed only for a few hours during the night, in order that they might form the place from whence private prayers and supplications might continually be offered up. But of what use are these churches now? do their doors stand ever open to admit the devout? No; excepting the brief space of time set apart twice a-day to keep up the form of worship, the gates are fast closed, nor is it possible to obtain admittance within the edifice without a fee to the guardian of the keys. Ask the reason of this, and the answer will be, that if the churches were left open they would be completely defaced, and even become the scene of the grossest pollutions. If this be true, which I fear it is, what, I ask, must be the moral and religious state of a country, where the churches are obliged to be fastened up to prevent their being desecrated and destroyed by the people? how must the ancient devotion and piety have departed? Indeed, so utterly are all feelings of private devotion lost in these churches, that were an individual to kneel in any other time than that actually set apart for Divine service, or in any other part of the edifice but that which is inclosed, he would be considered as a person not sound in his intellects, and probably be ordered out of the building. No; cathedrals are visited from far different motives, by the different classes of persons who go to them. The first are those who, being connected with or living near a cathedral, attend regularly every Sunday by rote; the second are those who, not having any taste for prayers, but who have some ear for music, drop in, as it is termed, to hear the anthem; the third class are persons who go to see the church. They are tourists; they go to see everything that is to be seen; therefore they see the church,—*id est*, they walk round, read the epitaphs, think it very pretty, very romantic, very old, suppose it was built in superstitious times, pace the length of the nave, write their names on a pillar, and whisk out, as they have a great deal more to see and very little time.

The fourth class are those who, during assize and fair times, go to see the big church built by the old Romans, after they have been to see all the other sights and shows. They are generally a good many together, to make it worth the verger's while to send a satellite round with them to show the wonderful things, and tell them wonderful stories about the monks and nuns; and after they have gaped round they go out, and the sight serves for talk till they see some fun they like a good deal better.

Such are most of the classes of visitors to these wondrous fabrics, not one of whom feels in the slightest degree the sanctity of the place or the majesty of the design, and small indeed is the number of those on whom these mutilated but still admirable designs produce their whole and great effect. Few are there who, amid the general change and destruction they have undergone, can conjure up in their minds the glories of their departed greatness, and who, while they bitterly despise the heartless throng that gaze about the sacred aisles, mourn for the remembrance of those ages of faith now passed and gone, which produced minds to conceive and zeal to execute such mighty, glorious works. 'Tis such minds as these that feel acutely the barren, meagre, and inappropriate use to which these edifices have been put; and to them does the neat and modern churchman appear truly despicable, as he trips from the door to the vestry, goes through the prayers, then returns from the vestry to the door, forming the greatest contrast of all with the noble works which surround him. What part has he, I say, what connexion of soul with the ecclesiastic of ancient days? Do we see him, when the public service is concluded, kneeling in silent devotion in the quiet retreat of some chapel? Do we see him perambulating in study and contemplation those vaulted cloisters, which were erected solely for the meditation of ecclesiastical persons? No; he only enters the church when his duty compels him; he quits it the instant he is able; he regards the fabric but as the source of his income; he lives by religion—'tis his trade. And yet these men of cold and callous hearts, insensible to every spark of ancient zeal and devotion, will dare to speak with contempt and ridicule of those glorious spirits by whose mighty minds and liberal hearts those establishments have been founded, and from whose pious munificence they derive every shilling they possess.

Have they not common decent gratitude? No; daily do they put forth revilings, gross falsehoods, and libels, on that religion and faith which instigated the foundation and endowments which they enjoy, and under whose incitement alone could the fabrics have been raised which they pretend to admire, while they condemn and ridicule the cause which produced them.

Can we hope for any good results while such men as these use, or rather possess, these glorious piles? men who either leave the churches to perish through neglect, or when they conceive they have a little taste, and do lay out some money, commit far greater havoc than even time itself, by the unfitness and absurdity of their alterations. Of this description those made by Bishop Barrington at Salisbury, and conducted by James Wyatt, of execrable memory, deserve the severest censure. During this improvement, as it was termed, the venerable bell-tower, a grand and imposing structure, which stood on the north-west side of the church, was demolished, and the bells and materials sold; the Hungerford and Beauchamp chapels pulled down, and the tombs set up in the most mutilated manner between the pillars of the nave; and a host of other barbarities and alterations too numerous to recite.

Nor less detestable was the removal of the ancient tracery and glass from the great eastern and aisle windows of St. George's Chapel, Windsor, and substituting copies of that tame and wooden painter, West;—designs which would be a disgrace in any situation, and, when thus substituted for the masterly arrangement of the ancient architect, become even more contemptible. In fine, wherever we go, we find that, whether the buildings have been treated with neglect, or attempted to be improved, both results are disastrous in the extreme.

The fact cannot for one moment be denied, that these edifices are totally unsuited for the present practices of the Establishment, quite deficient in what is now so much studied—comfort; and since the choir has been applied to the purpose of a parish church, totally wanting in actual sitting room, to gain which the ancient features are being rapidly swept away. What can be so disgusting as to enter the choir of a cathedral church, and to find the stalls nominally appropriated to the dignitaries of the Church, occupied by all classes of lay persons? and not unfrequently the bishop's throne, the cathedra itself, tenanted, during the absence of the bishop, by some consequential dame? Nay, so entirely is propriety of arrangement or decorum lost in these churches, that were it not for the presence of a few singing men and boys, and the head of a solitary residentiary peeping above his cushion, one would conclude the assembled group to be a congregation of independents, who had occupied the choir for a temporary preaching place. Then the concluding rush out, when singing men, choristers, vicars, and people, make a simultaneous movement to gain the choir-door, produces a scene of the most disgraceful confusion. All this has arisen from the alteration of the ancient arrangement of appropriating the choir solely to ecclesiastics; but this was abandoned by the new churchmen on the consideration that they could never muster a decent show, and so they let the people in to hide the deficiency of their absence.

This led to pewing choirs, one of the vilest mutilations of effect the cathedrals have ever suffered; for to what do all the alterations that have lately been effected in Peterborough and Norwich cathedrals tend, but utterly to destroy the appearance of a choir, filling up the centre with pews and seats, and contracting the grandeur of the open space into a paltry aisle leading to boxes.

It is in vain to cover the fronts of these seats with tracery and panelling; the principle of the thing is bad, and all that is done only renders the defect more glaring.

This picture of the modern state of cathedrals is forcible, but it is not overdrawn; any one may be satisfied of its truth by inspecting the edifices themselves, and the manner in which the services are conducted.

Go to that wonderful church at Ely, and see the result of neglect: the water, pouring through unclosed apertures in the covering, conveying ruin into the heart of the fabric; the opening fissures of the great western tower, which, unheeded and unobserved, are rapidly extending. Then look at what was once the chapter-house, but now filled with pews and vile fittings, brought from the parish church which the chapter refused to repair.*   See how the matchless canopies have been pared down and whitewashed.   Look on the decay of the whole church, and then re-member Ely is yet rich in its revenues.   What must be the hearts of those men forming the chapter?   And yet they are but a fair type of many of the others: I only cite them in particular, because Ely is one of the most interesting churches in existence, and it is decidedly in a vile state of repair.

The same observations will apply to most of the other great churches. Why, Westminster Abbey itself, by far the finest edifice in the metro-polis (if cleared of its incongruous and detestable monuments), is in a lamentable state of neglect, and is continually being disfigured by the erection of more vile masses of marble.   Having occasion lately to examine the interior of this wonderful church, I was disgusted beyond measure at perceiving that the chapel of St. Paul had been half filled up with a huge figure of James Watt, sitting in an arm-chair on an enormous square pedestal, with some tasteless ornaments, which, being totally unlike any Greek or Roman foliage, I suppose to have been intended by the sculptor to be Gothic.   This is the production of no less a personage than Sir F. Chantrey.   Surely this figure must have been originally intended for the centre of some great terrace-garden; it never could have been designed for the interior of the abbey: for so offensive is it in its present position, that if Sir Francis did really so design it, he deserves to be crushed under its great pedestal, to prevent him again committing so great an outrage on good taste.

But is this noble edifice for ever to be blocked up and mutilated by the continual erection of these most inappropriate and tasteless monu-ments?   Have not the dean and chapter sufficient authority to prevent their erection?   But what can we expect or hope for from them, when they suffer filthy dolls to be exhibited within the sacred walls, to render the show-place more attractive to the holiday visitors?   Oh, spirits of the departed abbots, could you behold this!   The mighty buildings you have raised, the tombs of the great men that lie within them—all is not attractive enough for the mob; a set of puppets are

* See Appendix, O.

added, the show draws, and the chapter collects the cash. Oh, vile desecration ! Yet this takes place in the largest church of the metropolis, the mausoleum of our kings ; a place rendered of the highest interest by the art of its construction, and the historical recollections attached to it.

Can we, then, wonder at what I before asserted,—and, I trust, have since proved,—that cathedral churches are become but show-places for the people, and considered only as sources of revenue by ecclesiastics ?

The neglected state of this once glorious church is a national disgrace. While tens of thousands are annually voted for comparatively trifling purposes, and hundreds of thousands have been very lately expended in mere architectural deformity, not even a small grant to keep the se- pulchral monuments of our ancient kings in repair, has ever been pro- posed ; and it is quite surprising to see the utter apathy that exists amongst those who, both by their birth and station, might be looked upon as the legitimate conservators of our national antiquities. Where can we find another spot, I will not say in England, but *in Europe,* which contains so many splendid monuments of ancient art—doubly interesting from the historical associations connected with them ? If we stand immediately behind the high altar screen, of exquisite tabernacle work and curious imagery,we have presented at one view the tombs of Edward I, invader of Scotland ; Henry III, rebuilder of the vast abbey itself ; the faithful and amiable Queen Eleanor ; Henry V, the conqueror of France ; Edward III and his queen Philippa ; King Richard II ; and last, but not least, the shrine of St. Edward, which, although despoiled of its rich and sumptuous ornaments, still contains the more precious deposit of the relics of that holy confessor, whose virtues have even survived the calumnies of the so-called Reformation, and still are held up to the imi- tation of our monarchs at the solemnity of their coronation.

Through the arched chantry of Henry V, are seen the massive brazen gates and grand entrance to the monumental chapel of the seventh Henry—a matchless example of the latter style. Beyond the tombs I have been describing, extend the aisles and lateral chapels, filled with monumental effigies of ecclesiastical and noble personages, all celebrated in English chronicles, and of surpassing beauty of execution ; and these

G

are contained at the *extreme end* of a church of immense length, and
whose groined canopy reaches more than one hundred feet from the tes-
selated pavement—a church whose history is interwoven with that of the
country itself, and should be inconceivably dear to us from its religious,
ancient, and national associations. It is not necessary for a man to be an
architect, an antiquary, an artist, to understand the vast claims which the
abbey of St. Peter's, Westminster, has upon his respect and veneration.
If he possess but one spark of that love of country and pride of nation
that ought to be found in every man's breast, he would view with religious
respect every stone of this noble structure; but it is soul-sickening to
sit day by day, as I have done, and see the class of people who come to
inspect this church, and the feelings with which they perambulate its
sacred aisles—a mere flock of holiday people who come to London to see
sights, and take the Abbey on their way to the Surrey Zoological
Gardens. It might naturally have been expected that, from its vicinity
to the Houses of Parliament, the Catholic members would occasionally enter its sacred walls, and try to imbibe some of the devotional
spirit of ancient days, which its venerable architecture and sepulchral memorials could hardly fail to impart, and which should be no
small consolation and relief to a Catholic mind, compelled to sit during
the noisy debates of political warfare. But I much question if these
gentlemen have ever penetrated westward of Henry the Seventh's Chapel.
The apathy of royalty towards this sacred fabric is truly melancholy; we
hear much of the interest certain distinguished personages take in the
performances of a learned monkey, or equestrian evolutions, but small
regard indeed do they pay to the resting-place of their ancestors.   Even
should they refuse to contribute a small sum out of the thousands which
they annually squander on trifles, towards so pious and worthy an object
as the restoration of the national monuments, a visit to the neglected and
desecrated pile of Westminster might teach them the instructive lesson
that royalty departed is easily forgotten; and if the memory of those
great kings of England, who, by their own personal valour and energy,
achieved the most important victories, and were foremost in camp and
council, is not sufficient to procure decent respect to their place of

sepulture, into what extreme oblivion and neglect must those sovereigns fall after their death, whose lives are a mere routine of fashionable luxury, their greatest achievement a pony drive, their principal occupation—to dine!

I am willing, however, to allow that there has been a vast improvement of late years in the partial restorations which have been effected in certain cathedral and other churches, as regards the accuracy of moulding and detail. The mechanical part of Gothic architecture is pretty well understood, but it is the principles which influenced ancient compositions, and the soul which appears in all the former works, which is so lamentably deficient; nor, as I have before stated, can they be regained but by a restoration of the ancient feelings and sentiments. 'Tis they alone that can restore pointed architecture to its former glorious state; without it all that is done will be a tame and heartless copy, true as far as the mechanism of the style goes, but utterly wanting in that sentiment and feeling that distinguishes ancient design.

It is for this reason that the modern alterations in the choirs of Peterborough and Norwich, above alluded to, have so bad an effect; the details individually are accurate and well worked, but the principle of the design is so contrary to the ancient arrangement, that I do not hesitate to say the effect is little short of detestable.

The same thing may be remarked at Canterbury, where I am happy to make honourable mention of the restorations. A great deal of money has been expended, and, I may add, judiciously; indeed, the rebuilding of the north-western tower is an undertaking quite worthy of ancient and better days.

In these works, as far as recutting mouldings, pateras, bosses, &c., and the repainting and gilding, nothing can be better executed; but when we come to see the new altar-screen, as it is termed, we are astonished that amid so much art as this vast church contains, some better idea had not suggested itself. It is meagre and poor in the extreme, and not one particle of ancient sentiment about it—it is a bare succession of panels; but this is the result of modern feelings. When this church was used for the ancient worship, the high altar was the great point of attraction: it was for the sacrifice continually there offered, that the church itself was raised; neither gold, jewels, nor silver, were spared in its decoration; on it the ancient artists, burning with zeal and devotion, expended their most glorious compositions and skill. The mass was gorgeous and imposing; each detail, exquisite and appropriate. Such a design as this was not produced by multiplying a panel till it reached across the choir, nor was it composed to back a common table. No; the artist felt the glory of the work he was called on to compose; it was no less than erecting an altar for the performance of the most solemn rites of the Church, and it was the glorious nature of the subject that filled his mind with excellence, and produced the splendid result. From such feelings as these all the ancient compositions emanated; and I repeat, that without them pointed architecture can never rise beyond the bare copy of the mechanical portions of the art.

There is no sympathy between these vast edifices and the Protestant worship. So conscious of it were the first propagators of the new doctrines, that they aimed all their malice and invectives against them. The new religion may suit the conventicle and the meeting-house, but it has no part in the glories of ancient days; the modern Anglican Establishment is the only one, among the many systems that sprung up, which retained the principle of cathedral establishments and episcopal jurisdiction: and so badly put together were these remains of ancient Church government with modern opinions and temporal jurisdiction, that they have ever proved the subject of popular clamour, and might be suppressed at any time by a legislative act.

Then what a prospect to look to! What new ordeal, what new destruction would these ill-fated fabrics undergo? The mind shudders at the thought. Would they be walled up as in Scotland, and divided into the preaching houses for the dissenters, the Unitarians, and the freethinkers? Would they be made into factories or storehouses, like the churches of France during the fatal revolution of 1790? or ruined, roofless, neglected, be left to decay like the many glorious fabrics that perished at the change of religion, of which only a few mouldering arches remain to indicate the site? One of these results would in all probability be produced if the present Establishment ceased to exist. One ray of hope alone darts through the dismal prospect; that, ere the fatal hour arrives, so many devout and thinking men may have returned to Catholic unity, that hearts and hands may be found willing and able to protect these glorious piles from further profanation, and, in the real spirit of former years, restore them to their original glory and worship.

If we turn from the cathedrals themselves, to examine the ecclesiastical buildings with which they are surrounded, we shall find the changes and destructions they have undergone, to suit the caprice and ideas of each new occupant, are so great, that it is with considerable difficulty anything like the original design can be traced.

All the ancient characteristic features have been totally changed, for after the clergy had left off ecclesiastical discipline for ease and comfort; exchanged old hospitality for formal visiting; and, indeed, become laymen in every other respect but in that of their income and title, they found the old buildings but ill suited to their altered style of living; what had served for the studious, retired priest, or the hospitable and munificent prelate of ancient days, was very unfit for a married, visiting, gay clergyman, or a modern bishop, whose lady must conform to the usages and movements of fashionable life.

Hence bishops' palaces have either been pulled down, and rebuilt on a mean and reduced scale, or their grandest features left to decay as useless portions of the building, and the inhabited part repaired in the worst possible taste. Nor have the rectories and canonries escaped even worse treatment: many of the old buildings have been entirely demolished, and some ugly square mass set up instead; and all have been miserably mutilated: the private chapel everywhere demolished, or applied to some menial purpose;* the old oak ceilings plastered up; the panelling removed, or papered over; mullioned windows cut out, and common sashes fixed in their stead; great plain brick buildings added, to get some large rooms for parties; a veranda, and perhaps a conservatory. And by such means as these the canonries are rendered habitable for the three months' residence.

* See Appendix, P.

Then, if we examine the buildings that were anciently erected for the residence of the vicars attached to cathedrals, as at Wells, what a lamentable change have they undergone! When these buildings were constructed, the vicars were a venerable body of priests, living in a collegiate manner within their close; each one had a lodging, or set of two chambers; a common hall where they assembled at meals, and a chapel (over which was a library stored with theological and historical learning), stood at opposite ends of the close. All these buildings were of the most beautiful description, and received great additions from the munificent Bishop Beckington; and so excellent is the arrangement of every part of this close, and its connexion with the cathedral by a cloister passing over a sumptuous gatehouse, and leading to the chapter-house stair, is so admirably managed, that, notwithstanding the vile repairs and mutilations it has suffered, and its present degraded condition, it is still one of the most interesting specimens of ecclesiastical buildings attached to cathedrals, and will give an excellent idea of the venerable character the residences of ecclesiastics formerly presented, and the unison of their appearance with that of the structures to which they formed the appendages.

But no sooner was the blasting influence of the new opinions felt, than this abode of piety and learning experienced a fatal change. The vicars were reduced to less than a third of their original number, and their lands so pillaged, that this ecclesiastical function was given to laymen, whose only qualification was a trifling skill in vocal music,—that the poor pittance they had left, although quite insufficient for the support of persons devoted to the duties of their office, might still induce the needy shopkeeper to leave his counter twice in the day, and hurry over the service, to return again to his half-served customers.

When the buildings, raised by the munificence of Roger de Salopia and Thomas de Beckington, fell into the hands of such men as these, the result may easily be imagined.

Gradually they sunk into neglect and decay; the dwellings were rented to various tenants, who altered and changed them to their pleasure;*

* Within four years *a baker's shop-front has been inserted in the end gable, adjoining the close gate,* by the *senior vicar;* who unites that useful but incompatible occupation with his choral duties.

and the great hall was used only when some newly-arrived mountebank required a large room to exhibit his feats of dexterity, when it was let out for the occasion, or to serve the even meaner purpose of a dancing academy.

The library was of little use to such men as these, who never required any other book but that of their shop-accounts; and who, if they ever handled an ancient author, it was only to convert the pages into wrappers for their parcels.

We cannot, therefore, feel surprised that a few odd leaves of manuscripts, and some imperfect and musty volumes of books, thrown into a corner of the muniment room, are all that remain of a collection, which the learning of its founders leaves us no hesitation in supposing to have been as useful as interesting and curious.

To such a degraded state are these lay vicars, as they are termed, fallen, that even the keeper of a public tavern is found among their number. Thus, this man, fresh from the fumes of the punch-bowl and tobacco-pipe, and with the boisterous calls of the tap ringing in his ears, may be seen running from the bar to the choir, there figuring away in a surplice, till the concluding prayer allows him to rush back, and mingle the response of " Coming, sir," to the amen that has hardly died away upon his lips.

How can we wonder at the contempt into which the Establishment has fallen, when such disgraceful scenes as these have arisen from its system? Where, I ask, are the often-boasted blessings which the mis-named Reformation has brought? where the splendid results so often asserted? Facts speak for themselves; and, I trust, I have brought forward a sufficient number to show how dreadfully all classes of ecclesiastical buildings and persons have been ruined and degraded by the introduction of the present system.

If the limits of this work permitted, I could fully show how baneful and disastrous to art were the effects produced by the Protestants in those foreign countries where they were, at one time, partially established; and even in France, where their ascendancy only lasted the brief space of a year, they committed such havoc, that the principal treasures of the churches, and most of the finest specimens of art, were plundered and demolished.*

Indeed, whether we regard the fanatic Knox in Scotland, the Huguenots of France, the concocters of the English Establishment, or the puritanic faction of Cromwell, we find that, divided as they were on points of their schismatical opinions, they were united, heart and hand, in robbery and destruction.† To them sanctity or art were alike indifferent; thirst of gold and wanton love of destroying all which exceeded their narrow comprehensions, mingled with the most savage fanaticism, led them to commit crimes and disorders harrowing to the soul, both on the score of common humanity and the love of noble art.‡

That these feelings have partially subsided, is purely owing to the lukewarm feelings with which religion is regarded by the majority in this country; since, only a few years back, the mere sight of a crucifix or a Madonna would have excited far greater horror, and caused more animadversion amongst the godly of the land, than the most obscene and filthy idol that the grossest superstition of paganism could produce;§ and I do not hesitate to say, that there are many, among the fanatical sects which come under the general denomination of dissenters, who would exult in the destruction not only of every noble religious edifice that remains, but glory in the extinction of all ecclesiastical authority whatever.

I cannot conclude this part of my subject without making a few observations on the present system of church and chapel building—a system so vile, so mercenary, and so derogatory to the reverence and honour that should be paid to Divine worship, that it is deserving of the severest censure; and I will say, that among the most grievous sins of the time, may be ranked those of trying for how small a sum religious edifices can be erected, and how great a per centage can be made, for money advanced for their erection, by the rental of pews. It is a trafficking in sacred things, that vastly resembles that profanation of the temple which drew such indignation from our Divine Redeemer, that, contrary to the mild

* See Appendix, Q.   † See Appendix, R.   ‡ See Appendix, S.
§ See Appendix, T.

forbearance he had ever before shown, he cast forth the polluters of the holy place with scourges and stripes.

Yes; the erection of churches, like all that was produced by zeal or art in ancient days, has dwindled down into a mere trade. No longer is the sanctity of the undertaking considered, or is the noblest composition of the architect, or the most curious skill of the artificer, to be employed in its erection; but the minimum it can be done for is calculated from allowing a trifling sum to the room occupied for each sitting; and the outline of the building, and each window, moulding, and ornament, must be made to correspond with this miserable pittance.

Of the feelings with which the old churchmen undertook the erection of their churches we can easily be acquainted, by referring to the solemn office of the dedication :—Domus quam aedificari volo Domino, talis esse debet, ut in cunctis regionibus nominetur; praeparabo, ergo, ei necessaria.

Magnus est Deus noster super omnes deos; quis, ergo, poterit praevalere ut aedificet dignam Deo domum. Domine Deus noster, omnis haec copia, quam parabimus ut aedificaretur domus nomini sancto tuo, de manu tua est. Quis prior Domino dedit, et retribuetur ei?

The Church commissioners' instructions are the very reverse of these noble sentiments. They require a structure as plain as possible, which can be built for a trifling sum, and of small dimensions, both for economy and facilities of hearing the preacher, the sermon being the only part of the service considered; and I hesitate not to say, that a more meagre, miserable display of architectural skill never was made, nor more improprieties and absurdities committed,* than in the mass of paltry churches erected under the auspices of the commissioners, and which are to be found scattered over every modern portion of the metropolis and its neighbourhood—a disgrace to the age, both on the score of their composition, and the miserable sums that have been allotted for their construction.

No kind of propriety or fitness has been considered in their composition. Some have porticoes of Greek temples, surmounted by steeples of miserable outline and worse detail. Others are a mixture of distorted Greek and Roman buildings; and a host have been built in perfectly nondescript styles, forming the most offensive masses of building. In

* See Appendix, U.

H

some cases, the architect has endeavoured to give the shell the appearance of an ancient pointed church, and, by dint of disguising all the internal arrangements, something like an old exterior has been obtained; but when the interior is seen the whole illusion vanishes, and we discover that what had somewhat the appearance of an old Catholic church, is, in reality, nothing but a modern preaching-house, with all its galleries, pews, and other fittings. In fine, so impossible is it to make a grand design suitable to the meagreness of the present worship, that to produce any effect at all, the churches are designed to represent any thing but what they really are; and hence, all the host of absurdities and incongruities, in form and decoration, which abound in modern places built for religious worship.

With respect to the style of that class of chapels built on speculation, it is below criticism. They are erected by men who ponder between a mortgage, a railroad, or a chapel, as the best investment of their money, and who, when they have resolved on relying on the persuasive eloquence of a cushion-thumping, popular preacher, erect four walls, with apertures for windows, cram the same full of seats, which they readily let; and so greedy after pelf are these chapel-raisers, that they form dry and spacious vaults underneath, which are soon occupied, at a good rent, by some wine and brandy merchant.

Of the horrible impiety of trading in religious edifices I have spoken more fully above; and I repeat, that no offence can sooner move the indignation of the Almighty, or provoke his vengeance, than such a prostitution of the name of religion to serve the private interests of individuals.

In conclusion, although I would not, for one instant, deny that prayers, offered from the humblest edifice that can be raised, would prove as available and acceptable as if proceeding from the most sumptuous fabric, if the means of the people could produce no better. Yet, when luxury is everywhere on the increase, and means and money more plentiful than ever, to see the paltry buildings erected everywhere for religious worship, and the neglected state of the ancient churches, it argues a total want of religious zeal, and a tepidity towards the glory of Divine worship, as disgraceful to the nation, as it must be offensive to the Almighty.

CONCLUSION.

REFLECTIONS ON THE PROBABLE STATE OF THE ENGLISH CHURCHES, HAD
THIS COUNTRY REMAINED IN COMMUNION WITH THE CATHOLIC CHURCH.

HAVING now shown the disastrous effects of the Protestant or destructive principle, on Catholic art and architecture in England, it may not be un-instructive to take into consideration the probable results which would have befallen the ancient churches, had Protestantism never been established in this country. Judging from what has occurred during the last three centuries on the Continent, it would be presuming far too much to suppose that England alone would have escaped the pestilential influence of Pagan ideas and taste which was spreading over Europe at the period of England's schism, and of which even some indications were perceptible* in the latter pointed erections; and there is but too great reason to believe that had the destructive spirit been suppressed, the restorative or classic rage would have been almost as fatal to Catholic art. As it is, everything glorious about the English churches is Catholic, everything debased and hideous, Protestant. This is certainly a melancholy superiority to the foreign churches, which present, in their solemn constructions, and paltry and incongruous fittings, a most lamentable contrast between the ancient spirit and modern practices of Catholicism, setting forth at one view the summit of excellence, and the lowest depth of degradation. A fine old Catholic church used for Protestant service,

---

* In Wolsey's palace of Hampton Court, the heads in terra-cotta on the turrets of the inner gatehouse, represent four of the Cæsars. Bishop Gardener's tomb at Winchester exhibits a variety of debased or Italian features and details.

In the Countess of Salisbury's chantry in the Priory church of Christ's Church, Hampshire, are several details in what is termed the *renaissance* style. Many instances might be cited to prove that germs of the revived pagan style existed in England previous to the separation of the English Church from Catholic communion.

H 2

is indeed a melancholy sight, but scarcely less melancholy is it to see modern Catholics with their own hands polluting and disfiguring, by pagan emblems and theatrical trumpery, the glorious structures raised by their ancestors in the faith.*   The consideration of modern

* What, indeed, can be more agonizing to a faithful Catholic, than to behold the clergy themselves (the legitimate guardians of these ancient fabrics, the successors of those holy and learned ecclesiastics who were at once the architects and ministers of the temple), filled with the most anti-Christian ideas of art, and united in the destruction of the venerable remains of Catholic dignity, to introduce the bastard pagan style, the very date of which is coeval with the decay of faith, and decline of their influence? Many churches in France have escaped the ravages of the Huguenots and Calvinists,—many the tremendous revolutions of 1790; but not one has been preserved from the innovating and paltry taste of the modern clergy. Were they to confine the display of their wretched ideas to mere fittings which could easily be removed, the case would not be so distressing, but the fabrics themselves are frequently mutilated past restoration, by these wholesale destructives. The Count de Montalembert gives a harrowing description of these barbarities, the truth of many of which I have confirmed by actual observation. Hundreds of stained windows have been either sold out, or destroyed, to be replaced by white panes; the most curious frescoes and rich painted ceilings have been mercilessly covered by thick coats of white and yellow wash, the usual modern decorations of ecclesiastical buildings. Every vestige of internal sculpture or ancient art has been destroyed, to be replaced by the odious productions of modern manufacturers—" d'objets d'églises," while the new altars present every possible combination of outrageous architecture and paltry ornament, and these are not unfrequently placed in such a position as to conceal the most interesting portions of the original buildings. It is quite impossible to enter a French church without being thoroughly disgusted with the extreme contempt of antiquity and degraded taste which their fittings and ornaments display. The result of this is truly lamentable; for few men are sufficiently instructed in these matters, to discriminate between really Catholic productions, and the wretched externals of modern paganism, which disguise the solemnities of the Church, or to draw the vast distinction between the ancient solemn celebration of the Eucharistic Sacrifice, and the theatrical trumpery of a modern fête. Many devout and well-intentioned persons, who are conscious of the insufficiency of the Protestant system, and are favourably disposed towards Catholic truth, go abroad full of expectation, and return utterly disheartened by what they have beheld, and which they attribute to the effect of Catholicism, instead of being the result of the opposite principle. Could they but have seen one of these very churches, now so disfigured, as it appeared in all its venerable grandeur during the ages of faith, how different would have been the result produced on their mind; but while the present childish and tinsel ornaments are mixed up with the most sacred rites, and bedizened dolls exhibited as representations of our blessed Lady, it is impossible for a mere observer to receive any but unfavourable impressions from the externals of religion; and to this cause may we principally attribute the very small number of conversions among the numerous travellers who annually visit Catholic countries.—See Appendix No. 3.

degeneracy tends to alleviate the sorrow we feel at Protestant ravages. Far better is it to see the great abbeys of England, ruined and roofless as they are, than to behold them degraded into mere means of revenue, and held *in commendam* by some tonsured child, or converted into a luxurious abode for a few nominal monks. Our English monasteries were cut off in their glory, in the midst of boundless hospitality and regular observance.* We can trace no sign of pagan novelties about their venerable ruins—all these breathe of faith, of charity, of contemplation, of austerity and prayer; and we can visit these solemn remains of ancient piety with unalloyed reverence and regret, but not so the abbatial remains of France, where the pointed arch and Christian sculpture of the St. Louis is mingled with the fantastic compositions of Francis the First, and the ultra-paganism of the "grand monarque." After the fatal Concordat, many of these once-famous houses lingered on till their final suppression in 1790. Large masses of hideous modern Italian buildings†

---

* In the very act by which the lesser monasteries were suppressed, the great houses were declared to be without blame.

It is truly edifying to see how exactly the rule was observed in Durham Abbey, one of the richest houses in England up to the time of its suppression. The vast wealth and possessions of the monks were entirely employed in charity, hospitality, and the advancement of learning and art, while they lived in a truly monastic state, sleeping in a common dormitory, rising at midnight to matins, remaining content with one fire in winter-time, and passing their whole time in devotion and study. I have printed some interesting extracts from a scarce book called *The Antiquities of Durham*, in the Appendix, which will fully illustrate these facts.—See Appendix No. 4.

† At the abbey of St. Ouen, Rouen, a sort of palace, now the Hôtel de Ville, was erected for the residence of the few monks, which resided in that famous house during the seventeenth century, who having abandoned all regular observances of the cloister, resided in separate suites of spacious apartments; and while they expended an immense sum for their own personal luxury, suffered the western end of their unrivalled church to remain in the unfinished state in which it was left before the Concordat, and which the amount they squandered away in this irregular lodging, would have amply sufficed to complete. The contrast between the abbatial church of St. Denis, near Paris, and the conventual buildings erected during the reign of Louis XIV, is painfully striking. The former is a noble specimen of monastic architecture, raised under the auspices of the illustrious Suger; the latter, a mere classic sort of barrack, undistinguishable by its architecture and arrangement from the hôtels of that period.

Even the venerable abbey of Jumièges was disfigured by similar erections, which are to be found in almost all the abbatial buildings of France. At St. Wandrille, an abbey near Candebec, on the Seine, whose foundations date of the highest Christian antiquity of Normandy, filled with vast apartments of pagan design, had either been added to, *or even replaced* the conventual refectory and dormitory ; and not unfrequently these degenerate monks had transformed their ancient and solemn church, as far as possible, into a semi-pagan or Italian building, by encasing the pillars with pilasters, inserting semies under the pointed arches, and disguising the original features by festoons, clouds, and similar monstrosities.

So fatal, indeed, has this rage for pagan novelties proved to Christian art, that after all the demolitions and destruction they have escaped, the old English churches have retained more of their original features, than most of those on the Continent.   They have had all *the advantages of neglect*, and to Protestant apathy we are not a little indebted,—for both of these are great preservatives of antiquity, when compared to either modern innovation or restoration.

Salisbury Cathedral suffered more under its pretended restoration by Bishop Barrington, than during the three preceding centuries, including the reigns of Henry VIII, Edward VI, and the rule of the usurper Cromwell.   It is not unfrequently remarked how glorious these ancient churches would appear if restored to Catholic worship ; and glorious indeed would they be could we but revive the old solemnity ; but, owing to the long persecution and other causes, to such a low ebb are the ancient ideas and feelings fallen, that I much question the probability of finding sufficient English Catholics in any one place who would understand the real use of one

the whole of the conventual buildings, with the exception of the cloisters, were reconstructed during the seventeenth century, in the worst style of French architecture ; and the ancient chapter-house, which contained the tombs of *several canonized abbots*, was demolished, to be replaced by a mere modern room, while the sacred remains of the illustrious and saintly dead were treated with almost Calvinistic irreverence, and scattered among the rubbish.   I have printed a full account of this proceeding in the Appendix, No. 5.

It is most interesting to observe the great similarity that exists between the proceedings of modern pagans and Protestants.   The Protestant canons of Durham only a few years since demolished the magnificent chapter-house of that abbey, and erected a common sitting-room, such as might be found in any ordinary inn, in its stead.   Both the chapter-houses of St. Wandrille and Durham were erected under the influence of the Catholic principle ; the former was demolished by degenerate monks acting under the revived pagan ideas ; the latter by degenerate canons instigated by Protestant principles.

of these vast piles, much better than their Protestant possessors ; and supposing they had them in their possession, it is not improbable that many
choir screens would be demolished, stalls removed, and after a host of other
barbarous innovations, as the people could not *see the high altar through
a pillar, or hear the preacher* at the extreme end of the nave, the buildings would be condemned as inconvenient and uncomfortable, and by no
means comparable to the new galleried assembly rooms used for Catholic
worship at the present day, and which have even been built, as if in
mockery, under the very walls of our venerable cathedrals.* Indeed a vast
change must take place in the minds of many modern Catholics, to render
them really worthy of these stupendous monuments of ancient piety,
and heaven forbid that they should ever be restored to *anything less
than their former glory ;* for who could wish to see the cathedrals, where
a St. Thomas or a St. Hugh celebrated the holy mysteries in ample chasuble and solemn chaunt, disgraced by buckram vestments of last Lyons
cut, a semi-pagan altar, and the theatrical quaverings of a Warwick-street
choir ? It is a most melancholy truth that there does not exist much
sympathy of idea between a great portion of the present Catholic body in
England and their glorious ancestors, and they have frequently abandoned
ancient traditions to follow the tide of innovations and paltry novelties.
Is there a worldly hollow expedient started by some half-fledged sect of
Protestants to collect cash,—it is often adopted. Does some hideous mass
of modern deformity rise under the name of a church,—it is not unfre-

---

* Hereford presents two striking examples of modern Catholic and Protestant degeneracy ;
the new church built close to the cathedral, is an attempt to adapt pagan architecture to
Christian purposes ; and although it has cost double the sum required for a Catholic parish
church, it is a miserable failure. The west end of the cathedral was rebuilt a few years
since by James Wyatt, of Salisbury-destroying notoriety, and at the same time a large room
was erected for concerts on the site of the west cloister, under the Protestant system,—both
vile burlesques of the pointed style. It is difficult to say which of these works exhibit the
greatest departure from true Catholic principles.

The new Catholic church at Bury St. Edmund's, is another semi-pagan abortion. Having
occasion lately to inspect the glorious remains of ancient art in that venerable town, I could
not avoid remarking, that, excepting the new hotel, it was the most uncatholic looking building
in the whole place.

quently preferred to an ancient and appropriate model. Nay, the holy mysteries themselves have been made a vehicle for raising temporary supplies, and their celebration has been placarded about walls as affording a musical treat to the lovers of harmony, who are admitted at so much per head. Now, although these things may pass muster in these days of charitable balls and steam excursions, Methodist Centenaries, Christian societies, York festivals, and the like, yet how do they accord with ancient Catholic practices ? and what an awful state of degeneracy do they attest among those who ought to be far in advance of all others in acting upon sound principle, and avoid even the semblance of modern expediency. . . Indeed, such is the total absence of solemnity in a great portion of modern Catholic buildings in England, that I do not hesitate to say, that a few crumbling walls and prostrate arches of a religious edifice raised during the days of faith, will convey a far stronger religious impression to the mind than the actual service of half the chapels in England.

Taking, therefore, these facts into consideration, as well as the prevailing rage for paganism during the last three centuries on the Continent, I do not think the architecture of our English churches would have fared much better under a Catholic hierarchy ; for, independent of the almost certain destruction of every screen in England, we might have had the lantern of Ely terminated by a miniature dome, and a Doric portico to front the nave of York.

But let no one imagine for a moment that the preservation of the choir screens and other ancient arrangements, was owing to any love or veneration for antiquity* on the part of the Protestant clergy. The difference

---

* The Protestant system of turning the cathedral choirs into pewed enclosures, has undoubtedly saved the rood screens at the entrance, and which have almost disappeared in the Continental churches, during the rage for innovation which prevailed during the last three centuries : and had not this miserable expedient of filling up the deserted stalls of the ecclesiastics been adopted, instead of the congregation being kept in their original place — the nave, it is most probable that the venerable images of saints and kings that still adorn the canopied and fretted screens of York and Canterbury, would long ere this have been demolished, *to throw the view of the church open,*—the reason assigned for the removal of screens by those modern churchmen who have destroyed this mystical separation between the people and the sacrifice that had existed for ages. The learned Father Thiers has written a most admirable

between them and their Catholic cotemporaries, is precisely this : they left many of the original features standing through indifference ; the latter removed them through a false idea of improvement. When Protestantism did anything *of itself*, it was ten times worse than their extravagances, since it embodied the same wretched pagan ideas, without either the scale or richness of the foreign architecture of the same period. Queen's College, Oxford ; the new quadrangle of Christ's Church ; Radcliffe Library ; St. Paul's Cathedral, London, and many other buildings of the same class, are utter departures from Catholic architecture, and meagre imitations of Italian paganism. It is most fortunate for English architecture, that during the greatest rage for classic art, the desire for church building was nearly extinct, in consequence of Protestant ascendancy. Hence many of our finest monuments remained comparatively safe in their neglect, while all the furor for the new style was diverted into mansions, palaces, and erections for luxury and temporal splendour.

And now I cannot dismiss this subject without a few remarks on those who seem to think, that, by restoring the details and accessories of pointed architecture, they are reviving Catholic art. Not at all. *Unless the ancient arrangement be restored,* and the *true principles carried out,* all mouldings, pinnacles, tracery, and details, be they ever so well executed, are a mere disguise. It is a great profanation to deck out Protestant monstrosities in the garb of Catholic antiquity ; pew and gallery fronts with tracery panels ; reading-desks with canopied tops, and carved communion-tables ; for however elaborate the ornaments — however costly the execution, and however correct the details may be in the abstract, unless a church be built on the ancient traditional form, it must appear a miserable failure. A follower of John Knox himself, as in the Scotch conventicle in London, may build a meeting-house with pointed windows, arches, and tolerably good detail, but these will always look

dissertation on the use and antiquity of these screens, in which he appropriately designates the modern innovators as Ambonoclasts, and sets forth in most powerful language and argument, the heinous offence of departing from the approved traditions of the Church in these matters.

like the scattered leaves of a precious volume that have been bound up by an unskilful hand, without connexion or relation to their meaning.

To apply these venerable forms to any but their real intention, is a perfect prostitution of this glorious style; a Catholic church not only requires pillars, arches, windows, screens, and niches, but it *requires them to be disposed according to a certain traditional form;* it demands a chancel set apart for sacrifice, and screened off from the people; it requires a stone altar, a sacrarium sedilia for the officiating priests, and an elevated roodloft from whence the Holy Gospel may be chaunted to the assembled faithful; it requires chapels for penance and prayer, a sacristy to contain the sacred vessels, a font for the holy sacrament of baptism, a southern porch for penitents and catechumens, a stoup for hallowed water, and a tower for bells;—and unless a building destined for a church possess all these requisites, however correctly its details may be copied from ancient authorities, it is a mere modern conventicle, and cannot by any means be accounted a revival of Catholic art.

APPENDIX.

APPENDIX.

A.

THEY (the visitors) represented their offences in such multiplying glasses, as made them seem both greater in number, and more horrid in nature, than indeed they were.—HEYLIN, p. 262.

The commissioners threatened the canons of Leicester that they would charge them with adultery and unnatural crimes, unless they would consent to give up their house.—*See Hist. Collect.* from 36 to 52.

Burnet owns that there were great complaints made of the violences and briberies of the visitors, and perhaps, says he, not without reason.—*Abrid.* p. 182.

The infamous Dr. London was appointed visitor to Godstowe Nunnery, of whose vile practices there, the abbess, Catherine Bukley, complains most feelingly, in a letter addressed to the king, which may be seen at length in Steven's Continuation to Dugdale, p. 537. This same Dr. London was so abominable a character, that he was afterwards convicted of perjury, and adjudged to ride with his face to the horse's tail at Windsor and Oakingham, with papers about his head.—STEVEN's *Continuation to Monasticon Anglicanum*, p. 538.

The learned and pious Abbot Whiting of Glastonbury, was condemned in consequence of a book against the king's divorce, which had been introduced without his knowledge, being found in the abbey. This book was brought in solely for the purpose of accomplishing the ruin of this abbot, who firmly opposed the surrender of his abbey,

B.

In the month of November, Hugh Farringdon, Abbot of Reading, with two priests, named Rug and Ongon, were hanged and quartered at Reading. The same day was Richard Whiting, Abbot of Glastonbury, hanged and quartered on the Torre Hill, beside his monastery. John Thorne and Roger James, monks, the one treasurer, the other under-treasurer, of Glastonbury church, were at the same time executed; and shortly after, John Beech, Abbot of Colchester, was executed at Colchester—all for denying the king's supremacy.—STOW's *Chronicle*, p. 576.

The 29th of April, John, prior of the charter-house, at London; Augustine Webster, Prior of Beuall; Thomas Laurence, Prior of Escham; Richard Reginalds, doctor, a monk of Sion; and John Hale, Vicar of Isleworth; were all condemned of treason, for the supremacy, and were drawn, hanged, and quartered at Tyburn, the 4th day of May 1538, their heads and quarters set on the gates of the city, all save one quarter, which was set on the Charter-house, London.—STOW.

K

The 18th of June, three monks of the charter-house at London, named Thomas Exmew, Humfrey Middlemore, and Sebastian Nidigate, were drawn to Tyburn, and there hanged and quartered for denying the king's supremacy.—*Ibid.*

The 22d of June, Doctor John Fisher, Bishop of Rochester, for denying the king's supremacy, was beheaded on the Tower Hill; his head was set on London bridge, and his body buried within Barking church-yard.—*Ibid.*

The 6th of July, Sir Thomas More was beheaded on the Tower Hill for the like denial of the king's supremacy; and then the body of Dr. Fisher, Bishop of Rochester, was taken up, and buried with Sir Thomas More, both in the Tower.

The 10th of April, Sir William Peterson, priest, late Commissary of Calais; and Sir William Richardson, priest of St. Marie's, in Calais, were both there hanged, drawn, and quartered, in the market-place, for the supremacy.—*Ibid.*

These are only a few of the many persons this monster of cruelty executed for denying his supremacy. Indeed, it was the means he ridded himself of all churchmen, whose firmness and constancy were a barrier to his innovations.

C.

Within this clochier of St. Paul's were four very great bells, called Jesus Bells, in regard they specially belonged to Jesus Chapel, situate at the east end of the undercroft of St. Paul's; as also, on the top of the spire, the image of St. Paul: all standing, till Sir Miles Partridge, knight, *temp.* Henry VIII., having won them of the king *at one cast of the dice*, pulled them down. Which Sir Miles afterwards, *temp.* Edward VI., suffered death on Tower Hill, for matters relating to the Duke of Somerset.—DUGDALE'S *St. Paul's Cathedral*, p. 128.

D.

Goodwin, speaking of a chapel which Stillington, Bishop of Wells, had built adjoining the east side of the cloister there, and in which he was buried says :—

" His body rested but a short time; for it is reported that diverse olde men, who in their youth had not only seene the celebration of his funeral, but also the building of his tombe, chapell and all, did also see tombe and chapell destroyed, and the bones of the bishop that built them turned out of the lead in which they were interred." This chapel was destroyed by Sir John Gates, in the time of Edward VI.

E.

The following are among the executions on the score of religion in Henry's reign :—

Twenty-second of July, 1534, John Frith, for denying the real presence in the sacrament, the first executed in England for this cause. November, 1538, was John Lambert burnt in Smithfield for the same opinion.

And Stow mentioned sixteen different persons burnt for heresy; that is, holding the present Protestant opinions. Fuller, Heylin, and other historians, show that Cranmer sat in judgment, and signed the condemnation of many of these, for the very opinions he held himself privately.

F.

In 1540, the king summoned a parliament, to be holden at Westminster the 28th of April; also a synod of prelates, in which six articles were concluded, touching matters of religion, commonly called " the whip with six strings."

Article 1, confirmed the real presence in the sacrament.

Article 2, against communion in both kinds.

Article 3, that priests might not marry after the order of priesthood received.

Article 4, that vows of chastity, made after twenty-one years of age, should be binding.

Article 5, the establishing of private masses.

Article 6, auricular confession to be expedient.

The punishment for the breach of the first article was burning without any abjuration, with loss of all goods and lands, as in case of treason; the default against the other five articles was felony, without benefit of clergy.—Fox's *Martyrs*, edit. 1589.

It will be seen from these articles what little differences of doctrine caused Henry's separation from the Catholic church, and proves that he was moved to that step from temporal motives only.

It is, also, worthy of remark, that the leading apostle of the Reformation, Archbishop Cranmer, subscribed to these articles, and proceeded on them by condemning others, when, in fact, he secretly violated every one of them himself.

G.

In order to show how soon the private interpretation of the Holy Scriptures was found to produce baneful results, I have transcribed a portion of Henry's speech to his parliament, made in 1545, which gives a true and lively picture of the state of religious discord that had already risen, and the rapid demoralisation that attended the departure from the ancient system.

" I see here daily you of the cleargie preach one against another, teach one contrary to another, inveigh one against the other, without charity or discretion; thus all men be in variety and discord, and few or none preacheth truly and sincerely the word of God. Alas! how can poor souls live in concord, when you preachers sow amongst them in your sermons debate and discord? if to you they look for light, and you bring them to darkness?

" Although I say the spiritual men be in fault, yet you of the temporality be not clear and unspotted of malice and envy, for you rail on bishops, speak slanderously of priests, and rebuke and taunt preachers: and, although you be permitted to read Holy Scriptures, and to have the word of God in your mother-tongue, you must understand it is licensed you so to do only to inform your own consciences, and to instruct your children and families, and not to dispute and make a railing and taunting stock of Scripture against priests and preachers, as many light persons do. I am very sorry to know and hear how irreverently the most precious jewel, the word of God, is *disputed, ruined, sung, and tangled, in every alehouse and tavern*, contrary to the true meaning of the same. I am even as much sorry that the readers of the same follow it, in doing, so faintly and coldly; for of this I am sure,

K 2

charity was never so faint among you, vertuous and godly living was never less used, nor God himself amongst Christians never less reverenced, honored, or served."—HOLINSHED'S *Chronicle*, vol. ii. p. 972.

H.

Poynet, first Protestant bishop of Winchester, passed away all the temporalities of his see conditionally to his preferment to it, in return for which he was to receive certain rectories.—STRYPE, *Mem. Ecc.* vol. iii. p. 272.

Ridley, within nine days after his promotion to the see of London, alienated four of its best manors to the king, to gratify some of the courtiers.—*Ibid.* p. 234.

Barlow, at Wells, 20th May, 1548, consigned by license to the king a very considerable portion of the demesnes and manors of his see.—COLLINSON.

I.

The following are notes relative to these barbarous demolitions :—

Neither the Bishops of Lichfield and Coventry, nor Llandaff, had any recompense for their demolished palaces, according to Spelman; but Hooper, who had been chaplain to the Protector, had a house granted him in Whitefriars.

In the year 1549, on the 10th of April, the chapel in Pardon churchyard, by commandment of the Duke of Somerset, was begun to be pulled down, with the whole cloystrie, the dance of death, the tombs and monuments, so that nothing was left but the bare plot of ground, which has since been converted into a garden for petty canons.—STOW'S *Survey*, p. 354.

In this chapel (standing on the north side of the churchyard) were buried Henry Barton, lord mayor of London, A.D. 1417, and Thomas Mirfin, mayor also in 1419, who had fair tombs therein, with their images in alabaster, strongly coped with iron; all which, with the chapel, were pulled down in A. D. 1549 (3 Edward VI.), by the Duke of Somerset's appointment, and made use of for his building at Somerset House in the Strand: the bones, which lay in the vault underneath, amounting to more than a thousand cart-loads, being conveyed into Finnesbury Fields, and there laid on a moorish place, with so much soil to cover them as did raise the ground for three windmills to stand on, which have since been built there.—DUGDALE'S *Hist. St. Paul's*, p. 130.

J.

In this month of April, and in May, commissioners were directed through England for all the church goods remaining in cathedral and parish churches—that is to say, jewels of gold and silver, silver crosses, candlesticks, censers, chalices, and such like, with their ready money, to be delivered to the master of the king's jewels in the Tower of London; all coapes and vestments of cloth of gold, cloth of tissue, and silver, to the master of the king's wardrobe in London; the other coapes, vestments, and ornaments, to be sold, and the money to be delivered to Sir Edward Peckham, knight: reserving church one chalice or cup, with table cloathes for the communion board, at the discretion of the commissioners, which were, for London, the lord mayor, the bishop, the lord chief justice, and other.—STOW'S *Chronicle*, p. 609.

K.

Harrington thus relates the ravages and spoliations at Wells :—Scarce were five years past after Bath's ruins, but as fast went the axes and hammers to work at Wells. The goodly hall, covered with lead (because the roofe might seeme too low for so large a roome), was uncovered; and now this roofe reaches to the sky. The chapell of our lady, late repaired by Stillington, a place of great reverence and antiquitie, was likewise defaced; and such was their thirst after lead (I would they had drank it scalding), that they took the *dead bodies of bishops out of their leaden coffins, and cast abroad the carcases scarce thoroughly putrified.* The statues of brass, and all the antient monuments of kings, benefactors to that goodly cathedral church, went all the same way, sold to an alderman of London.

Furthermore, says Stow (speaking of St. Leonard's, Shoreditch), one vicar there (of late time), for covetousness of the brasse, which hee converted into coyned silver, plucked up many plates fixed on the graves, and left no memory of such as had been buried under them—a great injury both to the living and the dead, forbidden by public proclamation in the reigne of our soveraigne lady Queen Elizabeth, *but not forborne by many,* that, either of a preposterous zeale, or of a greedie minde, spare not to satisfie themselves by so wicked a meanes.—Stow's *Survey,* p. 475.

L.

In order to do away, as much as possible, with the idea of an altar, the communion tables were placed away from the walls; and when the high church party, under Charles I, attempted to place them again altarwise, as they are set at present, the zeal and opposition of the low church party give rise to many disgraceful scenes and foolish pamphlets. A book called " The Holy Table, Name, and Thing," tells us that, when the vicar of Grantham fell upon removing the communion table from the upper part of the choir to the altar-place, as he called it, Mr. Wheatly, the Alderman, questioning him thereupon, what authority he had from the bishop, received this answer: that his authority was this—he had done it, and he would justify it. Mr. Wheatly commanded his officers to remove the place again, which they did accordingly, but not without STRIKING, much heat, and indiscretion, both of the one side and the other. The vicar said, he cared not what they did with their old tressel, for he would make him an altar of stone at his own charge, and fix it in the old altar place, and would never officiate at any other; the people replying, that he should set up no dresser of stone in their church.

A letter was addressed to the vicar of Grantham about setting his table altarwise.

In answer to the letter comes out a book, entitled " A Coal from the Altar," which was answered again by the " Quench Coal." And this knotty point, where the table should stand, engaged a host of writers of the time.

M.

There is no period of English history which has been more disguised than the reign of that female demon, Elizabeth; for while her unfortunate sister has been stigmatised as bloody Mary, and ever held up to odium as an intolerant persecuting bigot, Elizabeth has been loaded with encomiums, of which she is quite undeserving.   The parliament during her reign enacted most sanguinary laws equally directed against persons who professed the ancient religion, or those who carried Protestant principles further than the new churchmen thought advisable for the safety of their establishment.

During twenty years of her reign, a great number of persons were executed solely on the score of professing the Catholic faith.   Of these, many were in holy orders; three gentlewomen; and the remainder, esquires, gentlemen, and yeomen.   Besides several priests, and Catholic lay persons who died in prison, and great numbers who were sent into perpetual banishment; to say nothing of many more who were whipped, fined (the fine for recusancy was 20*l.* per month), or stripped of their property, to the utter ruin of their families.*

In one night, fifty Catholic gentlemen, in the county of Lancaster, were suddenly seized and committed to prison, on account of their non-attendance at church.   At the same time, an equal number of Yorkshire gentlemen were lying prisoners in York castle, on the same account, most of whom perished there.   These were every week dragged by main force to hear the established service performed in the castle chapel.—Dr. Milner's *Letters to a Prebendary.*

The torturing then in practice, Camden, in his Annals, confirms; who, speaking of the famous Father Campian, says, he was not so racked but that he was still able to write his name.

It appears from the account of one of these sufferers, that the following tortures were in use against the Catholics in the Tower:—1. The common rack, by which the limbs were stretched by levers; 2. The Scavenger's daughter, so called, being a hoop in which the body was bent till the head and feet met together; 3. The chamber Little-ease, being a hole so small, that a person could neither stand, sit, nor lie straight in it; 4. The iron gauntlet.— *Diar. Rar. Gest. in Turr. Lond.*

With what cruelty Catholics were racked, we may gather from the following passage in a letter from John Nicols to Cardinal Allen, by way of extenuating the guilt of his apostasy and perfidy in accusing his Catholic brethren :—" Non bona res est corpus, isto cruciatu, longius fieri per duos ferè pedes quam natura concessit."

The continual harassing the Catholics suffered is amply shown by the following extract :—

The 4th of April, being Palm Sunday, there was taken, saying of masse in the Lord Morleie's house, within Aldgate of London, one Albon Dolman, priest; and the Lady Morley, with her children, and divers others, were also taken for hearing the said masse.   There was also taken, the same day and houer, for saying masse at the Lady Gilford's in Trinitie Lane, one Oliver Heywood, priest ; and, for hearing the said masse, the Lady Gilford, with diverse other gentlewomen.   There was also taken, at the same instant, in the Lady Browne's house, in Cow Lane, for saying masse, one Thomas Heiwood, priest, and one John Couper, priest, with the Lady Browne ; and diverse others were likewise taken for hearing of the said masse. All which persons were for the said offences indicted, convicted, and had the law according to the statute in that case provided.   There were also found in their several chappels diverse

---

* For a full account of these cruel proceedings, see the third volume of Dodd's Church History, edited by the Rev. M. A. Tierney.

Latine books, beades, images, palms, chalices, crosses, vestments, pixes, paxes, and such like.—Stow's *Chronicle*, p. 1158.

Death by burning, on the score of religion, was likewise practised:—

The 22d July, 1576, two Dutchmen, anabaptists, were burnt in Smithfield, who died in great horror with roaring and crying.—Stow's *Chronicle*, p. 1162.

Mathew Hamont of Hetharset, by his trade a ploughwright, three miles from Norwich, was convened before the Bishop of Norwich, for that he denied Christ to be our Saviour, and other heresies.

For which he was condemned in the consistory, and sentence was read against him by the Bishop of Norwich, the 14th of April, 1578, and thereupon delivered to the sheriffs of Norwich; and because he spake words of blasphemie against the queen's majesty, and others of her counsell, he was, by the recorder, Master Sergeant Wyndham, and the major, Sir Robert Wood, condemned to lose both his eares, which were cut off, the 13th of May, in the market-place of Norwich; and afterwards, the 20th of May, he was burnt in the castle-ditch.—Stow's *Chronicle*, p. 1174.

Many more instances could be cited; but, I trust, sufficient has been shown to prove that the system on which the present establishment was founded and carried on, was the very acme of religious intolerance and persecution; and it is only very lately that Catholics have been relieved from degrading restrictions, which they continued to suffer after the more violent persecutions had ceased.

N.

The Earl of Leicester (favourite of Elizabeth) was at the head of those who said that no bishops ought to be tolerated in a Christian land, and that he had cast a covetous eye on Lambeth Palace.—Heylin's *Hist. of Eliz.* p. 168.

O.

The magnificent chapter-house of Ely, is now used as Trinity church, in consequence of the chapter assigning it to the parishioners, to save the expense of repairing the parish church, which they were bound to do; and the lamentable havoc that has been made in this once beautiful structure by the modern pewing, communion-screen, &c., and the fixing of some wretched monumental tablets, must be seen to be properly conceived. Owing to the same cause, three other cathedrals have been mutilated in a similar manner.

At Norwich cathedral, the ancient chapel of St. Luke, and the south aisle of the choir and apsis, have been inclosed and blocked up with pews, to serve as a parish church for St. Ethelbert's.

At Hereford, the north transept is inclosed and filled with pews, &c., to serve as a parochial church for the parishioners of St. John the Baptist.

At Chester, the south transept has been walled off, and serves for the parish church of St. Oswald's.

P.

Formerly not only the residences of ecclesiastics, but the houses of the laity, were all provided with a private chapel, suitable to the size of the dwelling; but, alas! how is this feeling now changed? In vain do we look, in modern mansions, for a chamber devoted to religious worship; and in those ancient dwellings, where the piety of our ancestors had directed chapels, in how few instances do we find them still employed for their primitive destination! how often do we find they have been levelled to the ground as useless portions of the building; or, if not so, desecrated to the meanest purposes!* Rarely, among the canonries, or ecclesiastical residences attached to cathedrals, can we find one that has been retained to its original use; and how can we imagine religion to dwell with those, who will not devote one small niche of their dwellings to her?

Domestic chapels and chaplains are alike falling into absolute disuse; they will soon be spoken of as things that used to be—as the remains of old superstition, and the relics of popery—the excuse made, whenever any of the ancient practices and regulations which had been preserved, are discontinued.

Q.

The excesses committed by the Huguenots and Calvinists in France, during the year 1562, are of so horrible and extensive a nature, that to give any thing like a narration of them would exceed the compass of a volume; but I have here subjoined a few notes, to prove to those who may be unacquainted with the subject, the truth of my assertion.

During the above-mentioned period, the whole of the rich ornaments belonging to the cathedral at Rouen were pillaged and melted, of which the high altar alone contained six hundred and eighty-two marks of silver, besides jewels, and twenty-seven marks of pure gold, all wrought into the most beautiful forms. Not only did these sacrilegious wretches plunder all that was valuable, but with fanatic fury they consumed all the holy relics contained in the shrines, and treated the remains of St. Romain with the most barbarous indignity.

The cathedral was filled with stores of ammunition, and the Divine service totally suspeded.—DOM. POM. *Hist. Cath. Rouen.*

At the same time the magnificent abbey of St. Ouen, in the same city, was ravaged completely: not only were all the precious ornaments and vestments pillaged, but the fury of these miserable heretics was vented on the finest efforts of art the church contained. The rood-loft, unrivalled as a specimen of elaborate and wonderful masonry, was totally demolished; the stalls burnt; all the brass work of the choir, which was of the finest description, torn down and melted; and even the tomb of the learned and munificent Abbé Marc d'Argent (founder and designer of this glorious church) fell a prey to their savage fury, and was totally destroyed.—*Histoire de l'Eglise de Saint Ouen, par* M. GILBERT. *Paris,* 1822.

July the 1st, a large party of Calvinists quitted Rouen for a predatory excursion, and, having burnt and pillaged several churches in the vicinity of Barentin, they re-entered Rouen in a sort of tumultuous triumph, some wearing chasubles, others copes, bearing the crosses in

* The ancient chapel of the Bishop of Ely's palace, at Ely, was used as a beer-cellar in 1834.

mockery, and tossing the chalices and thuribles in their hands by way of derision; some crying " Death to the mass ;" others, " Here's a death-blow to the Papists," and similar outrageous expressions.—Dom. POMERAYE, *Hist. Cath. Rouen. Rouen*, 1686, p. 126.

A manuscript chronicle of the Abbey of Jumièges relates, that two of the monks, going to Evreux to meet their abbot, Gabriel le Veneur, fell into the hands of a similar party ; when they twisted whipcord round their foreheads so tightly, to make them reveal the place where the treasures of their abbey were concealed, that, their eyes starting from their sockets, one died from excess of agony immediately, and the other, Father Caumont, remained a miserable object till his death.—Dom. POM. *Hist. Cath. Rouen*, p. 162.

The 10th of May, 1652, being Sunday, the Protestants of Bayeux and its vicinity entered the cathedral church armed ; and having instantly caused the cessation of high mass, then celebrating, they broke down the altars and images, and commenced pillaging the sacred vessels and ornaments. Those Catholic citizens and ecclesiastics who endeavoured to repress this outrage were immediately sacrificed, being either pistolled on the spot, or dragged to the walls, from which, after having their throats cut, they were immediately precipitated. The bishop, Charles de Humières, and Germain Duval, the dean, only escaped the massacre by gaining the haven, from whence they put to sea in a small fishing-boat that happened to be lying there.—BEZIER's *Histoire de la Ville de Bayeux*, p. 24.

The *procès verbal*, presented to the king by the bishop and clergy of Bayeux, on the reestablishment of the ecclesiastics in 1563, gives a detailed account of all the destructions and robberies committed on the cathedral, while in the possession of these fanatics. It is too long for insertion here, but the following facts may be gathered from it ;—That every precious ornament whatever, as well as vestments of all descriptions, had been pillaged and destroyed; that a great portion of the stained windows were dashed out. The stalls, bishop's throne, chapel-screens, organ-case, and every description of wood carving, had been broken up and carried away. The charters, all archives belonging to the cathedral, had been burned, as well as the library. That the bodies of the ancient ecclesiastics, including the Patriarch de Harcour, had been disinterred, the bodies left exposed, and their coffins melted down. That all the brass work, consisting of effigies on tombs, an immense crown of admirable workmanship that hung in the choir, and other curious ornaments, had likewise been melted. That all the scaffolding, cords, pulleys, and materials, that were employed about the repair of the edifice, had been sold and removed. The ten great bells had been broken and melted, as well as the organ pipes, and four thousand weight of lead from the roof, which had been cast into ammunition. Besides a great variety of other demolitions and acts of cruelty, practised on the ecclesiastics in the city, the whole of which are given at length in BEZIER's *Histoire de la Ville de Bayeux*, beginning at page 3 of the Appendix.

From these historical accounts of only a few of the very extensive outrages committed by the Protestants in France, I leave the candid and impartial reader to judge if I have gone too far in my assertion.

L

R.

To prove the truth of the great similarity of the various classes of Protestants in their out-rages, I wish to refer the reader to the description of the demolitions at Wells, described in this Appendix under the letter K. I have also subjoined some extracts from an account of the excesses committed by the Puritans, during the civil wars, at Peterborough cathedral.

" Espying that rare work of stone over the altar, admired by all travellers, they made all of it rubbish, breaking up, also, the rayles, of which they compiled bonfires; tumbling the communion table over and over. They were, also, so offended with the memorials of the dead, that not one monument in the church remained undefaced. When their unhallowed toylings had made them out of wind, they took breath afresh on two pair of organs, piping with the same about the market-place lascivious jigs, whilst their comrades danced after them in surplices. The clappers of the bells they sold, with the brass they had slaied from the grave-stones; nor was any window suffered to remain unshattered, or remarkable place unruined."

It is well worthy of remark, that the outrage at Wells was conducted by the advocates of the new opinions, in the time of Edward VI, and that this attack on Peterborough was carried on by the Puritans, another class of Protestants, one century after; so that those, who had been the abettors of schism, suffered by the very principles they had introduced: for these fanatics seem to have held the surplices of the establishment in as much abhorrence and derision as the others had formerly the vestments of the ancient church which they had plundered and destroyed.

The fact is, the present establishment, in its episcopacy and ancient form of church government, has too much of the old system about it to suit the levelling and destructive feelings produced by real Protestantism. At the time of the Commonwealth the establishment was overthrown, and is at present in a most insecure state, not from the combinations and cabals of Catholics, but from the extending principles of contempt for ecclesiastical authority, and the all-sufficient private judgment in matters of religion, which are inseparable from Protestant opinions.

The history of this country, since the change of religion, ought to convince the churchmen of this country of the utter impossibility of preserving a national church or unity of creed without Catholic communion. The daily extending sects of dissenters are ample evidences of this fact; all of which have been produced by the same principles as those which founded the establishment itself: but, either from inherent hatred against the ancient religion, or from infatuation and blindness, many modern clergymen continually preach against the Catholics of this country as unheeding the mass of zealous Protestant dissenters, who openly clamour against them, and the undermining effects of nine-tenths of their own brethren, who not only disbelieve, but openly condemn, various portions of the articles, creeds, and discipline, as they are at present by law established. For a confirmation of this assertion, see that admirable Letter of Dr. Milner to Dr. Sturges, of Winchester, demonstrating the low church principles to be entirely subversive of the original tenets of the Church of England.

S.

Wherever Vandemerk and Sonoi, both lieutenants to the Prince of Orange, carried their arms, they invariably put to death, in cold blood, all the priests and religious they could lay hands upon, as at Odenard, Ruremond, Dort, Middlebourg, Delft, and Shonoven.—See *Hist. Ref. des Pays Bas*, by the Protestant minister DE BRANT.

Of the horrible barbarities practised by this Sonoi, a copious account is given in *L'Abrégé de l'Histoire de la Hollande*, par M. KENOUX, a Protestant author, who draws a most frightful picture of the barbarities practised on the Catholic peasants of the Low Countries.

The reformation in Scotland began by the murder of Cardinal Beaton, in which Knox was a party ; and to which Fox, in his " Acts and Monuments," says, the murderers were actuated by the Spirit of God.

Numberless instances might be cited, to show the horrible excesses committed by these pretended reformers in the furtherance of their principles.

T.

Such was the detestation, only a few years since, to the bare representation of the cross (a symbol that has been used by Christians from the earliest periods), that, when the small Catholic chapel was erected at Lincoln, a plain cross having been formed in the gable by the omission of some bricks, the then mayor sent a message to the priest, desiring the same to be immediately defaced. To which mandate the worthy pastor replied, that he should by no means do so till the crosses on the cathedral, and other churches, were removed ; and owing to this spirited answer the cross was suffered to remain.

U.

To what miserable resources are not the designers of ecclesiastical decoration driven in the present day, when all those exquisite symbols and powerful representations of the sacraments and ceremonies of the Christian church, which formed an inexhaustible source for every class of artists, have been expelled and prohibited, as savouring of superstition—a name applied by modern churchmen to every religious truth that surpasses their own narrow comprehension, and every sacred rite which they find too irksome or expensive.

But, will it be believed, these pretended suppressors of superstition, these revilers of those sacred badges which had distinguished religious worship from the earliest period, fly to pagan rites and heathen worship for emblems to replace those they had so barbarously rejected ! Yes ; the sacrifice of rams and heifers is sculptured, in lieu of that of the divine Redeemer sacrificed for the whole world ; the images of the pagan priestesses have replaced those of the saints and martyrs, whose zeal and constancy laid the foundation of the great fabric of the Christian church : and, indeed, so infatuated have been the builders of modern preaching-houses in this new system, that, from the winged Osiris of the Egyptians to the votive wreaths dedicated to the god Mars, they have adopted all descriptions of ornaments relating to pagan rites, which they have introduced without the slightest consideration of their utter impropriety in the places of worship of any class of Christians. Yet, such is the blind prejudice of the mass of persons in this country, that, while such gross violations of propriety are daily taking place without comment, were any one to be found bold enough to erect an image of the crucified Redeemer within the walls of one of these edifices, an outcry would be immediately raised that popish idolatry was about to be revived ; nor would the zealots cease till the object of offence was removed; and should no appropriate Greek or Roman figure be found to supply its place, a neat king's arms, with some appropriate text, would be thought admirably suitable to fill the vacant space.

Not only has this mania of employing heathen emblems filled the churches with incongruities, but they are universally employed about the sepulchral monuments of persons professing to be Christians, and of which many have been erected at the expense of a nominally Christian country.

Let any candid person survey the monuments erected, during the last and present century, in those great edifices, St. Paul's and Westminster Abbey, and then pronounce, whether there is one sign or symbol by which he could have supposed that the persons, to whom they are erected, professed the Christian faith. Mars, Mercury, Neptune, Minerva, Apollo, and a host of heathen divinities, are sculptured either receiving the soul of the departed, or assisting him in the achievement of his exploits; and, when he regards the costume of the deceased, he is equally at a loss to distinguish the rank, profession, or the age in which he lived. Statesmen, warriors, and even ecclesiastics, have been alike enveloped in the Roman toga; and thus made to appear, both by costume and attributes, pagans of two thousand years ago.

No. I.

EXTRACT FROM DODD'S CHURCH HISTORY, BY THE REV. M. A. TIERNEY, VOL. II. PAGE 141-3.

It is not to be doubted, but that the reformation, set on foot by queen Elizabeth, was contrary to the inclinations of all the governing part of the clergy, or at least of a great majority; and that they protested against it. The bishops were all deprived, and imprisoned, on that account. The convocation met, as the reader has seen, and subscribed to a profession of faith, directly contrary to the reformed doctrine. Great numbers of the most eminent clergymen went abroad; and there was scarce any university, either in Flanders, France, or Italy, but one or more might be found in them, besides others, that were entertained as professors of divinity in foreign monasteries. A great many, indeed, still remained in England, and conformed for awhile, in hopes that the queen would relent, and things come about again. But their hopes vanishing, they forsook their benefices, and followed their countrymen over seas. There was not a province through all England, where several of queen Mary's clergy did not reside, and were commonly called the old priests. They served as chaplains in private families. Their names and places of residence I have frequently met with, in the manuscripts I perused in composing this work. Again, several Catholic clergymen found such friends, as to be permitted to enjoy sinecures, without being disturbed by oaths and other injunctions.

This non-compliance of so many of the clergy left the reformers unprovided with teachers, and persons proper for that function; in so much that Collier says, " that, upon the Catholic clergy throwing up their preferment, the necessities of the Church required the admitting of some mechanics into orders."* The strength of the party, that opposed the reformation,

---

* [Collier, ii. 465. See also Strype, Annal. i. 178, 179. Among other schemes adopted in consequence of this defection, it was proposed, in some instances, to unite several churches, and thus to carry on the duties of religion

appears still more from the account which the Protestant writers give of the desertion, that happened in our universities, and scarcity of persons sufficiently qualified to instruct the people." "It must be known," saith Anthony Wood, "that, in the beginning of the reign of queen Elizabeth, the university of Oxford was so empty, after the Catholics had left it, upon the alteration of religion, that there was very seldom a sermon preached in the university church called St. Mary." And, in another place, he adds, "there was not one then [an. 1564] in that society [of Merton college], that could, or would, preach any public sermon in the college turn; such was the scarcity of theologists, not only in that house, but generally throughout the university."* The same Oxford historian also gives us several particulars of this grand defection. He names twenty-two persons of note, ejected out of New college only; seven out of St. John's college; and great numbers out of the colleges of St. Mary Magdalen, Lincoln, and Trinity; so that the university seemed to be entirely destroyed. He tells us, moreover, that the persons left were few, and so illiterate, that an order came out for every one to con over the Bible, and lessons, being unable to read them distinctly otherwise: that a like order came out for liberty to make use of the Common-prayer in the Latin tongue, there being some danger of losing that language in the university: and that Thomas Sampson, and Dr. Humphrey, and perhaps a third, named Andrew Kingsmill, were the only persons that could preach with any reputation. Now these preachers being all puritans, they filled the university with Calvinistical notions.† This desolate condition of Oxford is, in like manner, taken notice of by Jewel, Parker, and others. "Our universities," saith Jewel, "are in a most lamentable condition: * * * there are not above two in Oxford of our sentiments."‡ Archbishop Parker tells the queen, "that there were not two men able or willing to read the lady Margaret's lecture; and, though they had a great many preachers, yet he was afraid several of them were but slenderly furnished for that employment." It appears from these accounts, that, whatever these might be as to the number in the whole, most of the clergy of character, upon account either of morals or of learning, stood firm in the belief of the old religion.

It may be readily imagined, that when the English churches were brought under the control of the new order of clergy (for the most part illiterate Puritans, and devoid of all sympathy for Catholic traditions and art), their ancient and appropriate arrangements were speedily destroyed, and they were used more as preaching conventicles, than as places consecrated to

---

with a smaller number of clergy. See a letter on this subject, from the bishop of Winchester to Cecil, in the Appendix, No. XLV.--*T.*]

* Wood, Athen. Oxon. i. 161, 429.

† Antiq. Oxon. 283, 284, 285. [He adds, that, after Sampson's departure, Humphrey was frequently absent, that sermons of the most ridiculous kind were constantly delivered, and that, on one occasion, no preacher making his appearance, Richard Taverner, the high sheriff of the county, decorated in the ensigns of his office, ascended the pulpit of St. Mary's church, and addressed his audience in a discourse, which thus commenced. " Arriving at the mount of St Mary's, in the stony stage (the pulpit was of stone), where I now stand, I have brought you some biscuits, baked in the oven of charity, carefully conserved for the chickens of the church, the sparrows of the spirit, and the sweet swallows of salvation." Ibid.—*T.*]

‡ [Apud Collier, ii. 432. Jewel's letter, however, is dated May 22, 1559, some months before the deprivation or removal of the Catholic members..—*T.*]

prayer and sacrifice. From the very commencement of the great schism, the *canons* of the establishment have been far more Catholic than her *practice ;* and, notwithstanding all that has been advanced to the contrary, the present position of the Church of England is a Protestant one. That many good Catholic-minded men, and witnesses of better things, have been found in her communion, even at the very worst periods, no one can doubt ; but these have ever formed a very small minority, and were, in fact, exceptions to the rule. The change of religion in England was compassed by crafty and avaricious statesmen, aided by Puritans and foreign heretics ; and no one can doubt this fact, who has attentively perused the works of Dodd, Heylin, Strype, Collier, and other old English historians. It is both false and absurd for certain modern writers to assert, that the present establishment has been a conservator of Catholic architecture, because Hooker, Laud, and a few other great men of the same school, protested against the destructions that were going on in every direction. There is not one sacred edifice in the whole country, that does not exhibit a lamentable series of innovations and demolitions, commencing with the so-called reformation, and continued at intervals to the present time ; indeed, as I have previously remarked, we may ascribe the preservation of the most interesting remains more to the feelings of apathy and neglect, than any veneration for their beauty. None but party men can endeavour to set up such pretensions in the face of existing facts ; all who are imbued with true Catholic feelings, must weep and deplore over the fallen state of Christian art and ideas for the last few centuries, not only in England but in Europe.

No. II.

The following glorious churches may be especially pointed out amongst a host of others, as being in a most lamentable state of decay and neglect.

1. The Cathedral Church of Durham.
2. The Cathedral Church of Ely.
3. The Cathedral Church of Carlisle.

In the Abbey Church of Westminster, although the fabric is being slowly and partially restored, the unrivalled sepulchral monuments are in a most miserable state.

The Abbey Church of Tewkesbury, one of the most solemn churches in England, containing tombs and chapels of the highest interest, at present wofully desecrated.

The Collegiate Church of Selby, the choir of which is a wonderful example of the fine period of the 1st Edward. In this wonderful building, the font with a magnificent canopy is disused. The chapels of the transepts are filled with rubbish, and one even used as *a coal-hole.* Two stove pipes of large diameter have been carried *right through the eastern aisle windows,* and up to the top of the eastern turrets. The nave is rendered useless, and galleries have been erected in the choir, and many fine foliage caps cut away to receive them. A description of the many barbarous mutilations that this glorious church has suffered would fill a volume.

N.B. The great tithes of this church are in the possession of a Catholic gentleman, who, instead of contributing funds towards saving this noble example of ancient piety from ruin, has actually affixed a most Protestant-looking tablet against one of the finely moulded pillars of the chancel ! ! !

In the parish church of Cromer, Norfolk, an edifice which could not be erected at the present time for £100,000, the eastern end has been suffered to go to utter ruin, and *side galleries are now being erected* in the nave. All the porches are in ruin. *This description will apply to nearly all the fine churches on the Norfolk coast, most of the chancels are in ruins,* and several of the transepts. These churches are for the most part noble edifices, erected by Catholic piety at an immense cost.

The disgust which the lamentable state of these neglected piles causes in the mind of the beholder, is not a little increased by the plantations, carriage-drives, stabling, and *villa-like* arrangements of the adjacent parsonage-houses.

The high church of Hull is a magnificent edifice, of immense size : a preaching place has been constructed by *walling up four compartments of the nave*, leaving the western end of nave, choir, chancel, eastern aisle, chapels, and transept, utterly bare and unoccupied . galleries have been erected with commodious staircases in the preaching place. It is most amusing to hear of a vestry meeting being called to consider the means of getting *increased accommodation* in a church of which only one third is occupied.

It is impossible even to hint at half of the enormities which have been perpetrated, *and are still tolerated* in many of our most glorious churches ; but an annual account of the proceedings of the destructives would do right good service ; as shame might in some instances have the effect of staying their sacrilegious hands. A great revival of Catholic feelings in respect to ecclesiastical architecture has already taken place, *but no one must relax for a moment ; innovations to an alarming extent, and I speak from actual observation, are yet going on.*

I cannot refrain from paying a just tribute of respect and gratitude to the labours of the Cambridge Camden Society, who have already done much, and are still going on admirably in the good cause.

I recommend to their special attention the edifices I have pointed out ; the remonstrances of a body will produce far greater results than can be achieved by any individual, and *immediate steps* should be taken to rescue these wonderful remains of ancient art from further destruction. The state of fonts require particular investigation. In the parish church of St. Helen's, York, on the 1st of May, 1841, the contents of the font were as follows : three dusters, a sponge, a hammer, several pieces of old rope, some portions of old books, a hand broom, several tin candle sockets and candle ends, besides a large deposit of dirt.

No. III.

ACCOUNT OF THE DESTRUCTIVE AND REVIVED PAGAN PRINCIPLE IN FRANCE, BY MGR. LE COMTE DE MONTALEMBERT.

Nous sommes engagés en ce moment dans une lutte qui ne sera pas sans quelque importance dans l'histoire, et qui tient, de près et de loin, à des intérêts et à des principes d'un ordre trop élevé pour être effleurés en passant. En fait, il s'agit simplement de savoir si la France arrêtera enfin le cours des dévastations qui s'effectuent chez elle depuis deux siècles, et spécialement depuis cinquante ans, avec un acharnement dont aucune autre nation et aucune autre époque n'a donné l'exemple ; ou bien si elle persévérera dans cette voie de ruines, jusqu'à ce que le dernier de ses anciens souvenirs soit effacé, le dernier de ses monumens nationaux rasé, et que, soumise sans réserve à la parure que lui préparent les ingénieurs et les architectes modernes, elle n'offre plus à l'étranger et à la postérité qu'une sorte de damier monotone peuplé de chiffres de la même valeur, ou de pions taillés sur le même modèle.

Quoi qu'il en soit, et quel que doive être le résultat des tentatives actuelles en faveur d'un meilleur ordre de choses, il est certain qu'il y a eu, depuis un petit nombre d'années, un point d'arrêt ; que si le fleuve du vandalisme n'en a pas moins continué ses ravages périodiques, du moins quelques faibles digues ont été indiquées plutôt qu'élevées, quelques clameurs énergiques ont interrompu le silence coupable et stupide qui régnait sous l'Empire et la Restauration. Cela suffit pour signaler notre époque dans l'histoire de l'art et des idées qui le dominent. C'est pourquoi j'ose croire qu'il peut n'être pas sans intérêt de continuer ce que j'ai commencé il y a cinq ans, de rassembler un certain nombre de faits caractéristiques qui puissent faire juger de l'étendue du mal et mesurer les progrès encore incertains du bien. J'ai grande confiance dans la publicité à cet égard ; c'est toujours un appel à l'avenir, alors que ce n'est point un remède pour le présent. Si chaque ami de l'histoire et de l'art national tenait note de ses souvenirs et de ses découvertes en fait de vandalisme, s'il soumettait ensuite avec courage et persévérance au jugement du public, au risque de le fatiguer quelquefois comme je vais le faire aujourd'hui, par une nomenclature monotone et souvent triviale, il est probable que le domaine de ce vandalisme se rétrécirait de jour en jour, et dans le même mesure où l'on verrait s'accroître cette réprobation morale qui, chez toute nation civilisée, doit stigmatiser le mépris du passé et la destruction de l'histoire.

Il est juste de commencer la revue trop incomplète que je me propose de faire, par le sommet de l'échelle sociale, c'est-à-dire par le gouvernement. Autant j'ai mis de violence à l'attaquer en 1833, autant je lui dois d'éloges aujourd'hui pour l'heureuse tendance qu'il manifeste in faveur de nos monumens historiques, pour la protection tardive, mais affectueuse, dont il les entoure. Ce sera un éternel honneur pour le gouvernement de juillet que cet arrêté de son premier ministre de l'intérieur, rendu presque au milieu de la confusion du combat et de toute l'effervescence de la victoire, par lequel on instituait un inspecteur-général des monumens historiques, à peu près au même moment où l'on inaugurait le roi de la révolution. C'était un admirable témoignage de confiance dans l'avenir, en même temps que de respect pour le passé. On déclarait ainsi que l'on pouvait désormais étudier et apprécier impunemment ce passé, parce que toute crainte de son retour était impossible. Cet arrêté nous a valu tout d'abord un excellent rapport* sur les monumens d'une portion notable de l'Ile-de-France, de l'Artois et du Hainaut, signé par le premier inspecteur-général, M. Vitet. C'était, si je ne me trompe, depuis les fameux rapports de Grégoire à la Convention, sur la destruction des monumens, la première marque officielle d'estime donnée par un fonctionnaire public aux souvenirs de notre histoire. A cette première impulsion ont succédé, il faut le dire, de l'insouciance et de l'oubli, que l'on peut, sans trop d'injustice, attribuer aux douloureuses préoccupations qui ont rempli les premières années de notre révolution. Cependant le progrès des études historiques, fortement organisé et poussé par M. Guizot, amenait nécessairement celui des études sur l'art. Aussi vit-on ces études former un des objets du second comité historique, institué au ministère de l'instruction publique en 1834. Avec le calme revint une sollicitude plus étendue et plus vigoureuse ; on demanda aux chambres et on obtint, quoique avec peine, une somme de 200,000 francs pour subvenir aux premiers besoins de l'entretien des monumens historiques. M. le comte de Montalivet a mis le sceau à cette heureuse réaction, en créant, le 29 septembre 1837, une commission spécialement chargée de veiller à la conservation des anciens monumens, et de répartir entre eux la modique allocation portée au budget sous ce titre. De son côté M. de Salvandy, étendant et complétant l'œuvre de M. Guizot, a créé ce comité historique des arts et monumens que la rapport de M. de Gaspardin a fait connaître au public, et qui, sous l'active et zélée direction de cet ancien ministre, s'occupe avec ardeur de la reproduction de nos chefs-d'œuvres, en même temps qu'il dénonce à l'opinion les actes de vandalisme qui parviennent à sa connaissance. Enfin, M. le garde-des-sceaux, en sa qualité de ministre des cultes, a publié une excellent circulaire sur les mesures à suivre pour la restauration des édifices religieux, circulaire à laquelle il ne manquera que d'être suffisamment connue et répandue dans le clergé. Il faut espérer maintenant que la chambre des députés renoncera à la parcimonie mesquine qui a jusqu'à présent présidé à ses votes en faveur de l'art, et qu'elle suivra l'impulsion donnée par le pouvoir.

Il y a là, avouons-le, un contraste heureux et remarquable avec ce qui se passait sous la Restauration. Loin de moi la pensée d'élever des récriminations inutiles contre un régime qui a si cruellement expié ses fautes, et à qui nous devons, après tout, et nos habitudes constitutionelles et la plupart de nos libertés ; mais, en bonne justice, il est impossible de ne pas signaler une différence si honorable pour notre époque et notre nouveau gouvernement. Chose étrange ! la Restauration, à qui son nom seul semblait imposer la mission spéciale de réparer et de conserver les monumens du passé, a été tout au contraire une époque de destruction sans limites ; et il n'a fallu rien moins qu'un changement de dynastie pour qu'on s'aperçût dans les régions du pouvoir qu'il y avait quelque chose à faire, au nom du gouvernement, pour sauver l'histoire et l'art national. Sous l'Empire, le ministre de l'intérieur, par une circulaire

* Rapport à M. le Ministre de l'Intérieur sur les monumens, etc., des départemens de l'Oise, de l'Aisne, de la Marne, du Nord et du Pas-de-Calais, par M. L. Vitet. Paris, de l'imprimerie royale, 1831. Depuis, M. Mérimée, qui a remplacé M. Vitet, a étendu la sphère de ses explorations et nous a donné deux volumes pleins de renseignemens curieux sur l'état des monumens dans l'ouest et le midi de la France.

M

du 4 juin 1810, fit demander à tous les préfets des renseignements sur les anciens châteaux et les anciennes abbayes de l'Empire. J'ai vu des copies de plusieurs mémoires fournis in exécution de cet ordre ; ils sont pleins de détails curieux sur l'état de ces monumens à cette époque, et il doit en exister un grand nombre au bureau de statistique. Sous la Restauration, M. Siméon, étant ministre de l'intérieur, adopta une mesure semblable, mais on ne voit pas qu'il ait produit des résultats. Le déplorable système d'insouciance qui a régné jusqu'en 1816 à 1830, se résume tout entier dans cette ordonnance, qu'on ne pourra jamais assez regretter, par laquelle le magnifique dépôt des monumens historiques, formé aux Petits-Augustins, fut détruits et dispersé, sous prétexte de restitution à des propriétaires qui n'existaient plus, ou qui ne savaient que faire de ce qu'on leur rendait. Je ne sache pas, en effet, un seul de ces monumens rendus à des particuliers qui soit conservé pour le pays, et je serais heureux qu'on pût me signaler des exceptions individuelles à cette funeste généralité. Et cependant, malgré la difficulté bien connue de disposer de ces glorieux débris, on ne voulut jamais permettre au fondateur de ce musée unique, homme illustre et trop peu apprécié par tous les pouvoirs, à M. Alexandre Lenoir, de former un restant de collection avec ce que personne ne réclamait. Ce mépris, cette impardonnable négligence de l'antiquité chez un gouvernement qui puisait sa principale force dans cette antiquité même, s'étendit jusqu'au Conservatoire de Musique, puisque l'on a été disperser ou vendre à vil prix la curieuse collection d'anciens instrumens de musique qui y avait été formée, ainsi que l'a révélé le savant bibliothécaire de cette établissement, M. Bottée de Toulmon, à une des dernières séances du Comité des Arts. Ce système de ruine, si puissant à Paris, se practiquait sur une échelle encore plus vaste dans les provinces. Qui pourrait croire que, sous un gouvernement religieux et moral, la municipalité d'Angers, présidée par un député de l'extrême droite, ait pu installer un théâtre dans l'église gothique de Saint-Pierre ? Qui pourrait croire qu'à Arles, l'église de Saint-Césaire, regardée par les plus savans antiquaires comme une des plus anciennes de France, ait été transformée en mauvais lieu, sans qu'aucun fonctionnaire ait réclamé ? Qui croirait que, au retour des rois très-chrétiens, il n'ait été rien fait pour arracher à sa profanation militaire le magnifique palais des papes d'Avignon ? Qui croirait enfin qu'à Clairvaux, dans ce sanctuaire si célèbre, et qui dépendait alors directement du pouvoir, l'église si belle, si vaste, d'un grandiose si complet ; cette église du douzième siècle que l'on disait grand comme Notre-Dame de Paris, l'église commencée par saint Bernard, et où reposaient, à côté de ses reliques, tant de reines, tant de princes, tant de pieuses générations de moines, et le cœur d'Isabelle, fille de saint Louis ; cette église qui avait traversé, debout et entière, la République et l'Empire, ait attendu, pour tomber, la première année de la Restauration ? Elle fut rasée alors, avec toutes ses chapelles attenantes, sans qu'il en restât pierre sur pierre, pas même la tombe de saint Bernard, et cela pour faire une place, plantée d'arbres, au centre de la prison, qui a remplacé le monastère.

Pour ne pas nous éloigner de Clairvaux et du département de l'Aube, il faut savoir qu'il s'est trouvé un préfet de la Restauration qui a fait vendre au poids sept cents livres pesant des archives de ce même Clairvaux, transportés à la préfecture de Troyes. Le reste est encore là, dans les greniers d'où il les a tirés pour faire cette belle spéculation : et j'ai marché en rougissant sur des tas de diplômes, parmi lesquels j'en ai ramassé, sous mes pieds, du pape Urbain IV, né à Troyes même, fils d'un cordonnier de cette ville, et probablement le plus illustre enfant de cette province. Ce même préfet a rasé les derniers débris du palais des anciens comtes de Champagne, de cette belle et poétique dynastie des Thibaud et des Henri-le-Large, parce qu'ils se trouvaient sur la ligne d'un chemin de ronde qu'il avait malheureusement imaginé. La charmante porte Saint-Jacques, construite sous Francis I ; la porte du Beffroy, ont eu le même sort. Un autre préfet de la Restauration, dans l'Eure-et-Loire, nous a-t-on dit, n'a éprouvé aucun scrupule à se laisser donner plusieurs vitraux de la cathédrale de Chartres, pour en orner la chapelle de son château. Ce qui est sûr, c'est qu'il n'y a pas un département de France où il ne se soit consommé, pendant les quinze années de la Restauration, plus d'irrémédiables dévastations, que pendant toute la durée de la République et de l'Empire ; non pas toujours, il s'en faut, par le fait direct de ce gouvernement, mais toujours sous ses yeux, avec sa tolérance, et sans éveiller la moindre marque de sa sollicitude.

Une pareille honte semble, Dieu merci, être écartée pour l'avenir, quoique dans les allures du gouvernement actuel tout ne soit pas également dignes d'éloges. Pourquoi faut-il, par exemple, qu'à côté des mesures utiles et intelligentes dont nous avons parlé plus haut, il y ait quelquefois des actes comme celui que nous allons citer ? Une société s'est formée en Normandie sous le titre de Société française, pour la conservation des monumens ; elle a pour créateur M. de Caumont, cet infatigable et savant archéologue qui a plus fait que personne pour populariser le goût et la science de l'art historique ; elle a réussi, après maintes difficultés, à enrégimenter dans ses rangs les propriétaires, les ecclésiastiques, les magistrats, les artistes, non seulement de la Normandie, mais encore des provinces voisines. Elle publie un recueil mensuel plein de faits et de renseignemens curieux, sous le titre de *Bulletin monumental* ; et ce qui vaut encore mieux, avec le produit des cotisations de ses membres, elle donne de secours aux fabriques des églises menacées, et obtient ainsi le droit d'arrêter beaucoup de destructions, et celui plus précieux encore d'intervenir dans les réparations. Voilà, on l'avouera, une société qui n'a pas sa rivale en France, ni peut-être en Europe, et qui méritait, à coup sûr, l'appui et la faveur du pouvoir. Or, devine-t-on quelle appui elle en a reçu ? M. le ministre de l'intérieur lui a alloué la somme de *trois cents* francs, à *titre d'encouragement !* Que penser d'un encouragement de ce genre ? Et n'est-ce pas plutôt une insulte, une véritable dérision, que de jeter cent écus à une association des hommes considérables dans leur pays, et dont le zèle et le dévouement sont propres à servir de modèles au gouvernement ? Espérons au moins que l'année prochaine ce délit contre l'art et l'histoire sera réparé d'une manière conforme au bons sens et à la justice.

Après le pouvoir central, il est juste de citer un certain nombre de magistrats et de corps constitués, qui ont noblement secondé son impulsion. Ainsi plusieurs préfets, parmi lesquels je dois spécialement désigner MM. les préfets du Calvados et de l'Eure ; M. Gabriel, préfet à Troyes, après l'avoir été à Auch ; M. Rivet, à Lyon ; M. Chaper, à Dijon, et surtout M. le comte de Rambuteau, à Paris, se montrent pleins de zèle pour la conservation des édifices anciens de leurs départemens. Ainsi, quelques conseils-généraux, et au premier rang ceux des

Deux-Sèvres,* de l'Yonne,† et de la Haute-Loire, ont voté des allocations destinées à racheter et à réparer des monumens qu'ils estiment, à juste titre, comme la gloire de leur contrée. Malheureusement ces exemples sont encore très peu nombreux, et se concentrent dans la sphère des fonctionnaires les plus élevés, et par conséquent les plus absorbés par d'autres devoirs. Partout, ou presque partout, les archives départementales et communales sont dans un état de grand désordre ; si dans quelques villes elles sont confiées à des hommes pleins de zèle et de science, comme, par exemple, à M. Maillard de Chambure, à Dijon ; ailleurs, à Perpignan, il y a peu d'années qu'on découpait les parchemins en couvercles de pots de confiture, et à Chaumont, on déchirait, tailladait et vendait à la livre tout ce qui ne paraissait pas être titre communal.   Mais comment s'étonner de cette négligence, lorsqu'on voit la chambre des députés refuser, dans sa séance du 30 mai dernier, une misérable somme de 25,000 francs, destinée à élever des bibliothèques administratives dans quelques préfectures.   Dans les administrations d'un ordre inférieur, dans le génie civil et militaire surtout, la ruine et le mépris des souvenirs historiques sont encore à l'ordre du jour.‡   Et lorsque nous mettons le pied sur le trop vaste domaine des autorités locales et municipales, nous retombons en plein dans la catégorie la plus vaste et la plus dangereuse du vandalisme destructeur.   Qu'on me permette de citer quelques exemples.

Ce sont sans doute de fort belles choses que l'alignement des rues et le redressement des routes, ainsi que la facilité des communications et l'assainissement qui doivent en résulter. Mais on ne viendra pas à bout de me persuader que les ingénieurs et les architectes ne doivent pas être arrêtés dans leur omnipotence, par la pensée d'enlever au pays qu'ils veulent servir, à la ville qu'ils veulent embellir, un de ces monumens qui en révèlent l'histoire, qui attirent les étrangers, et qui donnent à une localité ce caractère spécial qui ne peut pas plus l'être remplacé par les produits de leur génie et de leur savoir qu'un nom ne peut l'être par un chiffre. Je ne saurais admettre que cette amour désordonné de la ligne droite qui caractérise tous nos travaux d'art et de viabilité modernes, doive triompher de la beauté et de l'antiquité, comme il triomphe à peu près partout de l'économie.§   Je ne saurais croire que le progrès tant vanté

* La délibération de ce conseil-général, dans sa session de 1838, mérite d'être citée textuellement.   Après avoir voté 4,000 fr., au lieu de 3,000 que le préfet proposait, pour huit anciennes églises du departement, le conseil demande que ces sommes ne soient employées que sous la direction de l'architecte du département et les avis de M. de La Fontanelle, membre correspondant des comités historiques établis près le ministère de l'instruction publique. Il recommande à M. l'Architecte de veiller à ce qu'on ne fasse pas disparaître, comme il n'arrive que trop souvent, les parties de l'édifice qui rappellent l'état de l'art dans le pays, et qui méritent, par cela seul, d'être conservées de préférence par des réparations faites dans le même style.

† Celui-ci a sauvé, par sa généreuse intervention, deux églises aussi précieuses pour l'histoire que pour l'art : Vezelay, où saint Bernard prêcha le croisade, et Pontigny, qui servit d'asile à saint Thomas de Cantorbéry pendant son exil en France.

‡ Parmi les exploits du génie militaire, il faut citer le badigeonnage des vieilles fresques qui ornaient la chapelle de la citadelle de Perpignan, où a eu lieu le procès du général Brossard.

§ On pourrait citer de nombreuses localités où des chemins, empierrés à grands frais, ont été piochés et transformés en bourbier, les ressources des communes et des départemens scandaleusement gaspillées, et tous les besoins des sciences et des arts mécaniques doive aboutir en dernière analyse à niveler le pays sous le joug de cette ligne droite, c'est-à-dire de la forme la plus élémentaire et la plus stérile qui existe, au détriment de toutes les considérations de beauté et même de prudence. Ce ne serait vraiment pas la peine de se féliciter du talent des jeunes savans qui sortent de nos écoles, si ce talent se borne à tailler la surface de la France et de ses villes en carrés plus ou moins grands, et à renverser impitoyablement tout ce qui se trouve sur le chemin de leur règle. C'est cependant là le principe qui semble prévaloir dans tous les travaux publics de notre temps et qui amène chaque jour de nouvelles ruines. Ainsi à Dinan, dans une petite ville de Bretagne où il ne passe peut-être pas vingt voitures par jour, pour élargir une rue des moins passagères, n'a-t-on pas été détruire la belle façade de l'hospice de son église, l'un des monumens le plus curieux de ces contrées ? Le maire a essayé d'en faire transporter une partie contre le mur du cimetère, mais tout s'est brisé en route. C'est ainsi que naguère, à Dijon, l'église St. Jean, si curieuse par l'extrême hardiesse de sa voûte, qui s'appuie sur les murs de côté, sans aucune colonne, cette belle église, que le xviiie siècle lui-même avait remarquée, réduite aujourd'hui à servir de magasin de tonneaux, s'est vue honteusement mutilée : on a élagué son chœur, rien que cela, comme une branche d'arbre inutile, et un mur qui rejoint les deux transepts sépare la nef du pavé des voitures. On n'en agit ainsi qu'avec les monumens publics et surtout religieux : il en serait tout autrement s'il était question d'intérêts privés. Que les maisons voisines embarrassent autant et plus le voie publique, c'est un mal qu'on subit ; mais on se dit : "Commençons par ruiner l'église ; c'est toujours cela de gagné ;" et l'on peut affirmer hardiment que le moindre cabaret est aujourd'hui plus à l'abri des prétentions élargisseurs que le plus curieux monument du moyen âge. A Dieppe, toujours pour élargir, n'a-t-on pas détruit la belle porte de la Barre, avec ses deux grosses tours, par laquelle on arrivait de Paris ; et cela sans doute, pour la remplacer par une de ces grilles monotones, flanquées de deux hideux pavillons d'octroi, avec porche et fronton, cet idéal de l'entrée d'une ville moderne, au dessus duquel le génie de nos architectes n'a pas encore pu s'élever. A Thouars, le vaste et magnifique château des La Tremoille va être démoli pour ouvrir un passage à la grande route : ce château date presque entièrement du moyen âge, et l'on sait que les monumens militaires de cette époque sont d'une rareté désespérante. A Paris, nous approuvons de tout notre cœur les nouvelles rues de la Cité, mais sans admettre la nécessité absolue de détruire ce qui restait des anciennes églises de Saint-Landry et de Saint Pierre-aux-Bœufs, dont les noms se rattachent aux premiers jours de l'histoire de la capitale ; et si le prolongement de la rue Racine eût porté un peu plus à droite ou à gauche, de manière à ne pas produire une ligne absolument droite de l'Odéon à la rue de La Harpe, il nous semble qu'on eût trouvé une compensation suffisante dans la conservation de la précieuse église de Saint-Côme, qui, bien que souillée par son usage moderne, n'en était pas moins l'unique de sa date et de son style à Paris. A Poitiers, la fureur de l'alignement est poussée si loin, que M. Vitet s'est attiré toute l'animadversion du conseil municipal, pour avoir insisté, en sa qualité d'inspecteur-général, pour le maintien du monument le plus ancien de cette ville, le baptistère de Saint-Jean, dont on place l'origine

des populations méconnus, parce que le pédantisme de quelque jeune ingénieur aura exigé la rectification, non pas d'une pente, mais une innocente et insensible courbe d'un ou deux pieds.

entre le vie et le viiie siècle : malheureusement ce temple se trouve entre le pont et le marché aux veaux et aux poissons, et quoiqu'il y ait toute la largeur convenable pour que lesdits veaux et poissons soient voiturés tout à leur aise autour du vénérable débris d'architecture franke, il n'en est pas moins désagréable aux yeux éclairés de ces magistrats, déjà renommés par la destruction de leurs remparts et de leurs anciennes portes.   Ils se sont révoltés contre la prétension de leur faire conserver malgré eux un *obstacle à la circulation* ; de là des pamphlets contre l'audacieux M. Vitet, dans lesquels il était dénoncé aux bouchers et aux poissardes comme coupable d'encombrer les abords de leur marché ; de là, demande au gouvernement d'une somme de douze mille francs, pour compenser cette irréparable dommage ; de là, plainte jusque devant le conseil d'état, où la cause de l'histoire, de l'art et de la raison, n'a pu triompher, dit-on, qu'à la majorité d'une seule voix.   Terminons l'histoire de ces funestes alignements, en rappelant qu'au moment même où nous écrivons, Valenciennes voit disparaître la dernière arcade gothique qui ornait ses rues, qui lui rappelait son ancienne splendeur, alors qu'elle partageait avec Mons l'honneur d'être la capitale de cette glorieuse race des comtes de Hainaut, qui alla régner à Constantinople.   On y détruit la portion la plus curieuse de l'ancien Hôtel-Dieu, fondé en 1431 par Gérard de Pirfontaine, chanoine d'Anthoing, avec l'autorisation de Jacqueline de Bavière, et le secours de Philippe-le-Bon.   On voit que les plus grands noms de l'histoire locale ne trouvent pas grâce devant le municipalité de Valenciennes.   Il faut, du reste, s'étonner de l'intensité tout-à-fait spéciale de l'esprit vandale, dans ces anciennes provinces des Pays-Bas espagnols, qui pouvaient naguère s'enorgueillir de posséder les produits les plus nombreux et les plus brillans de l'art gothique.   Ce n'est guère que là, à ce qu'il nous semble, qu'on a vu des villes s'acharner après leurs vastes et illustres cathédrales, au point d'en faire disparaître jusqu'à la dernière pierre pour leur substituer une place, comme cela s'est fait à Bruges pour la cathédrale de Saint-Donat ; à Liège, pour celle de Saint-Lambert ; à Arras, pour celle de Notre-Dame ; à Cambray, pour celle de Notre-Dame aussi, avec sa merveilleuse flèche !   Ce n'est que là qu'on a vu, comme à Saint-Omer, la brutalité municipale poussée assez loin pour démolir, sous prétexte de *donner travail aux ouvriers*, les plus belles ruines de l'Europe centrale, celles de l'abbaye de Saint-Bertin, et marquer ainsi d'un ineffaçable deshonneur les annales de cette cité.

Combien de fois d'ailleurs ne voit-on pas la destruction organisée dans nos villes, sans qu'il y ait eu même l'ombre d'un prétexte ?   Ainsi à Troyes, n'a-t-on pas mieux aimé détruire la charmante chapelle de la Passion, au couvent des Cordeliers, changé en prison, et puis en reconstruire une nouvelle, que conserver l'ancienne pour l'usage de la prison ?   Ainsi à Paris, peut-on concevoir une opération plus ridicule que ce renouvellement de la grille de la Place-Royale, que la presse a déjà si généralement, mais si inutilement blâmé ?   Melé a cette affaire par les protestations inutiles que j'ai été chargé d'élever en commun avec M. du Somerard et M. le baron Taylor, à l'appui des argumens sans réplique, des calculs approfondis et consciencieux de M. Victor Hugo, j'ai pu voir de près tout ce qu'il y a encore de haine aveugle du passé, de considérations mesquines, d'ignorance volontaire et intéressée, dans la conduite des travaux d'arts sur le plus beau théâtre du monde actuel.   Cette vieille grille avait en elle-même bien peu de valeur artistique : mais elle représentait un principe, celui de la conservation.

Et les mêmes hommes qui se sont ainsi obstinés à affubler la Place-Royale d'une grille dont on avait nul besoin, ne rougissent pas de l'état ignominieux où se trouve Notre-Dame, par suite de l'absence de cette grille indispensable qu'on leur demande depuis sept années ! Peu leur importe, en vérité, que la cathédrale de Paris soit une *borne à immondices*, comme le dit avec tant de raison le rapport du comité des arts au ministre. Ils trouvent de l'argent en abondance pour planter un anachronisme au milieu de la plus curieuse place de Paris, et ils n'ont pas un centime à donner pour préserver des mutilations quotidiennes, d'outrages indicibles, la métropole du pays ; pour fermer cet horrible cloaque qui est pour Paris et la France entière, pour la population et surtout pour l'administration municipale, une flétrissure sans nom comme sans exemple en Europe.*

Lorsque l'on voit sortir des exemples pareils du sien de la capitale, c'est à peine si l'on se sent le courage de s'indigner contre les actes des municipalités subalternes : toutefois il peut être bon les signaler. Disons donc qu'à Laon, cette immense cathédrale, trop sévèrement jugée, ce nous semble, par M. Vitet,† l'une des plus vastes et des plus anciennes de France, si belle pour sa position unique, par ses quatre tours merveilleusement transparentes, par le symbolisme trinitaire de son abside carré, par le nombre prodigieux de ses chapelles, cette cathédrale inspire aux chefs de la cité à peu près autant de sympathie que Notre-Dame aux édiles parisiens. Ses abords, déjà encombrés d'une manière fâcheuse, le seront bientôt complètement par la construction d'un grand nombre de maisons sur l'emplacement du cloître, vendu pendant la révolution. Ce terrain pouvait être racheté par la ville pour une somme insignifiante ; mais, aux réclamations élevées par des personnes intelligentes et zélées, il a été répondu, par un magistrat, en ces termes : " Franchement, je ne m'intéresse pas aux édifices de ce genre ; c'est à ceux qui aiment le culte à l'appuyer." Réponse digne, comme on le voit, de cette municipalité qui a eu le privilège de détruire le plus ancien monument historique de France, le tour de Louis d'Outremer, et qui passera à la postérité, flagellée par l'impitoyable verve de M. Hugo.‡ Ailleurs, c'est encore le même indifférence, ou plutôt le même aversion pour tout ce qui tient à l'histoire ou à l'art. A Langres, quelques jeunes gens studieux avaient humblement demandé au conseil municipal l'octroi de l'abside de Saint-Didier, la plus ancienne église de la ville (aujourd'hui enlevée au culte), afin d'y commencer un musée d'antiquités locales, institution vraiment indispensable dans une contrée où chaque jour, en fouillant le sol, on découvre d'innombrables monumens de la domination romaine. Mais le sage conseil a refusé tout net, et a préféré transformer sa vieille église en dépôt de bois et pompes.—La guerre déclarée à une

* En 1837, lors de la discussion, à la chambre des pairs, sur la cession du terrain de l'archevêché à la ville, on éleva quelques objections sur cette cession à titre gratuit. Il fut répondu que l'état était suffisamment dédommagé par l'obligation que contractait la ville d'entourer ce terrain d'une grille ! On voit comme cette obligation a été bien remplie.

† Page 38 de son rapport au ministre.

‡ Ajoutons que le conseil-général de l'Aisne vote près de deux millions par an pour ses routes, qu'il ne parvient pas à employer toute cette somme : mais qu'il refuse d'en consacrer un vingtième, un cinquantième aux réparations urgentes de l'édifice le plus remarquable du département. Il se borne à exprimer le vœu que le gouvernement veuille bien le classer parmi les monumens nationaux ; comme si tous les autres départemens n'avaient pas des cathédrales dignes d'être rangées dans la même catégorie.

grande idée historique vaut bien la guerre faite à un monument ; voilà pourquoi nous allons encore parler de Dijon. Ce n'est pas assez pour cette ville d'avoir détruit, en 1803, sa Sainte-Chapelle, œuvre merveilleuse de la générosité des ducs de Bourgogne ; d'avoir transformé ses belles églises de Saint-Jean en magasin de tonneaux, de Saint-Etienne en marché couvert, et de Saint-Philibert en écuries de cavalerie ; nous allons citer un nouveau trait de son histoire. On sait que saint Bernard est né à Fontaines, village situé à peu près aussi loin de Dijon que Montmartre l'est de Paris. On y voit encore, à côté d'une curieuse église, le château de son père, transformé en couvent de feuillans, sous Louis XIII, et conservé avec soin par le propriétaire actuel, M. Girault.* On a ouvert dernièrement une nouvelle porte sur la route qui conduit à ce village : la voix publique, d'un commun accord, lui a donné le nom de *Porte Saint-Bernard*, et le lui conserve encore. Mais devant le conseil municipal il a en été autrement. Lorsque cette proposition y a été faite, il s'est trouvé un orateur assez intelligent pour déclarer que saint Bernard était un *fanatique* et un *mystique* dont les allures sentaient le carlisme et le jésuitisme, et qui, dans tous le cas, *n'avait rien fait pour la ville de Dijon ! !* Et le conseil municipal s'est rangé de cet avis. Je regrette, pour mon compte, que par voie d'amendement on n'ait pas nommé la porte d'après un homme aussi éclairé que cet orateur, mais, dans tous les cas, il aura été récompensé par la sympathie et l'approbation de M. Eusèbe Salverte, qui, dans la dernière session a si énergiquement blâmé le ministère d'avoir consacré quelques faibles sommes à l'entretien de l'église de Vézelay, où saint Bernard, en prêchant la seconde croisade, avait trouvé moyen de plonger les populations fanatisées plus avant dans *la stagnation féodale.*†

Si maintenant nous passons des autorités municipales à la troisième des catégories de vandales que j'ai autrefois établies, celle des propriétaires, il nous faut avouer que le mal, moins facile à connaître et à dénoncer, est peut-être la plus vaste encore que partout ailleurs. Nul ne saurait mesurer toute la portée de ces dévastations intimes : comme le travail de la taupe, elles échappent à l'examen et à l'opposition. Ce qu'il y a de plus fâcheux pour l'art dans les dispositions de la plupart des propriétaires français, c'est leur horreur des ruines. Autrefois on fabriquait des ruines artificielles dans les jardins à l'anglaise ; aujourd'hui on trouve aux ruines véritables des édifices les plus curieux un air *incomfortable*, que l'on s'empresse de faire disparaître, en achevant leur démolition. Celui qui aura sur ses domaines quelques débris du château de ses pères, ou d'un abbaye incendiée à la révolution, au lieu de comprendre tout ce qu'il peut y avoir d'intérêt historique ou de beauté pittoresque dans ces vieilles pierres, n'y verra qu'une carrière à exploiter. C'est ainsi qu'ont disparu notamment toutes les belles églises anciennes des monastères, dont on a quelquefois utilisé les bâtimens d'habitation : c'est ainsi, par exemple, que nous avons vu vendre il y a trois mois, jusqu'à la dernière pierre de l'église de Foigny en Thiérache, près la Capelle, église fondée par saint Bernard, qui avait quatre cent pieds de long, et qui subsistait encore, il y a quelques années, dans toute sa pure et native beauté ; et on a pu faire disparaître ce magnifique édifice, sans qu'une seule récla-

---

* Bien loin d'imiter tant de propriétaires vandales, ou pour le moins indifférens, M. Girault a publié un fort bon opuscule intitulé : *la Maison natale de Saint Bernard à Fontaine-lez-Dijon*, 1824.

† Discussion du budget de l'intérieur, en 1838.

mation se soit élevée pour conserver à la contrée environnante son plus bel ornement et une preuve vivante de son importance historique. Près de là, dans un site bien boisé et très solitaire, à Bonne-Fontaine, près d'Aubenton, abbaye fondée en 1153, on voit encore le transept méridional et six arcades de la nef de l'église qui est évidemment du xiie siècle : mais l'année prochaine on ne les verra peut-être plus, parce que l'acquéreur installé dans l'abbatiale, en arrache chaque jour quelques pierres pour les besoins de son ménage. Il y a quinze jours, un ouvrier était occupé à dépecer la grande rosace qui formait l'antéfixe du transept, et qui, laissée à nu par la destruction du pignon, se découpait à jour sur le ciel, et produisait un effet aussi original que pittoresque. On ne conçoit pas qu'un esprit de spéculation purement industriel n'inspire pas mieux, et qu'on ne songe jamais aux voyageurs nombreux qu'on éloigne en dépouillant le pays de toute sa parure, de tout ce qui peut distraire de l'ennui, éveiller la curiosité ou attirer l'étude. Quelle différence déplorable pour nous entre le système français et les soins scrupuleux qui ont valu à l'Angleterre la conservation des admirables ruines de Tintern, de Croyland, de Netley, de Fountains, et de tant d'autres abbayes qui, pour avoir été supprimées et à moitié démolies par la réforme, n'en offrent pas moins aujourd'hui d'inappréciables ressources à l'artiste et à l'antiquaire. Et s'il faut absolument descendre à des considérations aussi ignobles, qu'on aille demander aux aubergistes, aux voituriers, à la population en général des environs de ces monumens, s'ils ne trouvent pas leur compte à la conservation de ces vieilles pierres qui, situées en France, auraient depuis long-temps servi à réparer une route ou une écluse. Où en seraient les rives du Rhin, si fréquentées et si admirées, avec le mode d'exploitation des ruines que l'on emploie en France ? Il y a long-temps que les touristes et les artistes auraient abandonné ces parages, comme ils ont abandonné la France, cette France qui était naguère, de tous les pays de l'Europe, la plus richement pourvue en églises, en châteaux et en abbayes du moyen âge, et qui le serait encore si on avait pu arrêter, il y a vingt ans, le torrent des dévastations publiques et particulières. Aujourd'hui c'est à l'Allemagne qu'il faut céder la palme, grâce au zèle qui anime à la fois le gouvernement et les individus contre les progrès du vandalisme, lequel y a régné comme chez nous, mais bien moins long-temps. Les mesures administratives y sont appuyées par cette bonne volonté et cette intelligence des individus qui manquent si généralement en France. C'est ainsi qu'il s'est formé dans plusieurs villes des associations avec le but spécial de conserver tel ou tel monument voisin. Nous citerons celle créée à Bamberg pour racheter et entretenir Altenbourg, l'ancien château des évêques de Bamberg. M. le baron d'Aufsess, l'un des amis les plus zélés de l'art chrétien et historique en Allemagne, en a formé une autre pour sauver le beau château de Zwernitz, en Franconie, et la même mesure a été prise par une réunion de prêtres et de bourgeois dans l'intérêt de la vieille église située au pied du Hohenstaufen.

Peut-être verrons-nous en France des améliorations de ce genre : la société formée par M. de Caumont pour la *conservation des monumens*, dont nous avons parlé plus haut, pourra se propager et former des succursales : Dieu le veuille ! car en France, plus qu'ailleurs, l'homme isolé n'a presque jamais la conscience de l'étendue de sa mission. Pour un homme vraiment énergique et éclairé comme M. de Golbéry, qui, par l'influence que lui donne sa triple qualité de législateur, de magistrat et de savant très distingué, a rendu des services si éminens à l'art

N

chrétien en Alsace,* nous aurons encore pendant long-temps cinquante hommes comme M. Nicolas, architecte de Bourbon-l'Archambault, lequel, pour donner une preuve de ses connaissances architecturales, a fait démolir la Sainte-Chapelle de Bourbon-l'Archambault, l'ornement et la gloire du Bourbonnais, pour en vendre les matériaux. C'est en 1833 que le dernier débris en a disparu.

Mais comment qualifier le trait que je vais raconter, et dans quelle catégorie de vandales faut-il ranger ses auteurs? Il y avait à Montargis une tour antique qui faisait l'admiration des voyageurs. M. Cotelle, notaire à Paris et propriétaire à Montargis, jugeant utile de conserver ces vénérables restes, avait provoqué des souscriptions et obtenu même du ministère une somme de 1,200 francs pour réparations urgentes. Malheureusement, aux élections générales de 1837, M. Cotelle se présente comme candidat ministériel; aussitôt les meneurs de l'oppotion se sont cru parfaitement en droit d'exciter quelques individus à retirer petit à petit les pierres qui faisaient la base de l'édifice, et, à leur grande joie, la tour s'écroula avec un épouvantable fracas. La nouvelle de cette belle victoire fut aussitôt expédiée à Paris; le tour y fut jugé bon, et plus d'un journal *sérieux* le raconta avec éloge.† Je ne pense pas qu'il y ait un autre pays au monde où un pareil acte serait toléré, bien loin d'être encouragé.

En quittant le temporel pour le spirituel, si on examine l'état du vandalisme chez le clergé, on reconnaît que sa puissance y est toujours à peu près aussi étendue et aussi enracinée. Malgré les recommandations et les prescriptions de M. l'évêque du Puy et de plusieurs autres respectables évêques, il y a toujours dans la masse du clergé et dans les conseils de fabrique, la même manie d'enjolivemens profanes et ridicules, la même indifférence barbare pour les trop rares débris de l'antiquité chrétienne. J'ai dit l'année dernière‡ combien le système suivi dans les constructions récentes était déplorable: il me reste à parler de la manière dont on traite les édifices anciens. Je sais qu'il y a dans chaque diocèse d'honorables exceptions, et que le nombre de ces exceptions s'accroît chaque jour.§ Mais il est encore beaucoup trop petit pour lutter contre l'esprit général, pour empêcher qu'il n'y ait un contraste affligeant entre cet état stationnaire, cette halte dans la barbarie, et la réaction salutaire manifestée par le gouvernement et par des citoyens isolés. A l'appui de ce que j'avance ici, qu'il me soit permis de transcrire littéralement ce qu'on m'écrit à la fois des deux extrémités de la France: "Vous ne sauriez vous imaginer (c'est un prêtre breton qui parle) l'ardeur que l'on met dans le Finistère et les Côtes-du-Nord à salir de chaux ce qui restait encore intact. La passion de

* Entre autres églises, M. de Golbéry a sauvé celle d'Ottmarshein, qui date, selon la tradition, des temps païens; la belle église de Geberschwir, et celle de Sigolsheim, fondée par l'impératrice sainte Richarde au neuvième siècle. Dans cette dernière église, il a eu le mérite de faire prolonger la nef de plusieurs arcades en conservant tout-à-fait le style de l'original, et en reportant sur la nouvelle façade le portail du neuvième siècle, au lieu de laisser plaquer contre l'antique édifice une sorte de coffre en platras moderne, avec un péristyle à triangle obtus, comme cela se pratique partout où les besoins de la population exigent l'agrandissement d'une vieille église. Entre mille exemples de cette absurdité, nous citerons Saint-Vallier, sur le Rhône.

† Voyez *le Courrier* et *le Siècle* des premiers jours de Novembre 1837.

‡ Voyez *De l'Etat actuel de l'Art religieux.*

§ Aux noms que j'ai eu occasion de citer ailleurs, je dois ajouter M. Pascal, curé de la Ferté, dans le diocèse de Blois, qui, dans sa polémique avec M. Didron, publiée par *l'Univers*, a donné des preuves de science et de zèle.

batir de nouvelles églises s'est emparée d'un grand nombre de mes confrères ; malheureusement elle n'est point éclairée. On veut partout du nouveau, de l'élégant à la manière des païens : pour ne pas ressembler à nos pères, pour ne pas imiter leur religieuse architecture, on nous fait ou des salles de spectacle, ou de misérables masures sans dignité, sans élégance, sans aucun cachet religieux, où le symbolisme chrétien est tout-à-fait sacrifié au caprice de MM. les ingénieurs. Ce n'est pas que l'on ne fasse quelquefois des réclamations, mais comme elles ne sont dictées que par le bon sens et la religion, et que, pour avoir des fonds, il faut suivre servilement les plans des architectes officiels, on passe à l'ordre du jour." D'un autre côté, on m'écrit de Langres : " Le clergé de notre diocèse est tellement éloigné de tout sentiment de l'art religieux, qu'il *s'oppose généralement aux réparations faites dans le caractère des monumens gothiques*, et qu'il n'est presque pas de prêtre qui ne préfère une église à colonnes et à pilastres grecs, à fenêtres carrées ou en demi-cercle, garnies de rideaux de couleur, aux monumens gothiques. Et chaque jour on voit, quand une église est trop petite, qu'au lieu de l'agrandir en suivant son architecture primitive, on la détruit, et on la remplace par une salle aux murs badigeonnés de jaune et de blanc."

Je pourrais citer vingt lettres semblables, qui ne contiennent toutes que l'exacte vérité, comme peut s'en assurer quiconque est doué de l'instinct le plus élémentaire en matière d'art religieux, et qui veut se donner la peine d'interroger les hommes et les lieux. Partout il trouvera des curés qui se reposent sur leurs lauriers, après avoir recouvert leurs vieilles églises d'un épais badigeon beurre-frais, relevé par des tranches de rouge ou de bleu, après avoir jeté aux gravois les menaux de leurs fenêtres ogivales, et échangé contre les produits de pacotille religieuse qu'on exporte de Paris, les trop rares monumens d'art chrétien que le temps avait épargnés. Je prends au hasard quelques traits parmi ceux que me fournit une trop triste expérience de ce qu'il faut bien nommer le vandalisme fabricien et sacerdotal. Quelquefois c'est une profonde insouciance qui fait la généreuse aux dépens de l'église. Ainsi plusieurs tonnes de vitraux provenant de l'église d'Epernay ont été donnés à un grand-vicaire de Châlons, pour orner la chapelle de son château ; ainsi une paix en ivoire du XIVᵉ siècle, appartenant à Saint-Jacques de Rheims, a été donnée par l'avant-dernier curé de cette paroisse, à un antiquaire de la ville. Ailleurs, c'est un esprit de mercantile avidité qui spécule sur les débris de l'antiquité chrétienne, comme sur une proie assurée. On se rappelle la mise en vente de l'ancienne église de Châtillon, l'une des plus curieuses de la Champagne, par la fabrique, sur la mise à prix de 4,000 fr., heureusement arrêtée par le zèle infatigable de M. Didron, et le rapport qu'il adressa au ministre de l'instruction publique sur cette honteuse dilapidation. Mais là où on ne saurait vendre en gros, on se rabat sur le détail. A Amiens, on a vendu trois beaux et curieux tableaux sur bois du XVIᵉ siècle, qui se trouvaient à la cathédrale, moyennant le badigeonnage d'une des chapelles. Il y en a d'autres qui servent en ce moment de portes au poulailler d'un jeune abbé ! C'est dans cette même église qu'un des chanoines disait naguère à M. du Sommerard en lui montrant des stalles du chœur, monument admirable d'ancienne boiserie : " Voyez ce *grenier à poussière !* Il nous empêche d'être vus ; qui nous en débarrassera ?" Dans la collection de ce savant archéologue, on voit de curieux émaux byzantins, qu'il avait d'abord admirés à la cathédrale de Sens, et qui lui ont été apportés, il y a trois ou quatre ans, par un brocanteur, qui les avait achetés à l'église, toujours moyennant le badigeonnage d'une chapelle.   A Troyes, la fabrique de la Madeleine a fait tailler, dans les bases et les fûts des colonnes, un certain nombre de places, que l'on loue à trois ou quatre francs par an, au risque de faire écrouler l'édifice tout entier.   C'est, du reste, la même fabrique qui voulait absolument abattre le fameux jubé de cette église, regardé comme le plus beau de France, sous prétexte que ce n'était plus de mode, et qui ne l'a épargné qu'à condition de pouvoir l'empâter sous une épaisse couche de badigeon.*   Rien n'échappe à ce mépris systématique de la vénérable antiquité; mais ce qui semble spécialement exposé à ses coups, ce sont les anciens fonts baptismaux, objets de l'étude et de l'appréciation toute particulière de nos voisins les Anglais.   A Lagery, près Reims, le curé a fait briser des fonts romains pour les remplacer par des fonts modernes.   Il en est de même dans presque toutes les églises du nord et de l'est de la France; partout les fonts sont brisés ou relégués dans un coin obscur, pour faire place à quelque conque païenne.   De l'autre côté de la France, près Poitiers, dans une église dont j'ai le tort d'avoir oublié le nom, il y avait un ancien font baptismal *par immersion*.   Cette particularité si rare et si curieuse n'a pas suffi pour lui faire trouver grâce devant le curé, qui l'a fait détruire.   Ailleurs ce sont ces vieilles tapisseries, si estimées aujourd'hui des antiquaires, surtout depuis que le bel ouvrage de M. Achille Jubinal est venu révéler toute la beauté et toute l'importance.   A Clermont en Auvergne, il y a dans la cathédrale douze tapisseries provenant de l'ancien évêché, et faites de 1505 à 1511, sous la direction de Jacques d'Amboise, membre de cette illustre famille si généreusement amie des arts; elles sont toutes déchirées, moisies et abîmées de poussière.   M. Thévenot, membre du comité des arts, avait offert de les nettoyer à ses frais et d'en prendre un calque; mais le chapitre lui a répondu par un refus.   A Notre-Dame de Reims, il y a encore d'autres tapisseries du XIVᵉ siècle, qui sont découpées, et servent de tapis de pied au trône épiscopal.   En revanche, quand on aura besoin de ce genre de parures pour certaines fêtes de l'Eglise, comme c'est encore l'usage à Paris pour la semaine sainte, soyez sûr qu'on ira chercher au hasard, dans quelque garde-meuble, tout ce qu'il y aura de plus ridiculement contradictoire avec la sainteté du lieu et du temps; c'est ainsi que le vendredi saint de cette année 1838, tout le monde a pu voir au *tombeau* de Saint-Sulpice, le *Festin d'Antoine et Cléopâtre* (Cléopâtre dans le costume le plus léger), et à celui de Saint-Germain l'Auxerrois, *Vénus amenant l'Amour aux nymphes de Calypso!*   Terminons cette série par un dernier trait de ce genre: à Saint-Guilhem, entre Montpellier et Lodève, il y a une église bâtie, selon la tradition, par Charlemagne, et dont l'autel a été donné par saint Grégoire VII; cet autel a été arraché, relégué dans un coin, par le curé qui y a substitué un autel en bois peint, oubliant sans doute qu'il outrageait ainsi les deux plus grands noms du moyen âge catholique, Charlemagne et Grégoire VII !

Quand on a ainsi disposé de la partie mobilière, il reste l'immeuble, que l'on s'évertue le mieux que l'on peut à revêtir d'un déguisement moderne.   Quelle est l'église de France qui ne porte les traces de ces anachronismes trop souvent irréparables?   Hélas! il n'y en a littéralement pas une seule.   Là où la pioche et la râpe n'ont pas labouré ces saintes pierres, l'ignoble badigeon les a toujours souillées.   Qu'ils parlent, ceux qui ont eu le bonheur de voir une de nos cathédrales du premier ordre, Chartres, par exemple, il y a quelques dix ans, avant qu'elle

---

* Arnaud, *Antiquités de Troyes*, 1827.

ne fût jaunie de cet ocre blafard que l'évêque a mis tant de zèle à obtenir, et qu'ils nous disent, si la parole leur suffi pour cela, tout ce qu'une église peut perdre en grandeur, en majesté, en sainteté, à ce sot travestissement ! Statues, bas-reliefs, chapiteaux, rinceaux, fresques, pierres tombales, épitaphes, inscriptions pieuses, rien n'est épargné : il faut que tout y passe ; il faut cacher tout ce qui peut rappeler les siècles de foi et d'enthousiasme religieux, ou du moins rendre méconnaissable ce qu'on ne peut complètement anéantir. D'où il résultera cet autre avantage, que les murs de l'église seront plus éclatans que le jour qui doit pénétrer par les fenêtres, même quand celles-ci seront dégarnies de leurs vitraux, et que par conséquent les conducteurs naturels de la lumière auront l'air de lui faire obstacle. Faire l'histoire des ravages du badigeon, ce serait faire la statistique ecclésiastique de la France ; je me borne à invoquer la vengeance de la publicité contre les derniers attentats qui sont parvenus à ma connaissance. A Coutances, dans cette fameuse cathédrale qui a si long-temps occupé les archéologues, le dernier évêque a fait peindre en jaune les deux collatéraux, et la nef du milieu en blanc, en même temps qu'il écrasait l'un des transepts sous la masse informe d'un autel dédié à saint Pierre, parce qu'il s'appelait Pierre. A Boury, village près Gisors, le curé a trouvé bon de donner à sa vieille église le costume suivant : les gros murs en *bleu*, les colonnes en *rose*, le tout relevé par des plinthes et des corniches en *jaune*. A Laon, l'église romane de la fameuse abbaye de Saint-Martin a été badigeonnée en ocre des pieds à la tête, par son curé, et dans la cathédrale, cette charmante chapelle de la Vierge qui a germé comme une fleur sur les lignes sévères du transept septentrional, a été recouverte d'un jaune épais, et ornée d'une série d'arcades à rez-terre, en *vert marbré*, relevées par des colonnes orange ; cette mascarade est due à un ecclésiastique de la paroisse, et il n'y a de plus affreux que la longue balustrade qui coupe par le milieu l'extrémité carrée du chœur, et qui est peint en noir parce que le mur auquel elle s'appuie, est peinte en blanc. A la grande collégiale de Saint-Quentin, il y a autour du chœur cinq chapelles que M. Vitet a qualifiées avec raison de " ravissantes, d'un goût et d'un dessin tout-à-fait mauresque."* Mais je ne sais si, de son temps, celle du chevet était décorée avec des bandes de papier peint marbré, absolument comme l'antichambre d'un hôtel garni, avec un prétendu vitrail en petits carrés de verre bleus et rouges, à travers lesquels les enfans peuvent s'amuser à voir trembloter le feuillage d'un arbre planté au chevet de l'église. On n'a pas respecté davantage la curieuse église de l'abbaye de Saint-Michel en Thiérache, que je recommande vivement aux antiquaires qui seront chargés de la statistique si importante du département de l'Aisne ; dans une position charmante et presque cachée au bord des vastes forêts qui longent la frontière belge, elle offre le plus grand intérêt par la disposition tout-à-fait excentrique de ses cinq absides, et par son transept du XIIᵉ siècle. Les moines l'avaient refaite à moitié dans le XVIIᵉ siècle, et avaient plaqué beaucoup de marbre sur ce qui restait d'ancien. Mais il y a deux ans que sa solitude et sa beauté n'ont pu la mettre à l'abri d'une couche générale de jaune, d'orange et de blanc qui en alourdit et altère les proportions. Dans le midi on doit déplorer les badigeonnages récens de St.-André-le-Bas à Vienne, de Notre-Dame d'Orcival en Auvergne, de St.-Michel au Puy-en-Velay, enfin de la cathédrale de Lyon ; cette dernière œuvre est du fait de M. Chenavard, architecte à qui des juges plus

* Rapport au ministre de l'intérieur, page 61.

compétens que moi ont déjà imputé l'écroulement de l'ancienne nef de la cathédrale de Belley, ainsi que des restaurations et constructions très affligeantes, à Saint-Vincent de Châlons-sur-Saône.* Quant à ce qui se passe dans Paris, j'emprunte l'énergique langage du rapport de M. de Gasparin : " On empâte, dit-il, de peinture, et on cache sous le stuc deux chapelles de Saint-Germain-des-Prés, en attendant qu'on ait assez d'argent pour habiller ainsi l'église entière. On déguise, sous des couleurs vert-pomme et bleu-pâle détrempées dans l'huile, l'église Saint-Laurent, et on en transforme en ce moment les chapelles en armoires. Enfin l'on badigeonne et l'on gratte tout à la fois la grande église de Saint-Sulpice qu'une vieille teinte grise commençait déjà à rendre respectable."†

Ce n'est pas au clergé, c'est au conseil des bâtimens civils, siégeant à Paris, qu'il faut attribuer et reprocher l'odieux système que l'on suit partout à l'encontre des clochers d'églises rurales. Il est à peu près reconnu par tout le monde que les flèches gothiques, ou en pointe, sont le plus bel ornement des horizons de nos campagnes. Mais malheur à celle qui exige des réparations. Fût-elle la plus antique, la plus noble, la plus gracieuse du monde, point de pitié. Dès qu'on y touche, il faut la remplacer par deux pans coupés, ou par une sorte de calotte ou chaudière. C'est la règle prescrite par le conseil des bâtimens, qui ne souffre pas qu'on s'en écarte, quand même on aurait tout l'argent nécessaire pour payer quelque chose de mieux. La ville de Charmes, dans les Vosges, avait près de cent mille francs de fonds municipaux disponibles, pour une réparation de cette nature : on ne l'en a pas moins forcée à remplacer, par un capuchon en forme de marmite renversée, sa flèche élégante et fière, qui de trois lieues à la ronde ornait le paysage. On pourrait citer une foule d'autres exemples de ce genre. Le résultat général de cette sorte de progrès consiste à abaisser partout les croix de village de trente à quarante pieds. Belle victoire pour la civilisation.

Enfin, avant de sortir des églises, il faut bien consacrer quelques mots à une classe spéciale de vandales qui y ont élu domicile, c'est-à-dire aux organistes. Si c'est un crime d'offenser les yeux par des constructions baroques et ridicules, c'en est un, assurément, que d'outrager des oreilles raisonnables par une prétendue musique religieuse qui excite dans l'âme tout ce qu'on veut, excepté des sentimens religieux, et d'employer à cette profanation le roi des instrumens, l'*organe* intime et majestueux des harmonies chrétiennes. Or, dans toute la France, et spécialement à Paris, les organistes se rendent coupables de ce crime. Règle générale, toutes les fois qu'on invoquera le secours si puissant et si nécessaire de l'orgue pour compléter les cérémonies du culte, toutes les fois qu'on verra affiché sur le programme de quelque fête que *l'orgue sera touché par M.* * * *, on peut être d'avance sûr d'entendre quelques airs du nouvel opéra, des valses, des contredanses, des tours de force, si l'on veut, mais jamais un motet vraiment empreint de sentiment religieux, jamais une de ces grandes compositions des anciens maîtres d'Allemagne ou d'Italie ; jamais surtout une de ces vieilles mélodies catholiques, faites pour l'orgue, et pour lesquelles seules l'orgue lui-même est fait. Je ne conçois rien de plus grotesque et de plus profane à la fois que le système suivi par les organistes de Paris. Leur

* Cet architecte vandale est justement jugé dans la lettre de M. de Guilhermy au ministre de l'instruction publique, sur les monumens du Lyonnais, insérée dans *le Journal de l'Instruction publique* de Novembre 1838.

† *Moniteur* du 3 Août 1838.

but semble être de montrer que l'orgue, sous des mains habiles comme les leurs, peut rivaliser avec le piano de la demoiselle du coin, ou avec la musique du régiment qu'on entend passer dans la rue. Quelquefois ils descendent plus bas, et le jour de Pâques de cette année 1838, on a entendu au salut de Saint-Etienne-du-Mont, un air fort connu des buveurs, dont les premières paroles sont :

> Mes amis, quand je bois,
> Je suis plus heureux qu'un roi.

On voit que ce n'est guère la peine pour Mgr. l'archévêque de Paris d'interdire la musique de théâtre dans les églises, puisque les organistes y introduisent de la musique de cabaret. Il y a longtemps cependant que ces abus, si patiemment tolérés aujourd'hui, sont proscrits par l'autorité compétente ; et, pour me mettre à l'abri du reproche d'être un novateur audacieux, je veux citer deux anciens canons qu'on trouve dans le Bréviaire de Paris. Le premier est du concile de Paris, en 1528, décret 17 : " Les saints Pères n'ont introduit dans l'Eglise l'usage des orgues que pour le culte et le service de Dieu. Ainsi, nous défendons qu'on joue dans l'église sur ces instrumens des chants lascifs ; nous ne permettons que des sons doux, dont la mélodie ne représente que de saintes hymnes et des cantiques spirituels." Le second est de l'archévêque François de Harlay, article 32 des statuts du synode de 1674 : " Nous défendons expressément d'introduire dans les églises et chapelles des musiques profanes et séculières, *avec des modulations vives et sautillantes* ; de jouer sur les orgues des chansons ou autres airs indignes de la modestie et de la gravité du chant ecclésiastique. . . . Enfin, nous défendons d'envoyer ou d'afficher des programmes pour inviter les fidèles à des musiques dans les églises, comme à des pièces de théâtre ou à des spectacles."

Pour pardonner tout ce qu'on fait et tout ce qui se laisse faire dans les églises, il faut se souvenir qu'on se borne à suivre la route tracée par la plupart de nos savans et de nos artistes attitrés, dont tout le génie consiste à mépriser et à ignorer l'art chrétien ; il faut se souvenir que l'un des architectes les plus renommés de la capitale, et qui postule aujourd'hui une importante restauration gothique, qualifie l'architecture du moyen âge *d'architecture à chauve-souris*, et qu'une des lumières de l'Académie des Beaux-Arts déplore partout l'appui donné par le gouvernement à *la seule tendance qu'il importe de décourager*.

Je ne puis terminer cette invective sans faire une rétractation exigée par la justice. J'ai dit naguère, que partout, excepté en France, les monumens d'art ancien étaient respectés, et j'ai nommé la Belgique parmi les pays qui lui donnaient cette salutaire leçon. Après avoir pris une connaissance plus approfondie des faits, je suis obligé de dire qu'il n'en est rien, et que, si le gouvernement et la législation belge sont plus avancés que les nôtres sous ce rapport, en revanche, les dispositions générales du pays sont plutôt en arrière de celles de la France. Par une contradiction remarquable, la Belgique, qui avait su se garantir plus qu'un autre pays des doctrines gallicanes et philosophiques du XVIIIe siècle, comme l'a démontré son insurrection contre Joseph II, avait cependant subi à un degré incroyable l'influence de l'art dégénéré des époques de Louis XIV et de Louis XV. Je ne connais rien en France de comparable aux gaînes colossales par lesquelles on a trouvé moyen de défigurer la nef de la cathédrale de Malines ; à la façade de Notre-Dame-de-Finistère à Bruxelles, véritable passoir à café flanquée de deux bilboquets ; aux miroirs, aux plâtres et aux marbrures qui déshonorent Saint-Paul et

Saint-Jacques à Liège ; à ces autels monstres en marbre noir, inventés exprès pour détruire, comme à Anvers, l'effet de la plus belle église gothique. La Belgique n'a pas encore su se dégager de ses langes grotesques. Et, chez elle, le vandalisme restaurateur marche fièrement à côté du vandalisme destructeur. Ce dernier lui fut apporté par la conquête française, qui fit disparaître presque toutes ses magnifiques abbayes et deux de ses plus anciennes cathédrales. Le règne de la maison d'Orange fut aussi une époque de dévastation et d'abandon systématique. Je ne veux en citer que deux traits. A l'époque où le roi Guillaume Ier mettait en vente à son profit pour 94 millions de domaines nationaux belges, et où il livrait à la hache d'impitoyables spéculateurs cette forêt de Soignes, la plus belle de l'Europe occidentale, l'ornement de Bruxelles et du pays tout entier, ce prince éclairé crut faire une bonne affaire en faisant vendre aux enchères l'ancien château de Vianden, dans le Luxembourg, édifice immense et admirable, sur un rocher qui domine l'Our, parfaitement conservé et habité,* et qui devait en outre avoir, à ses yeux, le mérite d'avoir été la première possession de la maison de Nassau dans les Pays-Bas.† Il fut adjugé pour *six mille* francs à un entrepreneur, qui en enleva les plombs, les bois, et le rendit ainsi aussi inhabitable que possible, jusqu'à ce que le roi, éveillé par les clameurs que faisait pousser cet acte de vandalisme inoui, racheta les ruines du château de ses pères moyennant 3,000 francs. C'étaient toujours 1,000 écus de profit, et une gloire de moins pour sa couronne et pour le pays ; et cependant voilà ce qu'on appellait une *restauration !* Ces ruines, dans leur état actuel, sont, de l'avis unanime des voyageurs, plus vastes et mieux conservées que tout ce qu'on voit de ce genre sur les bords du Rhin ; qu'on juge du prix qu'avait un pareil monument dans son intégrité. Sous ce même règne, en 1822, on voyait encore, à quatre lieues de Bruxelles, l'immense abbaye des Prémontrés de Ninove. Ses quatre façades offraient un vaste ensemble d'architecture classique, dans les proportions les plus imposantes et les plus régulières ; sa reconstruction, en 1718, avait coûté 3,500,000 francs. En 1822, elle était dans un état de conservation parfaite, et on la mettait en vente pour 80,000 francs. La province de la Flandre-Orientale voulut en faire l'acquisition pour l'offrir comme château au prince d'Orange, qui faisait alors bâtir à Bruxelles un palais dont toute l'étendue n'égale pas une seule des quatre façades de Ninove ; mais le roi refusa cette offre. Il n'eut pas davantage l'idée d'utiliser cet immense édifice, si voisin de sa capitale, pour en faire un hospice, un collége, ou une caserne ; et l'adjudication définitive eut lieu le 15 janvier, après l'affiche suivante que nous croyons devoir transcrire comme une curieuse pièce justificative de la future histoire du vandalisme : " Cette abbaye, dont la construction a coûté plus de 1,500,000 florins avant la révolution, offre, sous le rapport de la démolition, des avantages immenses. Tous les matériaux en sont de la plus grande beauté : le fer, le plomb, les ardoises fortes, les grès, le marble, n'y ont pas été épargnés ; la charpente en est énorme : aucune planche n'a été clouée. Pour le transport, la Dendre offre un moyen facile. Les fortifications de Termonde, les travaux à Bruxelles, etc., assurent le débit avantageux des matériaux. En un mot, cette vente se présente aux spéculateurs sous l'aspect et dans les circonstances les plus favorables."

Tous ces avantages ont été si bien saisis qu'aujourd'hui il ne reste pas pierre sur pierre de

---

* Le roi l'avait repris à M. de Marbœuf, qui l'avait reçu en dotation de Napoléon, et qui l'entretenait fort bien.

† En 1340, Marguerite de Spanheim, héritière du comte de Vianden, l'apporta en dot à Othon, comte de Nassau.

l'édifice. Seulement on peut en examiner les plans chez un menuisier de la ville, et vraiment c'est une visite qui vaut la peine d'être faite, pour voir jusqu'où la fureur de détruire peut aller, en pleine paix et sous un gouvernement régulier.

Depuis la révolution de 1830, le nouveau gouvernement s'est occupé avec quelque sollicitude de la conservation des monumens. La loi communale, tout en accordant aux municipalités des attributions plus larges qu'en aucun autre pays du monde, leur défend de procéder, sans *l'approbation du roi*, " à la démolition des monumens de l'antiquité et aux réparations à y faire, lorsque ces réparations sont de nature à changer le style ou le caractère des monumens."* Voilà de belles et sages paroles, dont l'absence se fait regretter dans notre loi municipale française ! Pour que l'approbation du roi ne soit jamais surprise, il a été institué une commission royale des monumens, présidée par le comte Amédée de Beauffort, et qui a déjà rendu de grands services. Il faut espérer que, grâce à ces précautions, on ne verra plus ce qui s'est passé il y a quelques années à Chimay, lorsque la pierre sépulcrale de l'historien Froissart (chanoine de la collégiale de Chimay) fut enlevée et brisée pour faire une entrée particulière dans la chapelle des fonts ! On est déjà parvenu à sauver, entre autres débris curieux, la vieille porte de Hall, à Bruxelles, qui renferme encore de très-belles salles, et que l'on s'acharnait à remplacer par deux de ces barraques à porche et à fronton obtus qui ornent toutes les autres entrées de la capitale. On a même été assez heureux pour rendre à Sainte-Gudule une portion notable de son ancienne beauté, en détruisant le maître-autel qui obstruait son chevet. M. Rogier, ancien ministre de l'intérieur, et actuellement gouverneur de la province d'Anvers, avait conçu et proposé la magnifique idée de faire terminer la flèche de la cathédrale de Malines, par une souscription populaire, afin de placer sous cette consécration religieuse et nationale, le souvenir de la révolution de 1830, et le point central du système des chemins de fer qui doit changer industriellement la face de la Belgique. Malheureusement on a cru s'apercevoir que les fondemens de la tour ne supporteraient pas une augmentation de poids aussi considérable. La ville de Malines mériterait, du reste, assez peu cet honneur, car

---

* Voici un arrêté du roi Léopold, qui montre comment cette loi excellente est exécutée. Il est daté du 28 novembre 1838. C'est un contraste humiliant pour nous que celui des mesures prises à Dinant en Belgique, avec les dévastations de Dinan en Bretagne, dont nous parlions plus haut.

" Vu l'arrêté du 25 août 1837, ordonnant le redressement de la route de première classe, n°. 3, de Namur vers Givet, dans la partie de la traverse de Dinant, comprise entre la place Saint-Nicolas et la sortie de la ville vers Givet ;

" Considérant que, par suite de ce redressement, la porte Saint-Nicolas devait être démolie ; que cependant, cette porte étant d'une belle construction et d'une grande antiquité, il est désirable qu'elle soit conservée intacte en la dégageant convenablement ; que, sous ce dernier rapport, de nouvelles dépenses deviennent nécessaires ; . . . .

" Considérant que la ville de Dinant est particulièrement intéressée à la conservation de la porte dont il s'agit, et que l'Etat, tout en prêtant son concours à la chose, n'est cependant déterminé que par un intérêt secondaire quant à la voirie ;

" Dispose :

" Art. 1er. Il est accordé à la ville de Dinant, à titre de subside, une somme de trois cents francs, pour contribuer à la dépense que nécessitera la conservation de la porte dite de Saint-Nicolas en cette ville.

" Art. 2. Les terrains nécessaires, et notamment celui qui se trouve au-delà de la porte et qui forme l'angle de séparation de l'ancienne route de la nouvelle, seront acquis et occupés conformément aux lois en matière d'expropriation pour cause d'utilité publique."

O

sa régence est occupée en ce moment à postuler avec acharnement la destruction de la belle
porte à tourelles qui conduit à Bruxelles ; et lorsqu'on leur reproche cette barbarie, ils
répondent : " Oh ! nous en avons détruit une, il y a quelques années, celle de Louvain, qui
était bien plus belle encore !" Et ils disent vrai, à leur plus grande honte. Mais si le
gouvernement a quelque prise sur les administrations provinciales et municipales, il n'en a point
sur les particuliers ni sur le clergé. La vente des vitraux et des chaires, de tous les fragmens
mobiliers d'art chrétien, à des Anglais ou à des brocanteurs de Paris, est organisée sur une
très-grande échelle ; il n'a fallu rien moins que l'intervention du roi protestant, pour empêcher
le curé catholique d'Alsemberg, de vendre la chaire gothique de son église à un Anglais.
A Alne, abbaye fondée par saint Bernard, sur les bords de la Sambre, il existe encore la plus
grande partie de la maison et une moitié environ de l'église, qui date de l'époque même du
fondateur. Croirait-on que ce sont les anciens religieux eux-mêmes, qui, ayant racheté ces
ruines, les vendent par charretées ! A Sainte-Gudule même, dont la restauration se fait, en
générale, avec beaucoup de zèle et de goût, il faut cependant dénoncer l'architecte qui a trouvé
bon de faire arracher un grand nombre de consoles richement sculptées sur les tours de la
façade, sous prétexte que ces consoles sans statues ne signifiaient rien. Quant au règne du
badigeon, il est encore bien plus universel et plus solidement établi qu'en France. Je ne crois
pas qu'à l'exception de Sainte-Waudru de Mons, il y ait une seule église de Belgique, grande
ou petite, qui ne soit pas périodiquement radoubée et mastiquée d'une pâte impitoyablement
épaisse ; il en résulte que la sculpture, si florissante au moyen âge en Belgique, est comme
annulée partout où il s'en trouve quelques monumens dans les églises : comment reconnaître
non seulement l'expression, mais jusqu'aux premières formes d'une figure qui est recouverte
d'au moins dix couches successives de plâtre ? On ne se figure pas le changement que subiraient
toutes les églises belges, si quelque chimiste tout-puissant trouvait le moyen de les dégager de
cette enveloppe déjà séculaire, et de les rendre à leur légèreté primitive. Il n'y a pas jusqu'au
délicieux jubé de Louvain, dont la transparence ne soit interceptée autant que possible par un
voile écailleux. Seulement au lieu du beurre frais et de l'ocre, usités en France, c'est le blanc
qui est universellement adopté en Belgique, un blanc vif, luisant, éblouissant, dont on ne se fait
pas une idée avant de l'avoir vu. On sort de là comme d'un moulin, avec la crainte d'être soi-
même blanchi. Puis si on jette un regard en arrière sur l'édifice, on se croit encore poursuivi
par la brosse fatale, car, par un raffinement barbare, ce n'est pas seulement l'intérieur qui est
métamorphosé en blanc de craie, ce sont encore les porches, les portails, tout ce qui peut se
relever sur la couleur sombre des pierres extérieures, et jusqu'aux meneaux et aux archivoltes
de toutes les fenêtres, qui sont passés au blanc par dehors, comme pour avertir le passant du
sort qui l'attend au dedans. Je n'ai vu nulle part le moindre germe de réforme sur ce point.

Pour en revenir à notre France, et pour qu'on ne me reproche pas de parler si long-temps
sans indiquer un remède, je finirai en insistant sur la nécessité de régulariser et de fortifier
l'action de l'inspecteur-général des monumens historiques, et celle de la commission qui délibère
sur ses propositions au ministère de l'intérieur : une loi, ou au moins une ordonnance royale,
est urgente pour leur donner un droit d'intervention légale et immédiate dans les décisions des
municipalités et des conseils de fabrique. J'ai déjà cité la loi belge à ce sujet ; en Prusse il y
a un édit royal qui interdit strictement la destruction de tout édifice quelconque revêtu

d'un caractère monumental ou se rattachant à un souvenir historique, et qui ordonne de conserver, dans toutes les réparations de ces édifices, le caractère et le style de l'architecture primitive. En Bavière la même prohibition existe, et s'étend, par une disposition récente, jusqu'aux chaumières des montagnes de la Haute-Bavière, si pittoresques, si bien calculées pour le climat et la localité, et auxquelles il est défendu de substituer les boîtes carrées que voulaient y importer certains architectes urbains. Il faut que quelque mesure sérieuse de ce genre soit adoptée en France ; c'est la seule chance de salut pour ce qui nous reste : c'est le seul moyen d'appuyer les progrès trop lents et trop timides de l'opinion.

Et, en vérité, il est temps d'arrêter les démolisseurs. A mesure que l'on approfondit l'étude de notre ancienne histoire et de la société telle qu'elle était organisée dans les siècles catholiques, on se fait, ce me semble, une idée plus nette et une appréciation plus sérieuse des formes matérielles que cette société avait créées, pour lui servir de manifestations extérieures. Il est impossible alors de n'être pas frappé du contraste que présente le monde actuel avec le monde d'alors, sous le rapport de la beauté. On a fait bien des progrès de tous genres ; je n'entends ni les contester, ni même les examiner ; il en est que j'adopte avec toute la ferveur de mon siècle ; mais je ne puis m'empêcher de déplorer que tous ces progrès n'aient pu être obtenus qu'aux dépens de la beauté, qu'ils aient intronisé le règne du laid, du plat et du monotone. Le beau est un des besoins de l'homme, de ses plus nobles besoins ; il est de jour en jour moins satisfait dans notre société moderne. Je m'imagine qu'un de nos *barbares* aïeux du XVe ou du XVIe siècle nous plaindrait amèrement si, revenant du tombeau parmi nous, il comparait la France telle qu'il l'avait laissée avec la France telle que nous l'avons faite ; son pays tout parsemé de monumens innombrables et aussi merveilleux par leur beauté que par leur inépuisable variété, avec sa surface actuelle de jour en jour plus uniforme et plus aplatie ; ces villes annoncées de loin par leur forêt de clochers, par des remparts et des portes si majestueuses, avec nos quartiers neufs qui s'élèvent, taillés sur les mêmes patrons, dans toutes les sous-préfectures du royaume ; ces châteaux sur chaque montagne, et ces abbayes dans chaque vallée, avec les masses informes de nos manufactures ; ces églises, ces chapelles dans chaque village, toujours remplies de sculptures et de tableaux d'une originalité complète, avec les hideux produits de l'architecture officielle de nos jours ; ces flèches à jour avec les noirs tuyaux de nos usines, et, en dernier lieu, son noble et gracieux costume avec notre habit à queue de morue.—Laissons au moins les choses telles qu'elles sont ; le monde est assez laid comme cela ; gardons au moins les trop rares vestiges de son ancienne beauté, et, pour cela, empêchons un vandalisme décrépit de continuer à mettre en coupe réglée les souvenirs de notre histoire et de défricher officiellement les monumens plantés sur le sol de la patrie par la forte main de nos aïeux.

No. IV.—DURHAM ABBEY.

THE NORTH ALLEY OF THE CLOISTERS.

In the north side of the cloisters, from the corner over-against the church door, to the corner opposite to the dormitory door, was all finely glazed, from the top to the bottom, within a little of the ground into the cloister-garth ; and in every window were three pews or carrels, where every one of the old monks had a carrel severally to himself, to which, after dinner, they resorted, and there studied their books, every one in his carrel, till the time of even-song; and thus they exercised themselves every day. These pews or carrels were finely wainscotted, and very close, except the fore-side, which was carved work, and admitted light through the carrel doors, in each of which was a desk to lay books on; and the carrels were no wider than from one stanchel of the window to an other.

Opposite to the carrels against the church wall, stood certain great almeries of wainscot, full of books, as well the old written doctors of the church, as other profane authors, with many other holy men's works; so that every one studied what doctor he pleased, having the library at all times open to resort to, and study in, as well as in their carrels.

THE DORTOR, DORTOIR, OR DORMITORY.

On the west side of the cloister was a large house, called the dortoir, where the monks and novices lay. Every monk had a little chamber to himself. Each chamber had a window towards the chapter, and the partition betwixt every chamber was close wainscotted, and in each window was a desk to support their books. On the west side of the said dortoir were the like chambers, with their windows and desks towards the infirmary and the water; the chambers being all well boarded.

The novices had likewise their chambers in the south end of the said dortoir, adjoining to the aforesaid chambers, having eight chambers on each side. Every novice had his chamber to himself, but neither so close nor so warm as the other chambers were; nor having any light but what came in at the foreside of their chambers, being quite close both above and on each side.

At each end of the dortoir was a square stone, wherein was a dozen of cressets wrought in each stone, being always filled and supplied by the cooks, as they needed, to afford light to the monks and novices, at their arising to their matins at midnight, and for their other necessary uses.

There was a large house and most decent place adjoining to the west side of the said dortoir, towards the water, for the monks and novices to resort unto, called the privies. Two great pillars of stone supported the whole floor thereof; and every seat and partition was wainscotted close on every side, so that they could not see one another when they were therein. There were as many seats on each side as little windows in the wall, to give light to the said seats; which afterwards were walled up, to make the house more close. In the west end were three beautiful glass windows; and on the south side above the seats, another fine glass window, which windows gave light to the whole.

In the dortoir every night a private search was made by the sub-prior, who called at every monk's chamber door, to see good order kept, and that none should be wanting. The middle part of it was paved with fine tile stones the whole length: the sub-prior's chamber was the first, as he was to see order kept.

The sub-prior always dined and supped with the convent, sitting at the upper end of the table; and supper being ended, which was always at five o'clock, upon ringing a bell to call one of the novices to say grace, they went to the chapter-house to meet the prior, there to remain in prayer and devotion till six o'clock. Then upon ringing a bell again they went to the salvi, and all the doors of the cells, the frater-house, the dortoir, and the cloisters, were locked, even at six o'clock, and the keys delivered to the sub-prior, till seven o'clock the next morning.

THE LOFT.

There was also a door in the west end of the frater-house, just within the frater-house door, at which the old monks or convent entered, and then ascended up a pair of stairs, having an iron rail to support themselves by, into a loft which was at the west end of the frater-house, above the cellar, where the convent and monks dined and supped together. The sub-prior sat at the upper end of the table, as chief; and they had their meat served from the great kitchen, in at the dresser-window, and brought through the frater-house: the said kitchen served both the prior and the whole convent, having two windows into the frater-house; the one was large for principal days, the other not so large for every day. At the foot of the stairs was another door, leading into the great cellar or buttery, where all the drink stood that served the prior, and the whole convent of monks.

This loft, since the dissolution of the monastry, was made the dining-room of the fifth prebendaries house.

The monks were accustomed every day after dinner, to go through the cloisters, in at the usher's door, and so through the entry under the prior's lodgings into the centry-garth where the monks were buried, where they all stood bareheaded a good space, praying among the tombs for the souls of their brethren who were buried there: and when they had done their prayers, they returned to the cloister, and stayed till three o'clock, that they went to evensong. This was their daily practice after dinner.

The monks were the only writers of the acts and deeds of the bishops and priors of the church of Durham, and of the other chronicles and histories: they likewise recorded other most valuable things, as what acts, what occurrences, what miracles performed every year, and in what month; being always virtuously employed, either in writing good and godly works, or studying the holy scriptures, to the setting forth the honour of God, and the edifying the people, as well in example of good life and conversation, as by preaching the word of God. Such were the labours of monks and religious men in ancient times.

THE COMMON HOUSE.

On the right hand at going out of the cloisters into the infirmary, was the common house. It was instituted to have a fire constantly by day in winter, for the use of the monks, who were allowed no other fire; but the master and officers of the house had their own several fires. A garden and bowling-alley belonged to the said house, towards the water, for the novices sometimes to recreate themselves, leave being first granted; their master attending to see to their good order. In this house once in the year, between Martinmas and Christmas, the master of it kept his O Sapientia, a solemn banquet, at which the prior and convent were entertained with figs, raisins, ale, and cakes, but not to superfluity or excess, being only a moderate scholastical congratulation among themselves.

THE GUEST-HALL.

A famous house of hospitality was kept within the Abbey-garth of Durham, called the guest-hall, and was situate on the west side towards the water. The terrer of the house was master thereof, as one appointed to give entertainment to all estates, noble, gentle, or what other degree soever, came thither as strangers. Their entertainment was not inferior to that of any place in England, both for the goodness of their diet, the clean and neat furniture of their lodgings, and generally all things necessary for travellers; and with all this entertainment, no man was required to depart, while he continued honest, and of good behaviour.

The houses belonging to the second, third, fourth, and tenth prebendaries, were erected out of the apartments and other offices belonging to the guest-hall, the hall itself being wholly demolished, nothing remaining except a part of the western wall: but nothing remains to let us know what was in the sixth and twelfth prebendaries houses.

This hall was a stately place, not unlike the body of a church, supported on each side by very fine pillars, and in the midst of the hall a large range for the fire. The chambers and lodgings belonging to it were kept very clean, and richly furnished. They were very pleasant to lie in, especially one chamber, called the king's chamber, well deserving that name; for the king himself might very well lie in it, such was the stateliness thereof.

The victuals the guests were entertained with came from the great kitchen of the prior, the bread and beer from his pantry and cellars. If they were honourable, they were served as honourably as the prior himself, otherwise according to their quality.

The terrer had certain men appointed to wait at his table, and to attend upon his guests and strangers; and for their better entertainment he had always a hogshead or two of wines kept in a cellar pertaining to the said hall.

The prior (whose hospitality was such as that, in reality, there was no need of the guest-hall, but that the convent was desirous to abound in all liberal and free almsgivings) kept a most splendid and noble house, being attended by the best gentlemen and yeomen in the country, and the magnificent service of his house deserved no less; so great were the liberalities and benevolences of his house-keeping, that constant relief and alms were daily given, not only to the poor of the city, but to those of the country round about.

The lord prior had two porters, one at the hall door, called Robert Smith, the other at the usher-door, at going from the great chamber to the church, called Robert Clark; which two were the last porters to the last prior.

There were certain poor children, called the children of the almery, who only were educated in learning, and relieved with the alms and benevolence of the whole house, having their meat and drink in a loft on the north side of the Abbey gates, before the suppression of the said house. This loft had a long slated porch over the stair-head, and at each side of the said porch were stairs to go up to the loft, with a stable underneath it, and a door into it, under the stair-head, to go into the said stable. This edifice, at the suppression of the house, became Mr. Stephen Marley's lodging. Soon after the suppression he altered it, and took down the porch and stairs that went up to the loft, and made a kitchen where the stable was, and his buttery above where the loft was. The children went to school at the infirmary school without the Abbey-gates, which was founded by the priors of the Abbey, at the charge of the house.

The last schoolmaster was Sir Robert Hartburne, who continued master till the suppression of the house. He was bound to say mass twice a week at Magdalen's chapel, near Kepier, and once a week at Kimblesworth. The meat and drink these children had, was what the monks and novices with their master had left. It was carried in at a door adjoining the great kitchen window into a little vault at the west end of the frater-house, like a pantry, called the covie, kept by a man. Within it was a window, at which some of the children received the meat and drink of the said man, called the clerk of the covie, out of the covie or pantry window, and carried it to the loft. This clerk waited on them at every meal to keep good order.

There were four aged women who lived in the infirmary, without the south gates of the Abbey of Durham, each having her several chamber to lie in, being supplied and fed only with the victuals that came from the prior's own table.

In the infirmary was a chapel, where the schoolmaster of the infirmary (having his chamber and school above it) or some other priest for him, was appointed to say mass to these aged women every holiday and Friday.

No. V.

ABBEY OF ST. WANDRILLE, NORMANDY. ESSAI PAR E. H. LANGLOIS.

AVEC Guillaume de la Douillie, mort en 1341, cessèrent, jusqu'au dix-septième siècle, les reconstructions les plus remarquables auxquelles la basilique de Fontenelle ait jamais donné lieu; et depuis cet abbé jusqu'à nos jours, ce vaste et beau monument demeura toujours imparfait. Ce fut en vain que Clément VII, pape d'Avignon, comme l'appelle D. Duplessis, octroya aux religieux, à la prière de Charles VI, la réunion à leur abbaye du prieuré de Quitri, dans le Vexin normand. La modicité de ce secours, les évènemens déplorables qui signalèrent ces époques de crimes, de deuil et de sang, la peste enfin, semblèrent de concert s'opposer à l'achèvement de cette entreprise. Peut-être pourrions-nous citer encore une raison un peu postérieure et bien différente, mais non moins puissante: le découragement et l'humeur assez fondés des moines qui, depuis le fameux concordat de Léon X et de François Ier, voyaient avec dépit les deux tiers de leurs revenus passer dans les mains des commendataires, hommes du siècle, qui souvent les honoraient de la plus profonde indifférence, quand ils ne les accablaient pas de ruineuses procédures.* Aussi, à dater de cette époque, sauf quelques

----

* Il est certain que les religieux véritablement attachés à leurs institutions primitives, regardèrent toujours les commendataires comme des espèces d'intrus, et ne virent jamais de bon œil la révolution que le concordat avait opérée dans le régime monastique. Près de deux siècles encore après cet évènement, le P. Bréard, historien de Saint-Wandrille, exprimait à cet égard sans la moindre réserve son chagrin, ses regrets et ses espérances. En parlant, dans ses *Vies des Hommes illustres de Fontenelle*, de Jacques Hommet, dernier abbé régulier de ce monastère, " son corps fut enterré, dit-il, devant l'autel matutinal de la grande église, et avec lui la dignité abbatiale de Fontenelle, dignité qui ne subsiste plus que de nom, *le véritable pasteur de cette abbaye ne portant que le titre de prieur, tandis que, les commendataires et œconomes s'arrogent les vénérables noms d'abbés.*

" Louons nostre bon Dieu, poursuit le zélé religieux, parmi ces désordres, et portons courageusement les iniquités ou plus-tost les fruits des péchés de nos pères. Peut-estre que ce débonnaire seigneur ne sera pas toujours fasché, et qu'il se servira, pour remettre les abbayes en règle, de ceux-là mesme dont il a usé pour en donner l'administration aux laïqs et séculiers. Ainsi soit-il."

notables exceptions, soit pénurie, soit refroidissement de zèle, s'accupa-t-on beaucoup plus, au fond des cloîtres, des commodités de la vie et d'un vain luxe même, que de ce qui pouvait ajouter à la magnificence, à la majesté des lieux saints.   *   *   *

Je ne puis passer sous silence quelques extraits de la relation de ces évènemens inséréé dans l'*Histoire* (MSS.) *de Saint-Wandrille, depuis la réforme.*   Ces détails se rattachent d'ailleurs à la destruction de deux édifices les plus importans de ce monastère, après la basilique, et qui, sans contredit, présentaient un bien plus haut degré d'intérêt sous le rapport de l'archéologie.   C'étaient l'ancien dortoir et le vieux chapitre.   Le premier était construit par Herlève, femme de Robert de Normandie, archévêque de Rouen, qui depuis y fut inhumée. Il avait trente-cinq pieds de haut sur cent vingt de large.   Au-dessus de ce monument régnait, également édifiée par Herlève, la première partie du chapitre, qui n'avait que douze pieds d'élévation ; mais celle qui l'excédait en portait trente de hauteur et autant en longueur et en largeur.   Cette deuxième partie, ouvrage de Maynard, vingt-sixième abbé et restaurateur de Fontenelle dans le dixième siècle, était éclairée par quatre grandes croisées, deux à l'orient et deux au septentrion ; mais il est présumable que ces grandes croisées avaient été percées à une époque postérieure à l'érection de cet édifice, ou qu'on avait considérablement agrandi les anciennes, dont les baies devaient être, selon le style du temps, d'une très-médiocre dimension.   Malgré la singularité de sa disposition, ce double chapitre, pris dans son ensemble, était regardé comme un chef-d'œuvre de l'architecture de ces temps reculés.   Cependant, malgré tout ce qui devait le rendre respectable, D. Laurent Hunault, prieur, entreprit et consomma sa perte, ainsi que celle du vieux dortoir, en 1671.   Il paraît que ce moine, doué d'un zèle actif, mais souvent mal entendu, était un de ces hommes qui ne balancent pas à réaliser leurs aveugles conceptions, aux dépens de ce que les siècles passés nous ont transmis de plus admirable.   Son insensibilité fit, au rapport de l'auteur qui me fournit ces détails, verser bien des larmes à l'estimable D. Alexis Bréard, l'infatigable historien de cette abbaye, et à tous ceux qui pensaient comme lui.   L'obstiné prieur n'en poursuivit pas moins son entreprise.

Déjà les ouvriers étaient près de défoncer le chapitre et de le démolir jusqu'aux fondemens, lorsqu'en creusant la terre à son entrée, on rencontra quatre sépulcres de pierre, dont toutes les parties étaient si bien unies et si entières, qu'on aurait cru que l'ouvrier venait d'y mettre la dernière main.   Quand on les eut ouverts, on trouva dans tous, sans exception, des bottines d'un cuir si excellent qu'on pouvait encore s'en servir.   On remarqua de plus, dans le premier, une baguette de coudrier, de la longueur du tombeau.   La chevelure blonde de la tête du troisième corps, s'était aussi conservée sans altération.   Mais le quatrième sépulcre renfermait ce qu'il avait de plus remarquable et de plus intéressant pour l'histoire : je veux dire une épitaphe en vers gravée sur une lame de plomb.   Il est certainement fâcheux que cette inscription n'ait pas été entièrement déchiffrée.   La voici telle que les PP. Bonnefont et Bréard nous l'ont laissée dans leurs écrits.   Comme ils ne s'accordent pas entre eux dans la manière de la lire, nous renvoyons dans les notes les variantes du dernier.

Hic inhumatus* jacet Willelmus† nomine. . . .
Nobilium de stirpe parentum nascitur esse

* Breardus legit *inhumata*.   † *Willelmus* deest apud Breardum.

Ricardi ducis Malgerius unde refulsit:
Ad cujus lævam requiescit filius ejus
Nomine Rodolphus, major natu fuit inquam II.
Hic III. jdus junii obiit, et uxor ejus Arectrix. . . .
Quæ juxta eum quiescit Malgero*

. . . .

. . . . . iis succedentibus sibi tribus
In laicali† (minor natu Fontanella. . . .
Est consecratus divino) numini monachili‡ habitu.

Telle est l'épitaphe qu'on découvrit dans le quatrième monument. Voici maintenant les conjectures de D. Alexis Bréard. Selon lui, Mauger comte d'Evreux, fils de Richard II comte de la même ville, de la nation des Normands, choisit sa sépulture, en 1118, à l'entrée du chapitre de Fontenelle, auprès de son père ; et dans la suite Raoul, ou Rodulphe, fils de Mauger, et sa femme Arectrix, furent aussi inhumés au même lieu. Cela supposé, D. Bréard soupçonne qu'il y a une méprise dans le *Neustria pia* du P. Artus du Moutier, qui aura confondu Mauger avec Guillaume, lorsqu'il prétend que ce comte d'Evreux fut enterré à Saint-Wandrille, dans le tombeau de Richard son père, en 1118. Le P. Mabillon néanmoins, dans ses *Annales*, à l'année 1108, dit que le comte Guillaume fut inhumé à Fontenelle, auprès de son père. S'il faut lire avec D. Bonnefont *hic inhumatus jacet Willelmus*, la difficulté sera levée, mais non pas à l'avantage du P. Bréard.

Ce dernier auteur va néanmoins encore plus loin : il croit que Richard, Mauger et Rodulphe sont trois comtes d'Evreux qui se sont succédés les uns aux autres ; que les quatre tombeaux défoncés sont ceux de ces trois comtes, et d'Arectrix, épouse de Rodulphe ; qu'ainsi ceux qui ont dressé les divers catalogues des comtes d'Evreux, ont eu grand tort d'en exclure ce dernier. Au reste, on ne peut que louer la modestie de notre auteur, qui s'est contenté de nous donner toutes ces observations historiques pour de fortes conjectures sans vouloir les ériger en faits certains.

Quant à D. Benoît Bonnefont, il est plus hardi et plus décisif ; il dit nettement que la lame de plomb fit connaître aux religieux de Saint-Wandrille " que Richard, comte d'Evreux, avec sa femme et ses deux enfans, avaient été ensevelis audit lieu en l'année 1118." Mais dans son troisième volume des *Vies des Saints de Fontenelle*, page 156, il rapporte un autre sentiment, suivant lequel " le Richard dont il est parlé dans l'épitaphe était comte d'Evreux, auquel succéda son fils, appelé Guillaume ; tous deux furent ensevelis à Saint-Wandrille avec la femme du second et un de leurs enfans, qui avait été revêtu de l'habit de la sainte religion, et était décédé dans ce monastère."

Peut-être qu'en examinant de plus près l'épitaphe en elle-même, et en la comparant à l'histoire du temps, on eût pu dire quelque chose de plus net et de plus exact que ces auteurs.

Les ouvriers, continuant à creuser la terre, rencontrèrent, proche d'un gros pillier qui soutenait le devant du chapitre, un cercueil d'une seule pierre. On ne douta point que ce ne fût

---

* Apud Breardum sic habetur : *M. . . . oro. . . .*   † Quæ includuntur uncinis, desunt apud Breardum.

‡ Breard. *monachali.*

P

celui de Girard II, trente-cinquième abbé de Fontenelle, qui, en 1126, avait été enterré précisément en ce lieu-là, comme on l'apprend par un ancien catalogue anonyme des abbés de ce monastère. La tête de cet abbé était si entière, qu'il ne lui était pas tombé une seule dent. Il avait une crosse de bois fort légère, et qui était très-bien conservée : sa grosseur était de trois pouces et sa longueur de cinq pieds.

Au côté gauche de l'abbé Girard, parut, bientôt après, un autre tombeau de pierre : c'était celui de Gerbert ou Girbert-le-Teutonique, trente-troisième abbé de Fontenelle, compté parmi les saints, et que Guillaume-le-Conquérant ne fit point difficulté de mettre en parallèle avec saint Anselme et le bienheureux Lanfranc. On ne trouva dans son sépulture qu'un bâton noir, un peu plat, et une lame de plomb, avec ces paroles : In nomine Domini hic jacet Gerbertus natione Teutonicus. D. Bonnefont semble supposer que ce n'était qu'une partie de l'épitaphe, et qu'on n'avait pu lire le reste. Il avance même, comme un fait certain, que ce saint abbé n'avait point de crosse, quoique D. Bréard n'en convienne point.

Enfin, les ouvriers pénétrèrent dans le chapitre même. Après en avoir déplacé le cercueil d'un religieux ancien, mort depuis l'introduction de la réforme, ils rencontrèrent cinq sépulcres sur une même ligne. Quand on eut fait l'ouverture du premier, on fut surpris de voir, au lieu d'ossemens, un habit de la même forme que ceux des bénédictins de la congrégation de Saint-Maur, quoique d'une étoffe plus grossière, et d'une couleur tirant sur le minime. On aperçut aussi une ceinture de cuir avec une boucle de fer. Le capuchon avait été abaissé sur le visage et le couvrait tout-à-fait. Mais lorsqu'on voulut le relever, les habits et la ceinture s'en allèrent presque entièrement en poussière.

On ne doute point que ce ne fût le sépulcre de Roger, trente-huitième abbé de Fontenelle, mort en 1165. Quoiqu'en exhaussant le chapitre de quelques pieds, un an avant l'introduction de la réforme, on eût négligé, au rapport de D. Bréard, de relever les briques sur lesquelles était son épitaphe, en quoi l'on fut plus attentif à l'égard des quatre autres abbés dont les sépulcres, aussi bien que celui de Roger, étaient devant la chaise du supérieur ; on ne profita pas néanmoins de cette attention dans le défoncement du chapitre : tous les pavés furent confondus et jetés pêle-mêle, sans nulle précaution ; en sorte qu'on fut obligé de recourir à d'autres moyens pour avoir connaissance de ces cinq abbés. Du reste, l'admiration redoubla à l'ouverture des quatre autres tombeaux. Tous ces abbés, sans en excepter le premier, avaient des bottines qui leur montaient jusqu'au-dessus des genoux. Trois avaient des crosses parmi lesquelles il s'en trouva une garnie de clous dorés et de quantité de fausses pierres précieuses de diverses couleurs. Un serpent replié en formait le sommet, et une pomme d'or en terminait le bout. Ces corps, ou plutôt ces ossemens, étaient revêtus de chasubles semblables à celles dont on se servait dans le douzième siècle. Il y en avait deux parmi elles qui jetaient beaucoup d'éclat. Mais outre des bracelets de drap d'or très-artistement travaillés, la chasuble et l'étole du troisième surpassaient tous les autres ornemens par leur prix et la vivacité de leurs couleurs. D. Bonnefont, qui avait eu les bracelets quelque temps entre les mains, les fit remettre dans le trésor de Saint-Wandrille.

Nous avons déjà remarqué que Roger était le premier des cinq abbés ; le deuxième était Anfroy, ou Anfrède, trente-neuvième abbé ; le troisième, Geoffroy Ier ou Gaufride, quarante-et-unième abbé : c'est celui qui portait des ornemens si magnifiques ; le quatrième était Pierre Mauviel, quarante-septième abbé ; et le cinquième, Geoffroy III, surnommé Savary, cinquante-quatrième abbé de ce monastère. Les cinq abbés furent, avec Girard II, transférés dans l'église principale et enterrés au pied du grand autel.

Après avoir défoncé le chapitre et l'avoir creusé deux pieds plus bas que les fondemens de l'église, les travailleurs se mirent en devoir d'en enlever les terres. Dans cette action, ils sentirent un nouveau sépulcre, que D. Bonnefont prend pour celui de saint Anségise, dix-neuvième abbé de Fontenelle, au milieu du neuvième siècle. Vis-à-vis celui-ci, on trouva un autre sépulcre de pierre, trois pieds au-dessous de la place où l'on avait découvert les tombeaux que l'on avait jugé pouvoir renfermer les comtes d'Evreux. D'abord, on n'y aperçut que des ossemens d'une blancheur extraordinaire. On y trouva aussi néanmoins une lame de plomb si rouillée, que personne ne pouvait la lire. Elle fut portée au P. prieur, qui négligea quelques jours d'en faire détacher la rouille. Enfin on y lut cette inscription :

HÌC REQUIESCIT ABBAS GERARDUS IV.
KAL. DECEMBRIS
AB INJUSTO INJUSTE INTERFECTUS.*

On reconnut alors que cet abbé n'était autre chose que le saint-Gérard, martyr, dont on célébrait la fête à Saint-Wandrille le 9 novembre, et que Gerbert-le-Teutonique était le saint Girbert ou Gilbert dont on chômait aussi la fête le 4 septembre. Il n'était plus temps néanmoins de recueillir précieusement ces reliques, ni même de les distinguer. D. Pierre Lastelle, dépositaire de l'abbaye, choqué du concours de peuple que la dévotion attirait dans ces lieux depuis la découverte de ces tombeaux, et pour plusieurs autres raisons, avait malicieusement mêlé les ossemens de ces deux saints avec ceux d'un ancien religieux et des comtes d'Evreux. Il n'avait pas plus favorablement traité le corps qu'on présumait être celui de saint Anségise.

Tous ces débris humains furent inhumés pêle-mêle, et confondus derrière le grand autel de l'église abbatiale, au milieu des plaintes amères des religieux.

On ne sera point surpris de la découverte de ces divers étages de sépultures dans l'ancien chapitre, s'il est constant, comme le prétend D. Bréard, que cet édifice subsistait au même lieu que les précédens, et que son aire avait été exhaussée deux ou trois fois.

Dans l'année 1671, qui précéda celle de cet évènement, en réparant les fondemens des murs de l'église, du côté du midi, qui dépérissaient par l'humidité, on avait trouvé des fondemens fort épais que l'on regarda comme les restes de l'ancienne église de Saint-Servais, construite par saint Wandon, douzième abbé de ce monastère. L'on y découvrit aussi beaucoup de corps placés par étage, et dont quelques-uns étaient renfermés dans des cercueils de pierres maçonnées. Tous ces ossemens furent remis plus haut, presque contre la muraille dont on voulait prévenir la ruine.

La démolition du chapitre excita le mécontentement de plusieurs supérieurs et de beaucoup

---

* Saint Gérard fut tué d'un coup de hache, pendant son sommeil, par un moine indigné de ses remontrances.

de religieux de la province. Ce fut sans doute à cette occasion que le chapitre général de 1678 défendit de détruire les tombeaux et autres semblables monumens sans la permission du révérend père général. On croit aussi que ce fut par suite de la même entreprise que D. L. Hunault fut éloigné de Saint-Wandrille, en 1678. Il fut alors élevé au rang de visiteur de Bretagne, et mourut dans cette province en 1697, prieur de Saint-Nicolas-d'Angely.

FINIS.

LONDON: RICHARDS, PRINTER, ST. MARTIN'S LANE, CHARING CROSS.

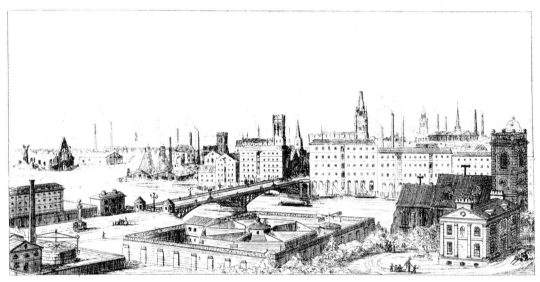

THE SAME TOWN IN 1840

1. St Michaels Tower, rebuilt in 1750. 2. New Parsonage House & Pleasure Grounds. 3. The New Jail. 4. Gas Works. 5. Lunatic Asylum. 6. Iron Works & Ruins of St Maries Abbey. 7. St Evans Chapel. 8. Baptist Chapel. 9. Unitarian Chapel. 10. New Church. 11. New Town Hall & Concert Room. 12. Wesleyan Centenary Chapel. 13. New Christian Society. 14. Quakers Meeting. 15. Socialist Hall of Science.

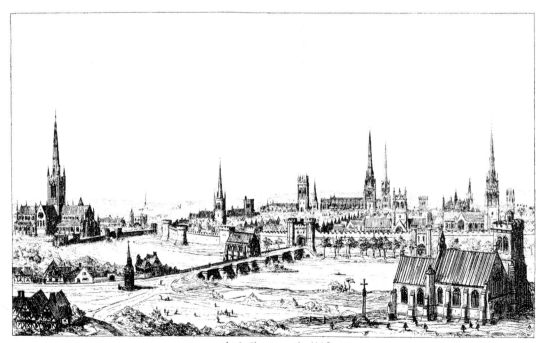

Catholic town in 1440.

1 St Michaels on the Hill. 2. Queens Cross. 3. St Thomas's Chapel. 4. St Maries Abbey. 5. All Saints. 6. St Johns. 7. St Peters. 8. St Alkmunds. 9. St Maries. 10. St Edmunds. 11. Grey Friars. 12. St Cuthberts. 13. Guild hall. 14. Trinity. 15. St Olaves. 16. St Botolphs.

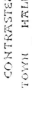

GVILDHALL   LONDON

George Dance Esq archt

CONTRASTED   HOTEL DE VILLE

TOWN HALLS

REDCLIFFE CHVRCH BRISTOL

CONTRASTED
PAROCHIAL CHVRCHES

AILSOVLS CHVRCH LANGHAM PLACE
JOHN NASH Esq! Arch!

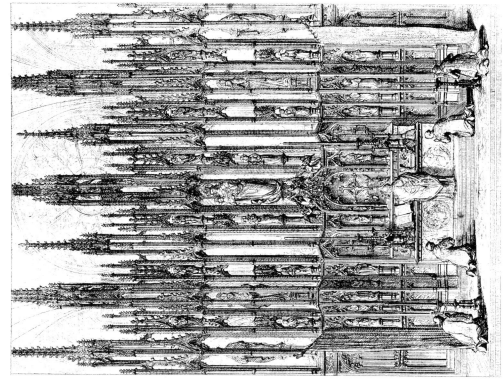

WYKHAM ABBEY c. 1430

CONTRASTED
ALTAR SCREENS

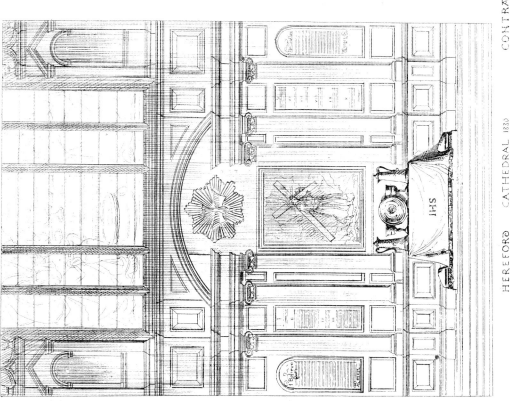

HEREFORD CATHEDRAL 1830

ST PANCRAS CHAPEL

Inwood Esq Arch.

CONTRASTED CHAPELS

BISHOP SKIRLAWS CHAPEL YORKSHIRE

ST GEORGE'S CHAPEL WINSOR

CHAPEL ROYAL BRIGHTON

CONTRASTED ROYAL CHAPELS

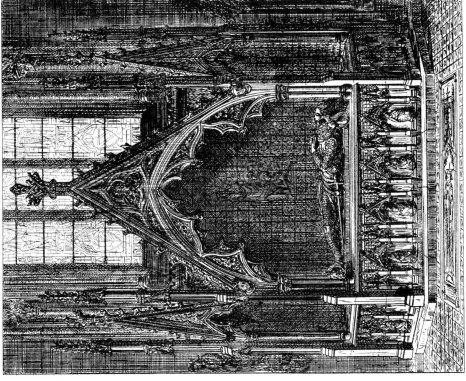

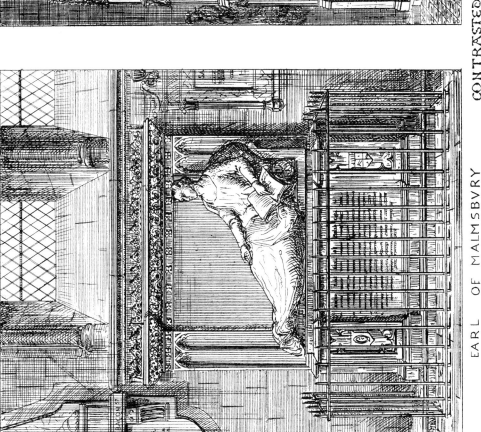

EARL OF MALMSBVRY   CONTRASTED   ADMIRAL GERVASE ALARD
SALISBVRY CATH   WINCHELSEA CHVRCH.
Chantrey 1823   (nu! effect

SEPVLCHRAL MONVMENTS

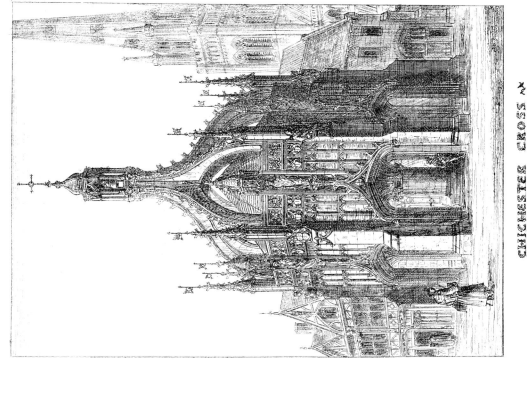

CHICHESTER CROSS

KINGS CROSS BATTLE BRIDGE

S Geary Arch.t

CONTRASTED CROSSES

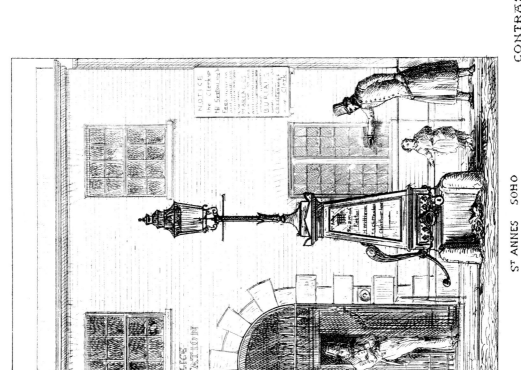

WEST CHEAP CONDVIT
THOMAS ILAM 1479

CONTRASTED
PVBLIC CONDVITS

S^T ANNES SOHO

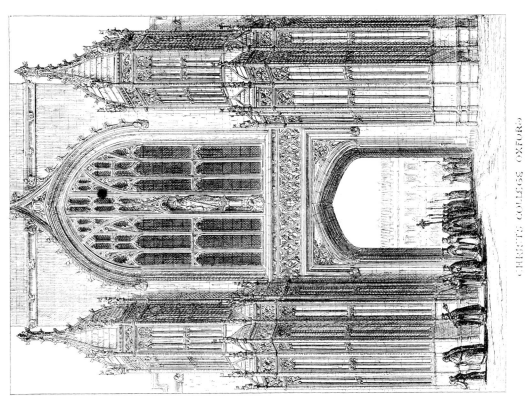

CHRISTS COLLEGE OXFORD

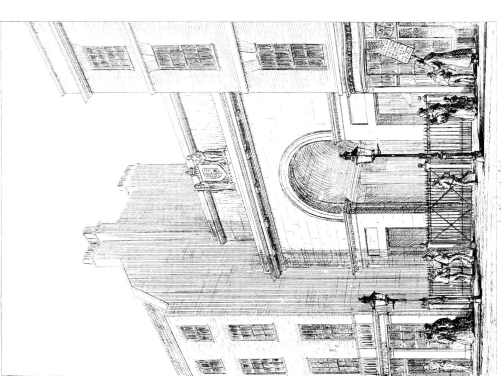

Jno R^d Smith del

KINGS COLLEGE STRAND

CONTRASTED COLLEGE GATEWAYS

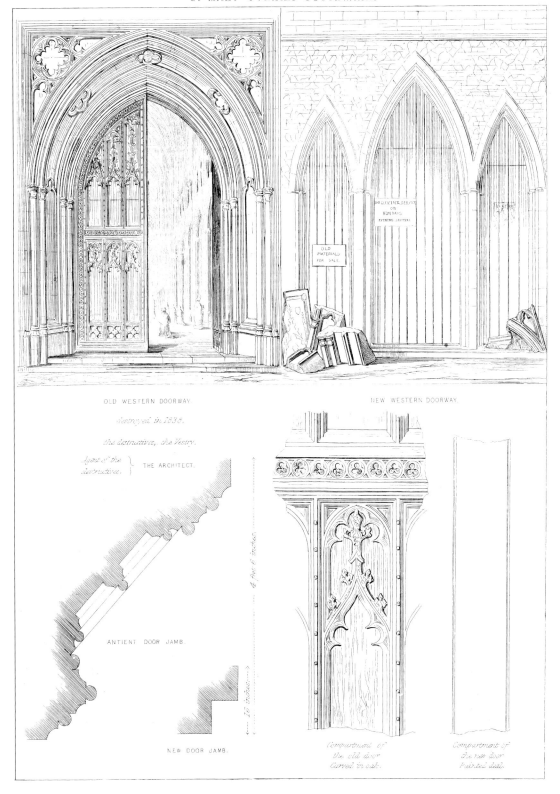

OLD WESTERN DOORWAY.

NEW WESTERN DOORWAY.

destroyed in 1838.

the destructives, the Vestry.

*Agent of the
destructives.* } THE ARCHITECT.

ANTIENT DOOR JAMB.

NEW DOOR JAMB.

*Compartment of
the old door
Carved in oak.*

*Compartment of
the new door
Painted deal.*

AAA. THE NVRSERY WINDOWS

B. AN ILL SHAPED MITER

CCC. THE DRAWING ROOM

D. THE STREET DOOR

EE THE PARLOVR

F THE WAY DOWN THE AREA

THIS HOVSE HAS BEEN BVILT WITH DVE

REGARD TO THE MODERN STYLE OF EPISCO-

-PAL ESTABLISHMENTS. ALL VSELESS BVILD-

-INGS SVCH AS. CHAPEL HALL OR LIBRARY

HAVE BEEN OMITTED, AND THE WHOLE

IS ON A SCALE TO COMBINE ECONOMY

WITH ELEGANCE !!!

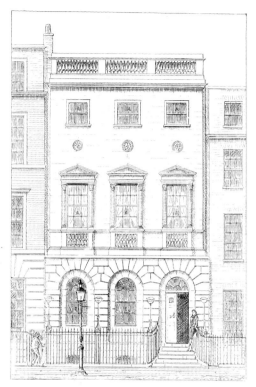

ELY HOVSE DOVER STREET
1836

CONTRASTED EPISCOPAL RESIDENCES

References to the
Old Palace ✠

a S'Etheldreda's chapel ✠

b Part of the library ✠

c The east cloister ✠

d Lodgings for guests ✠

e The great hall ✠

THIS VENERABLE PALACE WAS SOLD

TO THAT EMINENT SVRVEYOR C.COLE

WHO VTTERLY DESTROYED IT AND ON

ITS SCITE ERRECTED THE PRESENT

HANDSOME AND VNIFORM ✠ STREET WITH

ITS NEAT AND APPROPRIATE

IRON GATES IN. 1776.

✠ Bradleys Londiniana

ELY PALACE HOLBORN 1536.

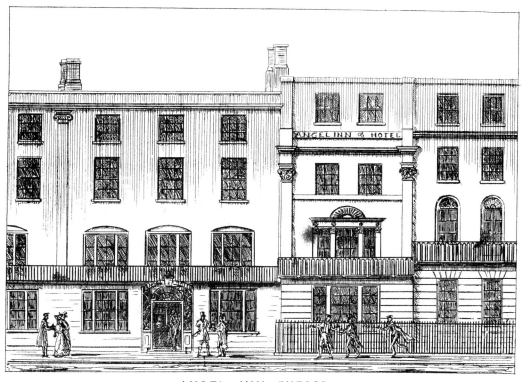

ANGEL INN OXFORD

ANGEL INN GRANTHAM

CONTRASTED PVBLIC INNS

MODERN POOR HOUSE

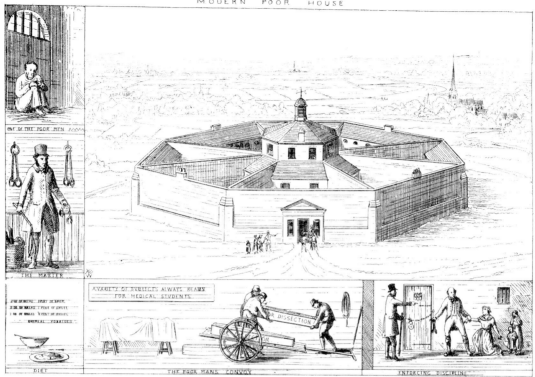

ONE OF THE POOR MEN

THE MASTER

DIET

A VARIETY OF SUBJECTS ALWAYS READY
FOR MEDICAL STUDENTS

FOR DISSECTION

THE POOR MANS CONVOY

ENFORCING DISCIPLINE

CONTRASTED RESIDENCES FOR THE POOR

ANTIENT · POOR · HOUSE

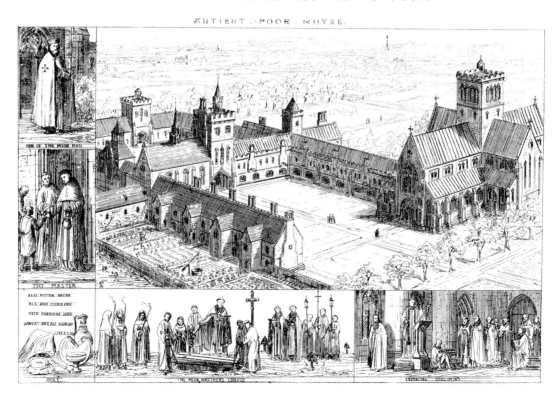

ONE OF THE POOR MEN

THE MASTER

DIET

THE POOR BROTHERS CONVOY

ENFORCING DISCIPLINE

PERSONS ARE DESIRED
NOT TO WALK ABOVE
AND TALK
DURING DIVINE SERVICE
NOR TO DEFACE
THE WALLS

SACRED
TO THE MEMORY OF
THE RIGHT REVEREND FATHER IN GOD
JOHN CLUTTERBUCK. DD
ÆTATIS SVÆ 73
ALSO DECAROLINE AND LYDIA
HIS TWO WIVES

The True Principles of Pointed
or Christian Architecture

Introduction

Timothy Brittain-Catlin

By comparison with the agitated reception that had attended the publication of A. W. N. Pugin's first edition of *Contrasts* five years beforehand, his next book, *The True Principles of Pointed or Christian Architecture*, received a surprisingly muted reaction when it was published on 3 July 1841. Neither the Oxford Movement's *British Critic* nor the *Dublin Review* of the Roman Catholic revival reviewed it: considering the interest generally shown by both in architectural matters, and Pugin's standing in the architectural world, it seems possible that their editors were unable to decide on what line to take. For Pugin had become a problematic figure, posing difficult questions to Anglican and Catholic builders alike, and had already achieved what some see as his most enduring contribution to all the subsequent history of Western architecture: the cementing of a moral stance to a specific architectural style.

Pugin had been a recent convert to Catholicism and a newcomer to architectural practice when he wrote his *Contrasts*; by the time of *True Principles* he was professor of ecclesiastical antiquities at St Mary's College, Oscott, the powerhouse of the Catholic Midlands. He gave a series of lectures on architecture there from December 1837 onwards: some of these were published in the *Catholic Magazine*. The fact that he was lecturing about design in a religious seminary is itself significant: an Anglican clergyman's education would not have included any reference to the applied arts, and the very existence of the lecture series testifies to the importance Pugin's patrons, particularly Oscott's president, Henry Weedall, accorded to the idea that the spiritual and aesthetic revival of England were two sides of the same coin.

Pugin's lectures were rewritten for publication in the form of a book in a coherent style that merged the polemical with the practical in every sentence. As a result, his message is immediately accessible and astonishingly memorable. This in itself distinguishes the text from the many others written in the first half of the nineteenth century, including those, such as Alfred Bartholomew's *Specifications* of 1840, which carried similar messages about the need for practical design, and the structural purity of mediaeval Gothic architecture. There are, however, two other reasons why *True Principles* is so important a text for any student of Pugin. The first is that Pugin wrote very little about the theory and practical method of design for modern uses, and next to nothing about his own work in the field of domestic and institutional architecture: and yet it is for his achievements in these fields that he came to be so revered during the late-Victorian and Arts and Crafts periods of English architecture. Secondly, many of Pugin's own buildings other than his churches were until recently inaccessible even to architects: the private houses of the Catholic clergy, and the monastic and conventual institutions, were by definition out of bounds to laymen.

The greatest architects are not generally renowned for their ability to explain their work in writing. In *True Principles*, however, Pugin provides a refreshing exception. The book is organised in the form of two lectures. The first begins with a definition of what Pugin calls 'great principles', and, indeed, if the architecture student were to read no further than the first page, he or she would already have found the most important passage of the book. Here Pugin sets out the two 'great rules for design': that *'there should be no features about a building which are not necessary for convenience, construction, or propriety'*; and that *'all ornament should consist of enrichment of the essential construction of the building'*. To this he adds: 'In pure architecture the smallest detail should *have a meaning or serve a purpose*; and even the construction itself *should vary with the material employed'* (italics as in the 1841 edition throughout).

These 'rules' are worth considerable reflection. Almost every word in them is significant. Sir Henry Wotton had in 1624 paraphrased the canonical Roman architect-writer Vitruvius and defined architecture in terms of 'firmness, commodity and delight'. In replacing 'delight' with 'propriety', Pugin was transferring architecture from the realm of the senses to that of moral judgment: the propriety of architecture is the quality of its being proper for the function being housed. With that one word, a classical architecture such as that of Pugin's time, which applied similar façades to churches, theatres, lunatic asylums and railway stations, becomes unsupportable. By claiming that ornament must be cut away from the constructional material of the building, Pugin was disposing of a whole realm of conventional practice; by requiring that a detail was to have 'meaning', he was implying that there must be a consistent architectural method applicable to the small as well as to the great parts of a building; and by varying constructional method according to the materials to hand, he was calling for a reverse of the practice of, for example, John Nash, whose professional methods had been discredited by parliamentary enquiries from 1828 and whose jerry-built terraces had, in Pugin's day, created a monumental stage-set delusion of grandeur around the Regent's Park in London.

The greater part of the text that follows is a lively illustration of these 'great principles'. Pugin starts by demonstrating the structural logic and achievements of Gothic church architecture, showing how a great Gothic cathedral provides an onlooker with what we would nowadays call a 'narrative' display of its structural form: the building is telling us what it is made of, and how it is built. It should be remembered that in 1841 it was a comparatively recent development that the technology of Gothic arches and vaults was understood. It was not until the appearance of a stream of books published, edited, or otherwise promoted by John Britton, mainly from the 1820s and 1830s, that even architects understood what determined the curve of an arch, the function of a rib, or the thrust of a buttress. Britton had employed the best draughtsmen of his day, most notably Pugin's father Auguste Charles, to illustrate the surviving remains of English Gothic architecture, and to analyse and reconstruct their original form, thus turning the romantic pursuit of antiquarians into a scientific study for professionals, and also enabling the Gothic to be compared with the classical on equally scholarly terms. The opening pages of *True Principles* are therefore a remarkably effective précis of Britton's lifetime's achievement, the adept packaging of more than twenty years of research into a form which even the laziest architect could appreciate.

In addition, Pugin's effective use of graphic material here (the appearance of which concerned him very greatly) marks another significant distinction between this book and, for example, Bartholomew's. He himself prepared the etchings for the full-page plates in his own lively style, and he, with the aid of at least two first-rate contemporary engravers, Orlando Jewitt and Thomas Talbot Bury, prepared other illustrations (including woodcuts) to be interspersed with the text in imitation of his favoured mid-seventeenth-century author, William Dugdale, who had used Wenceslaus Hollar's work in this way. But Pugin's adoption of Britton's scientific approach and his consciously archaising graphic style should not detract from the originality of his message. The transformation of the methods of Gothic church architecture into practical illustrations of metalwork, and wallpaper and fabric design, are entirely his, and it is this adept translation of the sublime into the everyday, and then back again into the elevated world of church furnishing, that made readers understand that their daily process of specifying doorknobs, hinges, and draperies could draw them into an elevated state of intercourse with the greatest achievements of the Gothic world. Furthermore, in explaining how modern industrial processes, particularly the mass production of cast-iron, ran counter to the inherent physical qualities of materials that could be teased out and given expression by hand, Pugin was also establishing in writing for the first time what he was already achieving in practice, the revival of lost craft skills.

By 1841 his association with the Hardman family, craft metalworkers of Birmingham, was nearly four years old. He had made his first contact with

Herbert Minton, the innovative Staffordshire potter; and he was on the verge of starting his lengthy association with the decorator J.G. Crace. *True Principles* gave him an opportunity to display his abilities to a professional audience, and these illustrations demonstrated that there was a coherent architectural method behind the myriad achievements of the 29-year-old prodigy, who had designed some ten churches (including a cathedral and a bishop's house) that already were complete or under construction; and whose residential architecture, although controversial, was certainly original.

The second lecture is launched with a discussion of open timber roofs, an apt point at which to begin, since the subject is applicable to all types of building, ancient and modern, and furthermore, the structural complexity of a great trussed roof provides an effective illustration of Pugin's principles: not only do the structural properties of the timber influence the form, but it is inherently absurd to hang heavy plaster ceilings from a necessary structure. This proceeds to a description of logical and illogical timber construction, an interesting section in the book, because not only was Pugin an original designer of functional timber furniture, but also his sketches and unexecuted designs show that he was fascinated by half-timbered architecture and yet never attempted it in practice. He then provides a satirical drawing on the type of modern 'gothick' furniture that he himself designed as a teenager for Windsor Castle, and returns to architecture with a memorable vignette of a plain brick box of a church, with a fancy front held up with iron rods. He explains how a Greek temple required a different type of structure to a Christian church, and how the former would appear absurd if the angle of its pediments were adapted to suit the heavy rainfall of northern Europe. One by one, the great sequence of rules and paradigms that came to forge the new architecture of the late nineteenth and early twentieth centuries can be detected across these pages. A row of bold chimneystacks, like those of the surviving mediaeval collegiate structures, is used to demonstrate four points of commonsense design, the forerunner of the Modernist concept of expressing externally the services and functions of a building. The spuriousness of modern decoration and the cheapness of popular building materials are lampooned. The Englishness of English design, disappearing under a heap of foreign imports, Swiss cottages and Hindu temples, is mourned; and all these are contrasted with an explanation of how the varying functions of an old English manor contributed to the richness of its appearance.

Some of the ideas expressed in *True Principles* had appeared in print before. In particular, John Loudon had in his many publications, such as his *Encyclopaedia* of 1833, and in his *Architectural Magazine*, called for practical planning in modern houses. But to look for the 'first' appearance of these arguments is to miss the point. Not Loudon, nor his architectural draftsman Edward B. Lamb, nor Bartholomew, nor any of the various academics or even poets who had expressed views similar to Pugin had been able to design in a way that put these ideas into practice, or to write about them from experience.

The evidence of his primacy as the designer and theoretician of a new kind of building can be found wherever mid- or late-Victorian architects are writing about where they found their inspiration. It is Pugin's name that appears in George Gilbert Scott's *Remarks on Secular and Domestic Architecture, Present and Future* of 1853, and in his later *Personal and Professional Recollections*; it is Pugin alone of his generation who is favoured with a mention in T. G. Jackson's *Modern Gothic Architecture* of 1873; and twenty years later, the architect John Dando Sedding declared that 'We should have had no Morris, no Street, no Burges, no Shaw, no Webb, no Bodley, no Rossetti, no Burne-Jones, no Crane, but for Pugin.' It was '*der geniale Architekt*' Pugin who was the first of the 'shining stars in the firmament of English nineteenth-century architectural history' in Hermann Muthesius' *Stilarchitektur und Baukunst* in 1902, and it is Pugin who emerges as the hero of C. F. A. Voysey's *Individuality* of 1915. The *Architectural Review*, almost since its foundation, has held Pugin's standard aloft, starting with a sympathetic (and beautifully illustrated) monograph by Paul Waterhouse in 1897-8, and continuing through the rediscovery of Pugin by Nikolaus Pevsner, his pupil Phoebe Stanton, John Summerson, and John Piper, amongst others, in the 1940s and 1950s; and in the 1980s Peter Davey continued the tradition with an article entitled 'Pugin Pointed the Way', that re-established Pugin's reputation, for better and for worse, as the father of England's contemporary architectural schools, the High Tech and the Romantic Pragmatic.

The Pugin of all these architect-writers and historians was the Pugin of *True Principles*: it is from these pages that a coherent theory of architectural design was gleaned. It is also the Pugin of *True Principles* who stands at the centre of an argument that has surfaced over the last twenty years – that as a romantic craftsman-architect, as a reviver of ancient glories, he cannot have been one of the founders of twentieth-century Modernism, with its industrialised buildings, its celebration of innovation, and its indifference to its geographical, if not its immediate, location. The answer to that charge is contained within these pages: here he sets out a functional view of architecture in a funny, concise, original, sharp way that architects could understand and enjoy; he establishes a theoretical concept of architectural design which was applicable to all styles, all climates and all materials; and he expands the horizons of the architect, by bringing him back into contact with forgotten craftsmanship, and thus making him responsible for every part of the design of the building. *True Principles* is undoubtedly, in Pevsner's words, Pugin's 'most influential statement'. Even a leading voice from the other side of the Gothic–classical divide, David Watkin, has seen it as such, writing in *Morality and Architecture* in 1977 that, following the appearance of *True Principles*, 'subsequent generations of critics, up to the present day, who certainly have not attributed divine authority to any particular style, nevertheless have gone on believing in the possibility of a way of building that was not artificial, not marked by human imperfections, and that represented some inescapable reality.'

The text presented here is that of the original edition of 1841. An edited translation of parts of the book, combined with other writings and illustrations, appeared in Belgium in 1850 under the title *Les Vrais Principes*. A slightly altered English edition appeared in 1853, and in 1895 an Edinburgh edition responded to the contemporary revival of appreciation for Pugin. Two recent editions have been facsimiles, or near facsimiles: that of 1969 was taken from the 1853 edition; and that of 1973 from this 1841 edition, but with altered page numbers. On completing these pages, it is hoped that the reader will continue before too long with Pugin's *An Apology for the Revival of Christian Architecture in England* (1843) which sets out in further detail the way in which his architectural theory could be applied to the new challenges of modern life.

The true principles of pointed architecture

London Published by John Weale, 59, High Holborn, 1841.

THE TRUE PRINCIPLES

OF

Pointed or Christian Architecture:

SET FORTH IN

TWO LECTURES DELIVERED AT ST. MARIE'S, OSCOTT,

BY

A. WELBY PUGIN,

ARCHITECT,

AND PROFESSOR OF ECCLESIASTICAL ANTIQUITIES IN THAT COLLEGE.

LONDON: JOHN WEALE.

M.CCM.XLI.

London:

PRINTED BY W. HUGHES, KING'S HEAD COURT, GOUGH SQUARE.

THE INK SUPPLIED BY MESSRS. SHACKELL AND LYONS.

LIST OF PLATES.

---

47 WOOD-CUTS.

31 VIGNETTES.

——

78

PRINCIPLES

OF

POINTED OR CHRISTIAN ARCHITECTURE.

LECTURE I.

THE object of the present Lecture is to set forth and explain the true principles of Pointed or Christian Architecture, by the knowledge of which you may be enabled to test architectural excellence. The two great rules for design are these : 1*st, that there should be no features about a building which are not necessary for convenience, construction, or propriety ;* 2*nd, that all ornament should consist of enrichment of the essential construction of the building.* The neglect of these two rules is the cause of all the bad architecture of the present time. Architectural features are continually tacked on buildings with which they have no connexion, merely for the sake of what is termed effect; and ornaments are *actually constructed,* instead of forming the decoration of *construction,* to which in good taste they should be always subservient.

In pure architecture the smallest detail should *have a meaning or serve a purpose;* and even the construction itself *should vary with the material employed,* and the designs should be adapted to the material in which they are executed.

Strange as it may appear at first sight, it is in *pointed architecture alone that these great principles have been carried out;* and I shall be able to illustrate them from the vast cathedral to the simplest erection. Moreover, the architects of the middle ages were the first who *turned the natural properties of the various materials to their full account*, and made *their mechanism a vehicle for their art.*

We shall have therefore to consider ornament with reference to construction and convenience, and ornament with reference to architectural propriety. Construction must be subdivided and treated under three distinct heads,—stone, timber, and metal; brick might indeed be added, but as the principles of its construction are similar to those of stone, I shall not make any distinction; and as for plaster, when used for any other purpose than coating walls, it is a mere modern deception, and the trade is not worthy of a distinction.

To begin with stone. A pointed church is the masterpiece of masonry. It is essentially a stone building; its pillars, its arches, its vaults, its intricate intersections, its ramified tracery, are all peculiar to stone, and could not be consistently executed in any other material. Moreover, the ancient masons obtained great altitude and great extent with a surprising economy of wall and substance; the wonderful strength and solidity of their buildings are the result, not of the *quantity or size of the stones* employed, but of the *art of their disposition.* To exhibit the great excellence of these constructions, it will be here necessary to draw a comparison between them and those of the far-famed classic shores of Greece. Grecian architecture is essentially *wooden* in its construction; it originated in wooden buildings, and never did its professors possess either sufficient imagination or skill to conceive any departure from the original type. Vitruvius shows that their buildings were formerly composed of trunks of trees, with lintels or brestsummers laid across the top, and rafters again resting on them. This is at once the most ancient and barbarous mode of building that can be imagined; it is heavy, and, as I before said, essentially wooden; but is it not extraordinary that when the Greeks commenced building in stone, the *properties of this material did*

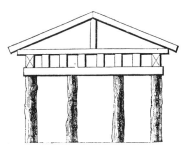

A Wooden Building the origin of Greek Temples.

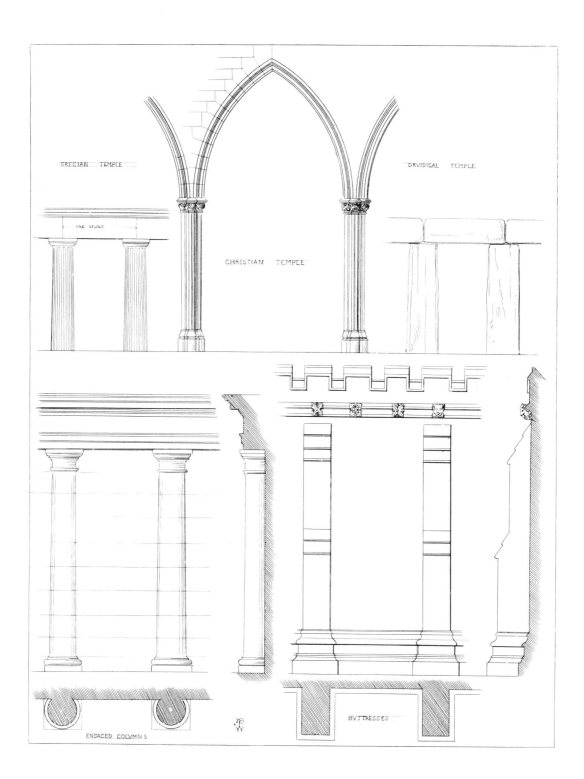

GRECIAN TEMPLE

DRVIDICAL TEMPLE

ONE STONE

CHRISTIAN TEMPLE

ENGAGED COLVMNS

BVTTRESSES

Plate I.

London Published by John Weale, 59 High Holborn 1844.

not suggest to them some different and improved mode of construction? Such, however, was not the case; they set up stone pillars as they had set up trunks of wood; they laid stone lintels as they had laid wood ones, *flat across;* they even made the construction appear still more similar to wood, by carving triglyphs, which are merely a representation of the beam ends. The finest temple of the Greeks is constructed on the *same principle* as a large wooden cabin. As illustrations of history they are extremely valuable; but as for their being held up as the standard of architectural excellence, and the types from which our present buildings are to be formed, it is a monstrous absurdity, which has originated in the blind admiration of modern times for every thing Pagan, to the prejudice and overthrow of Christian art and propriety.

The Greeks erected their columns, like the uprights of Stonehenge, just so far apart that the blocks *they laid on them would not break by their own weight.* The Christian architects, on the contrary, during the *dark ages,* with stone scarcely larger than ordinary bricks, threw their lofty vaults from slender pillars across a vast intermediate space, and that at an amazing height, where they had every difficulty of lateral pressure to contend with. This leads me to speak of buttresses, a distinguishing feature of Pointed Architecture, and the first we shall consider in detail.—Plate I.

It need hardly be remarked that buttresses are necessary supports to a lofty wall. A wall of three feet in thickness, with buttresses projecting three feet more at intervals, is much stronger than a wall of six feet thick without buttresses. A long unbroken mass of building without light and shade is monotonous and unsightly; it is evident, therefore, that both for strength and beauty, breaks or projections are necessary in architecture. We will now examine in which style, Christian or Pagan, these have been most successfully carried out. Pointed architecture does *not conceal her construction, but beautifies it:* classic architecture seeks to conceal instead of decorating it, and therefore has resorted to the use of engaged columns as breaks for strength and effect;—nothing can be worse. A column is an architectural member which should only be employed when a superincumbent weight is required to be sustained *without the obstruction of a solid wall;* but the moment a wall is built, the *necessity and propriety of columns cease,* and engaged columns always produce the effect of having once been detached, and the intermediate spaces blocked up afterwards.

A buttress in pointed architecture at once shows its purpose, and diminishes naturally as it rises and has less to resist. An engaged column, on the contrary, is overhung by a cornice. A buttress, by means of water tables, can be made to project such a distance as to produce a fine effect of light and shade. An engaged column can never project far on account of the cornice, and all the other members, neces-

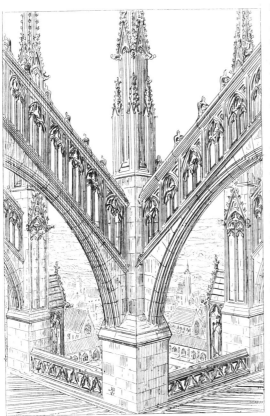

Flying Buttresses.

sarily according with the diameter of the column, would be increased beyond all proportion. I will now leave you to judge in which style the real intention of a buttress is best carried out.

I have yet to speak of flying buttresses, those bold archcs, as their name implies, by which the lateral thrust of the nave groining is thrown over the aisles and transferred to the massive lower buttresses. Here again we see the true principles of Christian architecture, by the conversion of an essential support of the building into a light and elegant decoration. Who can stand among the airy arches of Amiens, Cologne, Chartres, Beauvais, or Westminster, and not be filled with admiration at the mechanical skill and beautiful combination of form which are united in their construction? But, say the modern critics, they are only props, and a bungling contrivance. Let us examine this. Are the revived pagan buildings constructed with such superior skill as to dispense with these supports? By no means; the clumsy vaults of St. Paul's, London, mere coffered semi-arches, without ribs or intersections, *have their flying buttresses; but as this style of architecture does not admit of the great principle of decorating utility*, these buttresses, instead of being made *ornamental, are concealed by an enormous screen*, going entirely round *the building. So that in fact one half of the edifice is built to conceal the other.* Miserable expedient! worthy only of the debased style in which it has been resorted to.

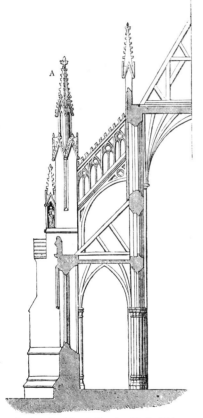
Section of a Pointed Church, with the Flying Buttresses decorated.

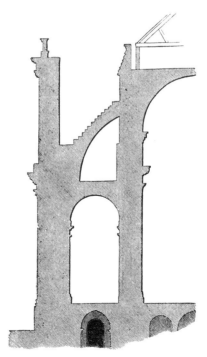
Section of St. Paul's, London, a Church built in the revived Pagan style, with the Flying Buttresses concealed by a Screen.

It is proper to remark that the cluster of pinnacles at A are not carried up for *mere ornament*, but, by their *weight*, to increase the resistance of the great pinnacle at the point of thrust.

We will now proceed, in the second place, to consider groining and vaulting, which are solely adapted to stone construction.

A groined ceiling is divided into compartments by means of ribs springing from caps or corbels, and uniting in bosses placed at the intersections; the spaces between the ribs are termed spandrils: the word boss signifies a spring of water, and has doubtless been applied to the key-stones of vaults, as the ribs seem to spring or separate from them.

Here again the great principle of decorating utility is to be observed. A stone ceiling is most essential in a large church, both for durability, security from fire,[1] and conveyance of sound. It is impossible to conceive stone ceilings better contrived than those of the ancient churches; they are at once light, substantial, beautiful, and lofty. 1st. They are light, because, their principal strength lying in the ribs, the intermediate spaces or spandrils are filled in with small light stones. 2nd. They are substantial, for all the stones being cut to a centre and forming portions of

a curve, when united they are capable of resisting immense pressure, the keys or bosses wedging all together. 3rd. They are beautiful, for no ceiling can be conceived more graceful and elegant than a long perspective of lines and arches radiating from exquisitely carved centres. 4th. They are lofty, not only on account of the elevation at which they are placed, but that their construction permits the clerestory windows to be carried up level with the crown of the arch in the intermediate spaces.

[1] Within the last few years the roofs have been burnt off the cathedrals of Rouen, Chartres, and Bruges; and, owing to the strength of the stone vaulting, the interiors of these churches have scarcely been injured; while York Minster has twice been completely

In the groining of the later styles we find a great departure from the severe and consistent principles I have been describing. Henry the Seventh's Chapel at Westminster is justly considered one of the most wonderful examples of ingenious construction and elaborate fan groining in the world, but at the same time it exhibits the commencement of the bad taste, by *constructing its ornament instead of confining it to the enrichment of its construction.* I allude to the stone pendants of the ceiling, which are certainly extravagances. A key-stone is *necessary* for

Pendant.

Boss.

the support of arched ribs; the older architects contented themselves with enriching it with foliage or figures, but those of the later styles allowed four or five feet of *unnecessary stone to hang down into the church,* and from it to branch other ribs upwards. This is at most an ingenious trick, and quite unworthy of the severity of Pointed or Christian architecture.[2]

gutted within a short period through the want of a stone groining; and yet a mere wood and plaster ceiling has been again constructed!

[2] This is one among many other symptoms of decline apparent in the later works in the pointed style. The moment the *flat* or *four-centred arch* was introduced, the spirit of Christian architecture was on the wane. *Height* or the *vertical principle,* emblematic of the resurrection, is the very essence of Christian architecture. It was to attain greater elevation with a given width that the pointed arch was employed; and the four-centred arch does not possess equal advantage in this respect with the old semi; and although some of the later buildings, as King's College Chapel, Cambridge, still retain the principle of internal height, with the use of the depressed arch, yet who can avoid being struck with the inconsistency of

In the third place, we will proceed to the use and intention of pinnacles and spiral terminations. I have little doubt that pinnacles are considered

---

running up walls to a prodigious elevation, and then, instead of *carrying out the principle, and springing a lofty groin,* losing a considerable increase of height by a flattened thrusting arched ceiling; the form of which is a sort of contradiction to the height at which it is commenced.

I do not make this observation by way of disparaging the merits of this stupendous building, but merely to show the early decay of the true principles of pointed architecture which may be traced even in that glorious pile.

We not unfrequently find the bulbous form employed in the Tudor period: this, which afterwards became the prevailing form of the Dresden and Flemish steeples,

 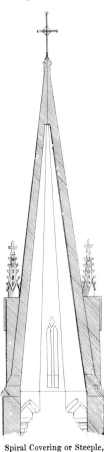

is of *the worst possible taste; and why?* Because *it is a form which does not result from any consistent mode of constructing a covering,* and, on the contrary, requires by its shape *to be constructed,* as will be seen by the annexed sketch; by the side of which I have placed a spire, the severe form and decoration of which are quite consistent with the true principles of rendering the necessary roof or covering of a tower elegant in appearance, without *departing* from *essential construction* for the sake of *ornament.*

One of the greatest defects of St. Paul's, London, is its fictitious dome. *The dome that is seen* is not *the dome of the church,* but a mere construction for effect. At St. Peter's the dome *is the actual covering of the building,* and is therefore constructed in that respect on the true principle; but, as will be perceived by the an-

Bulbous Covering or Steeple,
in the debased style.

Spiral Covering or Steeple,
in the Christian style.

by the majority of persons as mere ornamental excrescences, introduced solely for picturesque effect. The very reverse of these is the case ; and I shall be able to show you that their introduction is warranted by the soundest principles of construction and design. They should be regarded 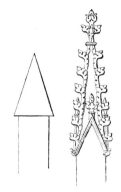 as answering a double intention, both mystical and natural : their mystical intention is, like other vertical lines and terminations of Christian architecture, to represent an emblem of the Resurrection ; their natural intention is that of an upper weathering, to throw off rain. The most useful covering for this purpose, and the one that would naturally suggest itself, is of the form represented in the annexed figure : only let this *essential form* be *decorated* with a finial and crockets, and we have at once a perfect pinnacle. Now the square piers of which these floriated tops form the terminations are all erected to answer a useful purpose ; when they rise

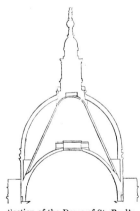
Section of the Dome of St. Paul's.

nexed section, the upper part of St. Paul's is mere imposing show, constructed at a vast expense without any legitimate reason.

From the various symptoms of decline which I have shown to have existed in the later pointed works, I feel convinced that Christian architecture had gone its length, and it must necessarily have destroyed itself by departing from its own principles in the pursuit of novelty, or it must have fallen back on its pure and ancient models. This is quite borne out by existing facts. Now that the pointed style is reviving, we cannot successfully suggest any thing new, but are obliged to return to the spirit of the ancient work. Indeed, if we view pointed architecture in its true light as Christian art, as the faith itself *is perfect, so are the principles on which it is founded.* We may indeed improve in mechanical contrivances to expedite its execution, we may even increase its scale and grandeur ; but we can *never successfully deviate one tittle from the spirit and principles* of pointed architecture. We must rest content to *follow,* not to *lead ;* we may indeed widen the road which our Catholic forefathers formed, but we can never depart from their track without a certainty of failure being the result of our presumption.

from the tops of wall buttresses, they serve as piers to strengthen the parapet, which would be exceedingly weak without some such support. Fig. S.

Their utility on the great piers which resist the flying buttresses has been already mentioned under the head of buttress. At the bases of great spires, the clusters of pinnacles are also placed to increase strength and resistance; in short, wherever pinnacles are introduced in pure pointed architecture, they will be found on examination to fulfil a useful end.

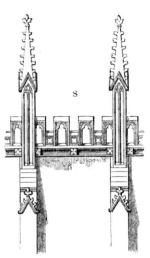

The same remarks will apply to the crocketed and floriated terminations of staircase and other turrets, which are in fact ornamented roofs; and I need hardly remark that turrets were not carried up without a legitimate reason.

Every tower built during the pure style of pointed architecture either was, or was intended to be, surmounted by a spire, which is the natural covering for a tower; a flat roof is both contrary to the spirit of the style, and it is also practically bad. There is no instance before the year 1400 of a church tower being erected without *the intention at least* of being covered or surmounted by a spire; and those towers antecedent to that period which we find without such terminations have either been left incomplete for want of funds, weakness in the sub-structure, or some casual impediment,—or the spires, which were often of timber covered with lead, have been pulled down for the sake of their material.[3] In fine, when towers were erected with flat embattled tops, *Christian architecture*

---

[3] The following glorious churches have been stripped of their spires since the views in Dugdale's Monasticon were taken:—Hereford Cathedral, Worcester Cathedral, Southwell Minster, Rochester Cathedral, Ely Cathedral, Ripon Minster, Finchal Abbey, and Lincoln Cathedral. It is to be remembered that these views were taken *above a century after the lead-stripping and spire-demolishing period commenced.*

was on the decline, and the omission of the ancient and appropriate termination was strong evidence of that fact. Towers surmounting gatehouses were never terminated by spires, for, being originally built for defence, the space at top was required for that purpose. This is the real reason why square-topped and embattled towers are said to be of a domestic character; so that even by persons unacquainted with the use and intentions of spires, they are associated with the idea of ecclesiastical architecture.

The pitch of roof in pointed architecture is another subject on which some useful observations may be made. It will be found, on examination, that the most beautiful pitch of a roof or gable end is an inclination sufficiently steep to throw off snow without giving the slate or lead covering *too perpendicular a strain,* which is formed by two sides on an equilateral triangle.

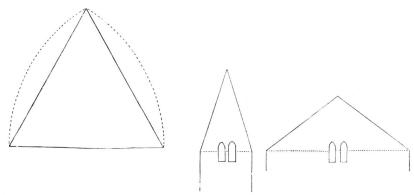

If this form be departed from, the gable appears either painfully acute or too widely spread. All really beautiful forms in architecture are based on the soundest principles of utility.

Practical men know that flat-pitched roofs, which are exceedingly ugly in appearance, are also but ill calculated to resist the action of weather. In slated roofs especially, gusts of wind actually blow under and lift up the covering: when the pitch is increased to its proper elevation, the whole pressure of the wind is *lateral,* and forces the covering closer to the roof.

I now come to speak, in the fourth place, of mouldings, on the judicious form and disposition of which a very considerable part of the effect of the building depends. Mouldings are the enrichment of splays of doorways, windows, arches, and piers, of base and string-courses, of weatherings and copings, and they are introduced solely on the principle of decorating the useful.

I will first point out the necessity of these splays and weatherings, and then proceed to consider the form and application of mouldings to them.

It will be readily seen that without a splay a considerable portion of light would be excluded, and that this form of jamb is necessary to the use and intention of a window.

In a doorway the convenience of splayed sides must be evident for ordinary ingress and egress. This form of jamb is therefore necessary to the use and intention of a doorway.

The advantage of piers splayed, or placed diagonally over square ones, both for elegance and convenience, must be evident to all; the arch mould over them

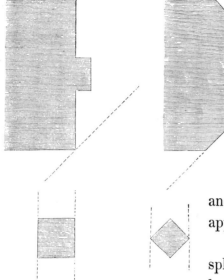

Square Piers supporting
Arches.
      Splayed Piers supporting
Arches.

is consequently splayed. This form of pier and arch mould is therefore necessary for both piers and arches.

Great increase of solidity and strength is gained by projections at the

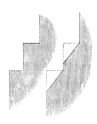

base of a building as sets-off; but were these projections left flat at top instead of being bevelled off, they would become lodgments for water.

The splayed or bevelled form is therefore necessary for base moulds. Strings and copings, the very intention of which is to throw off water, must be sloped, for the same reason.

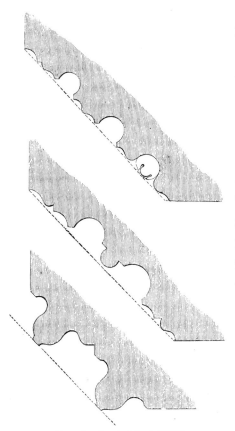

Examples of ancient Jamb Moulds.

The use of the splayed form being now demonstrated, I will proceed to consider the mouldings used to enrich it. All mouldings should be designed on the principle of light, shadow, and half tint; and the section of a moulding should be of such a form as to produce various and pleasing gradations of light and shadow. Monotony should be carefully avoided, also all cutting shadows near the outer edge, which have a meagre effect. The original splayed form should never be lost sight of in the sinkings of the mould, which ought not to be so extravagantly deep as to produce both a real and apparent weakness in the jamb.

All the mouldings of jamb are *invariably sunk from the face of the work*. A projecting mould in such a situation would be a useless excrescence, and contrary to the principles of pointed architecture, which do not admit of any unnecessary members. A hood mould projects immediately above the springing of the arch to receive the water running down the wall over the window, and convey it off on either side. This projection

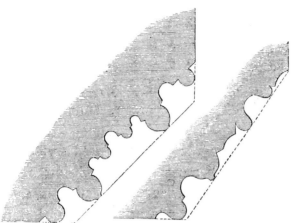

Examples of ancient Jamb Moulds.

answers a purpose, and therefore is not only allowable but indispensable in the pointed style; but a projection down the sides of jamb, where it would be utterly useless, is never found among the monuments of antiquity.

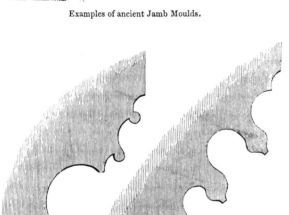

Modern Jamb Mould,
weak and wiry.

French Jamb Mould of the late
styles, *extravagantly* hollowed.

The mouldings round an arch are generally more sub-divided than those of the jamb. This is carrying out the same principle that may be observed in vegetation, where the solid trunk spreads and divides as it rises upwards. The use of caps at the springing of arches is to receive the different moulds of jamb and arch, which could not be successfully united by any better means than foliated and moulded projections. Hence, in the later pointed continental churches, where the same moulds run up the jambs and round the arches without interruption, caps are entirely omitted; and the same thing is observable, under similar circumstances, in the nave of Crowland Abbey, Lincolnshire.

The next class of mouldings I will notice are those belonging to base moulds, weatherings, and strings. I have shown above that the bevelled form is necessary for these projections; but when the weathering is of any depth, it is evident that the inclined plane cut by the horizontal joints of the masonry will produce what are technically called feather-edged joints, at A A A, which would be easily broken by the action of frost, and the joints themselves would be penetrated by water. To obviate this, all the varied and beautiful

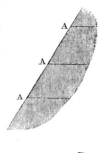

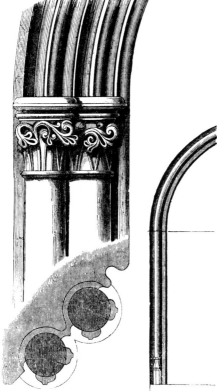

Caps at the transition from Jamb to Arch Mould.

Ancient examples of Base Moulds and Weatherings.

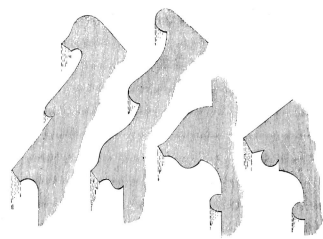

moulds of weatherings have been introduced, by the form of which the stones are strengthened at the joints, and they are protected from the action of water by the over-hanging mould throwing it off to the next bevel.

These observations will apply equally to string-courses and copings.

Another important consideration relative to mouldings, and by which their profile should in a great measure be regulated, is the position in which they are placed with relation to the eye of the spectator. The

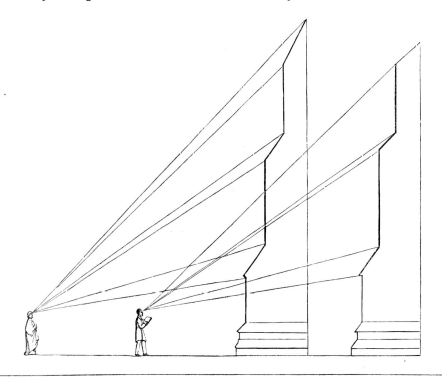

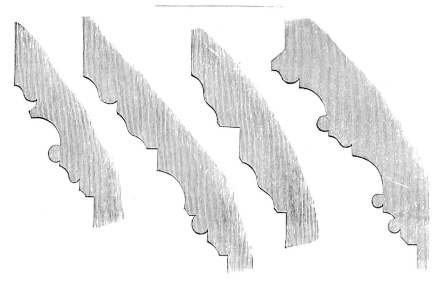

Ancient Profiles of Corbel Moulds.

slope of weatherings themselves is determined by this principle, the pitch increasing with the height that they are placed from the ground. Were this not attended to, the upper water table would be lost to a spectator, unless he was at a considerable distance from the building.

In corbel moulds the profile should *be so formed as to gain projection with strength,*

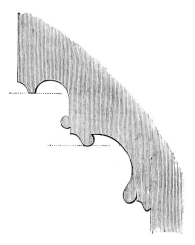

Modern and Weak Corbel Mould.

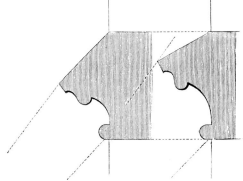

avoiding deep hollows and unnecessary nozings.

The apparent width of a stringcourse placed above the eye depends almost as much on the top bevel as on its actual width; for string-courses of equal width, with different bevels, will vary considerably to the eye.

Every moulding in a pointed building must be designed and shaped on these consistent principles. The severity of Christian architecture requires a *reasonable purpose for the introduction of the smallest detail*, and daily experience proves that those who attempt this glorious style without any fixed idea of its unalterable rules, are certain to end in miserable failures.

Another most important, but now most neglected part of masonry, is the jointing of the stones. All bond and solidity is frequently sacrificed for what is called a neat joint, by setting one stone on end to form a jamb (Plate II. fig. A), when the same space in good old constructions would have been occupied by five or six stones tailing into the wall, and *lying in their natural bed* (fig. B); a point which should be most strictly attended to.

Or, if the jambs are built in courses, they are made as uniform as possible, like rustics (fig. C). By this means the effect of the window is spoiled; the eye, owing to the regularity of these projections, *is carried from the line of jamb to them*, while in the old masonry (fig. D) the irregular outline of the stones does not interfere with the mouldings of the window.

Another point to be remarked in the ancient masonry is the smallness of the stones employed: now, independently of this being the strongest mode of construction, it adds considerably to the effect of the building by increasing its apparent scale. *Large stones destroy proportion;* and to illustrate this I have given two representations of the same piece of architecture differently jointed. Figs. E, F.

Not only are the stones which are used in the ancient buildings exceedingly small, but they are also very irregular in size, and for the same reason as I have before mentioned, that the jointing might *not appear a regular feature*, and by its *lines interfere* with those of the building.

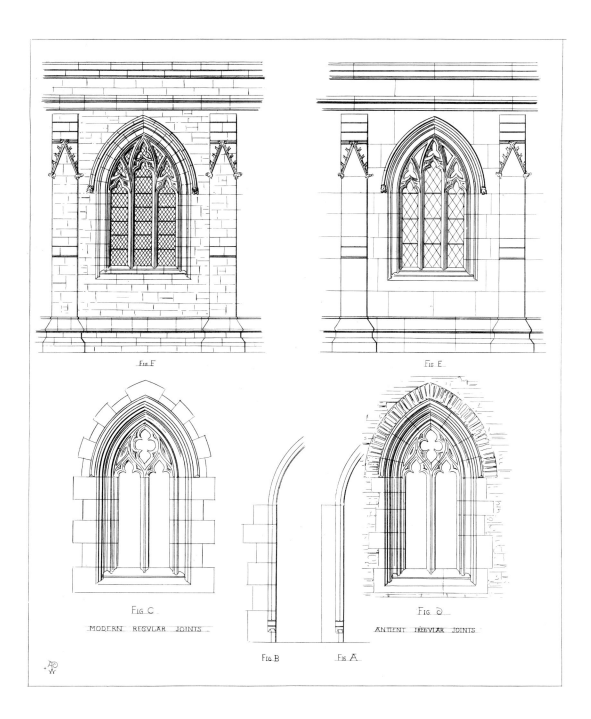

Fɪɢ F.

Fɪɢ E.

Fɪɢ C.

MODERN REGVLAR JOINTS

Fɪɢ B.

Fɪɢ A.

Fɪɢ D.

ANTIENT IREGVLAR JOINTS

Plate II.

London Published by John Weale, 59, High Holborn, 1841.

In the early buildings the work was carried up in regular beds: there were as many joints in a detached pillar as in the wall, and equal space was occupied by the mortar in every part of the building. The joints of stone tracery should always be cut to the centre of the curve where they fall; and if the joint crosses three or four different *curves, its bed should vary with those curves;* and without this is rigidly ad-hered to in the construction

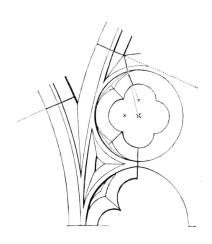

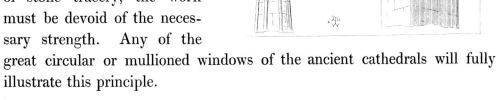

of stone tracery, the work must be devoid of the neces-sary strength. Any of the great circular or mullioned windows of the ancient cathedrals will fully illustrate this principle.

Images in these northern countries were, with some very few excep-tions, placed in niches under canopies. This is really necessary to pre-serve the sculpture from the injuries of weather, and it is much more consistent than leaving the venerable image of a saintly or royal personage exposed to all the pelting of the pitiless storm. Detached images, surmounting buildings, are characteristic of southern and Italian architecture, and are much better suited to the climate of Milan than that of England.

Having now, I trust, successfully shown that the ornamental parts of pointed stone buildings are merely the decorations of their essential construction, and that the formations of mouldings and details are regulated by practical utility, I will endeavour to illustrate the same principles in ancient metal and wood-work.

ON METAL-WORK.

We now come to the consideration of works in metal; and I shall be able to show that the same principles of suiting the design to the material and decorating construction were strictly adhered to by the artists of the middle ages in all their productions in metal, whether precious or common.

In the first place, hinges, locks, bolts, nails, &c., which are always *concealed in modern designs*, were rendered in pointed architecture *rich and beautiful decorations;* and this not only in the doors and fittings of buildings, but in cabinets and small articles of furniture.

The early hinges covered the whole face of the doors with varied and flowing scroll-work. Of this description are those of Notre Dame at Paris, St. Elizabeth's church at Marburg, the western doors of Litchfield Cathedral, the Chapter House at York, and hundreds of other churches, both in England and on the continent. Plate III. figs. 1 and 3.

Hinges of this kind are not only beautiful in design, but they are *practically good.* We all know that on the principle of a lever a door may be easily torn off its modern hinges by a strain applied at its outward edge, (fig. 2.) This could not be the case with the ancient hinges, which extended the whole width of the door, and were bolted through in various

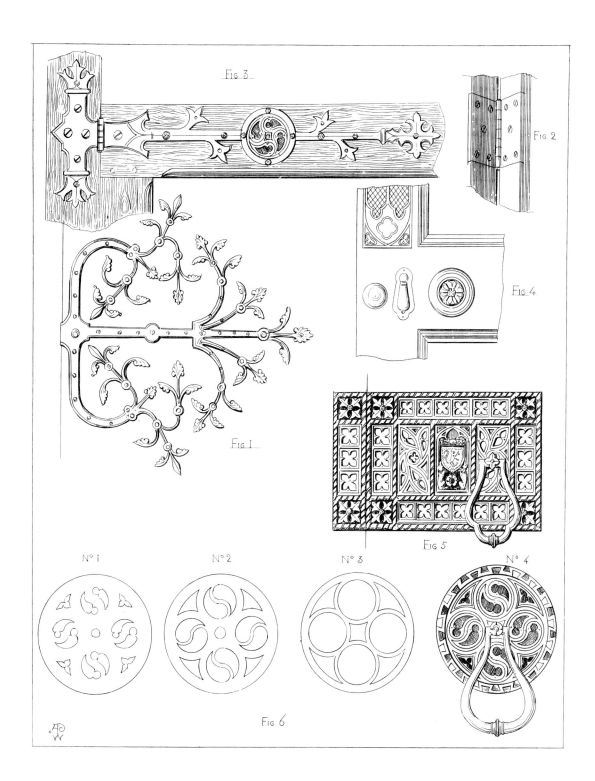

Fig 3

Fig 2

Fig 4

Fig 1

Fig 5

N° 1

N° 2

N° 3

N° 4

Fig 6

Plate III.

London Published by John Weale, 59 High Holborn, 1841.

FIG 1

FIG 2

FIG 3

FIG 6

FIG 7

MODERN CAST RAILING

FIG 4

ANTIENT RAILING

FIG 5

Plate IV.

London, Published by John Weale, 59 High Holborn, 1841.

places. In barn-doors and gates these hinges are still used, although devoid of any elegance of form; but they have been most religiously banished from public edifices as unsightly, merely on account of our present race of artists not exercising the same ingenuity as those of ancient times in rendering the *useful* a vehicle for the beautiful: the same remarks will apply to locks that are now concealed and let into the styles of doors, which are often more than half cut away to receive them. Plate III. fig. 4.

A lock was a subject on which the ancient smiths delighted to exercise the utmost resources of their art. The locks of chests were generally of a most elaborate and beautiful description. A splendid example of an old lock still remains at Beddington Manor House, Surrey, and is engraved in my father's work of Examples. In churches we not unfrequently find locks adorned with sacred subjects chased on them, with the most ingenious mechanical contrivances for concealing the key-hole. Keys were also highly ornamented with appropriate decorations referring to the locks to which they belonged; and even the wards turned into beautiful devices and initial letters. Fig. 5.

In all the ancient ornamental iron-work we may discern a peculiar manner of execution, admirably suited to the material, and quite distinct from that of stone or wood. For instance, tracery was produced by different thicknesses of pierced plates laid over each other. Fig. 6.

Leaves and crockets were not *carved* or *modelled*, and *then cast*, but cut out of thin metal plate, and twisted up with pliers (Plate IV. figs. 1, 2), and the lines of stems either engraved or soldered on. By these simple means all the lightness, ease, and sharpness of real vegetation is produced at a much less cost than the heavy flat foliage usually cast and chased up. It is likewise to be remarked, that the necessary fastenings for iron-work were always shown and ornamented. Bolts, nails, and rivets, so far from being unsightly, are beautiful studs and busy enrichments, if properly treated. Fig. 3.

Large tracery was either formed of round iron, like a stem twisted into intersections, or of flat iron bars of different thicknesses riveted together, and the edges chamfered by filing.

Well at Antwerp.

Railings were not *casts of meagre stone tracery* (Plate IV. fig. 4), but elegant combinations of metal bars, adjusted with due regard to strength and resistance. Fig. 5.*

There were many fine specimens of this style of railing round tombs, and Westminster Abbey was rich in such examples, but they were actually pulled down and sold for old iron by the order of the then Dean, and even the exquisite scroll-work belonging to the tomb of Queen Eleanor, of which I have here given a specimen (fig. 6), was not respected. The iron screen of King Edward the Fourth's tomb at St. George's Chapel, Windsor, is a splendid example of ancient iron-work.

The fire-dogs or Andirons (fig. 7), as they were called, which supported either the fuel-logs where wood was burnt, or grates for coal, were frequently of splendid design. The ornaments were generally heraldic, and

---

* The parts marked with a + in this figure are merely pierced out of *thin* plate, and riveted to the bars.

it was not unusual to work the finer parts in brass for relief of colour and richness of effect.

These form a striking contrast with the inconsistencies of modern grates, which are not unfrequently made to represent diminutive fronts of castellated or ecclesiastical buildings with turrets, loopholes, windows, and doorways, all in a space of forty inches.

New Sheffield pattern for a modern Castellated Grate.

The fender is a sort of embattled parapet, with a lodge-gate at each end ; the end of the poker is a sharp pointed finial ; and at the summit of the tongs is a saint. It is impossible to enumerate half the absurdities of modern metal-workers ; but all these proceed from the false notion of *disguising* instead of *beautifying* articles of utility. How many objects of ordinary use are rendered monstrous and ridiculous simply because the artist, instead of seeking the *most convenient form*, and *then decorating it*, has embodied some extravagance *to conceal the real purpose for which the article has been made!* If a clock is required, it is not unusual to cast a Roman warrior in a flying chariot, round one of the wheels of which, on close inspection, the hours may be descried ; or the whole front of a cathedral church reduced to a few inches in height, with the clock-face

Patterns of Brumagem Gothic.

occupying the position of a magnificent rose window. Surely the inventor
of this patent clock-case could never have reflected that according to the
scale on which the edifice was reduced, his clock would be about two
hundred feet in circumference, and that such a monster of a dial would
crush the proportions of almost any building that could be raised.   But
this is nothing when compared to what we see continually produced from
those inexhaustible mines of bad taste, Birmingham and Sheffield : staircase turrets for inkstands, monumental crosses for light-shades, gable
ends hung on handles for door-porters, and four doorways and a cluster of
pillars to support a French lamp ; while a pair of *pinnacles* supporting an
arch is called a Gothic-pattern scraper, and a wiry compound of quatrefoils
and fan tracery an abbey garden-seat.   Neither relative scale, form,
purpose, nor unity of style, is ever considered by those who design these

abominations; if they only introduce a quatrefoil or an acute arch, be the outline and style of the article ever so modern and debased, it is at once denominated and sold as Gothic.

While I am on this topic it may not be amiss to mention some other absurdities which may not be out of place, although they do not belong to metal-work. I will commence with what are termed Gothic-pattern papers, for hanging walls, where a wretched caricature of a pointed building is repeated from the skirting to the cornice in glorious confusion,—door over pinnacle, and pinnacle over door. This is a great favourite with hotel and tavern keepers. Again, those papers which are shaded are defective in principle; for, as a paper is hung round a room, the ornament must frequently be shadowed on the light side.

Pattern of Modern Gothic Paper.

The variety of these miserable patterns is quite surprising; and as the expense of cutting a block for a bad figure is equal if not greater than for a good one, there is not the shadow of an excuse for their continual reproduction. A moment's reflection must show the extreme absurdity of *repeating a perspective* over a large surface with some hundred different points of sight: a panel or wall may be enriched and decorated at pleasure, but it should always be treated in a consistent manner.

Flock papers are admirable substitutes for the ancient hangings, but then they must consist of a pattern *without shadow*, with the forms relieved by the introduction of harmonious colours. Illuminated manuscripts of the thirteenth, fourteenth, and fifteenth centuries would furnish an immense number of exquisite designs for this purpose.

Ancient Pattern for a Flock Paper.

These observations will apply to modern carpets, the patterns of which are generally *shaded*. Nothing can be more ridiculous than an apparently *reversed groining* to walk upon, or highly relieved foliage and perforated tracery for the decoration of a floor.

The ancient paving tiles are quite consistent with their purpose, being merely ornamented with a pattern not produced by any apparent relief, but only by *contrast of colour;* and carpets should be treated in precisely the same manner. Turkey carpets, which are by far the handsomest now manufactured, have no shadow in their pattern, but merely an intricate combination of coloured intersections.

Pattern of Ancient Paving Tiles.

Modern upholstery, again, is made a surprising vehicle for bad and paltry taste, especially when any thing very fine is attempted.

To arrange curtains consistently with true taste, their use and intention should always be considered: they are suspended across windows and other openings to exclude cold and wind, and as they are not always required to be drawn, they are hung to rings sliding on rods, to be opened or closed at pleasure: as there must necessarily be a space between this rod and the ceiling through which wind will pass, a boxing of wood has been contrived, in front of which a valance is suspended to exclude air.

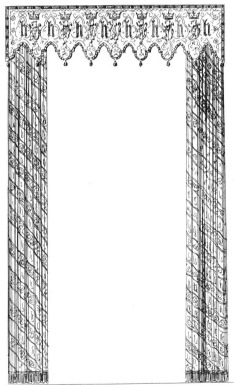

ANTIENT CVRTAIN HANGINGS

Now the materials of these curtains may be rich or plain, they may be heavily or lightly fringed, they may be embroidered with heraldic charges or not, according to the locality where they are to be hung, but their real use must be strictly maintained. Hence all the modern plans of suspending enormous folds of stuff over poles, as if for the purpose of sale or of being dried, is quite contrary to the use and intentions of curtains, and abominable in taste; and the only object that these endless festoons and bunchy tassels can answer is to swell the bills and profits of the upholsterers, who are the inventors of these extravagant and ugly draperies, which are not only useless in protecting the chamber from cold, but are the depositories of thick layers of dust, and in London not unfrequently become the strong-holds of vermin.

It is not less ridiculous to see canopies of tomb and altar screens set up

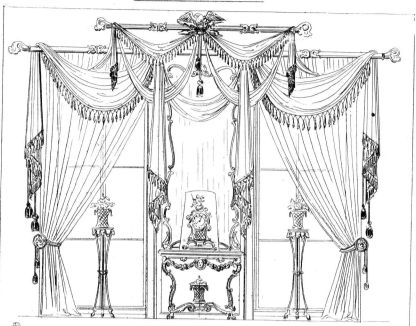

MODERN UPHOLSTERY

over windows, instead of the appropriate valance or baldaquin of the olden time. It is proper in this place to explain the origin and proper application of fringe, which is but little understood. Fringe was originally nothing more than the ragged edge of the stuff, tied into bunches to prevent it unravelling further. This suggested the idea of manufacturing fringe as an ornamental edging, but good taste requires that it should be both *designed and applied consistently*.

In the first place, fringe should never consist of *heavy parts*, but simply of threads tied into ornamental patterns.

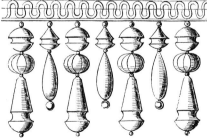

Modern Fringe, composed of turned
pieces of wood.

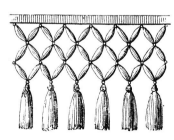

Ancient Fringe, composed of threads.

Secondly, a deep fringe should not be suspended to a narrow valance.

Thirdly, no valance should be formed entirely of fringe, as fringe can only be applied as an ornamental edging to some kind of stuff.

Fourthly, fringe should not be sewed *upon* stuff, but always *on the edges*. It is allowable at the very top, as it may be supposed to be the upper edge turned over.

A Modern Valance of Fringe.

But to return to metal-work. We have in the next place to consider the use of cast-iron. When viewed with reference to mechanical purposes, it must be considered as a most valuable invention, but it can but rarely be applied to ornamental purposes.

Iron is so much stronger a material than stone that it requires, of course, a much smaller substance to attain equal strength; hence, to be consistent, the mullions of cast-iron tracery must be so reduced as to look painfully thin, devoid of shadow, and out of all proportion to the openings in which they are fixed. If, to overcome these objections, the castings are made of the same dimensions as stone, a great inconsistency with respect to the material is incurred; and, what will be a much more powerful argument with most people, treble the cost of the usual material.

Moreover, all castings must be deficient of that play of light and shade consequent on bold relief and deep sinkings, so essential to produce a good effect.

Cast-iron is likewise a source of continual repetition, subversive of the variety and imagination exhibited in pointed design. A mould for casting is an expensive thing; once got, it must be worked out.

Cast-iron Mullion.   Stone Mullion.

Hence we see the same window in green-house, gate-house, church, and room; the same strawberry-leaf, sometimes perpendicular, sometimes horizontal, sometimes suspended, sometimes on end; although by the principles of pure design these various positions require to be differently treated.

Cast-iron is a deception; it is seldom or never left as iron. It is disguised by paint, either as stone, wood, or marble. This is a mere trick, and the severity of Christian or Pointed Architecture is utterly opposed to all deception: better is it to do a little substantially and consistently with truth than to produce a great but false show. Cheap deceptions of magnificence encourage persons to assume a semblance of decoration far beyond either their means or their station, and it is to this cause we may assign all that mockery of splendour which pervades even the dwellings of the lower classes of society. Glaring, showy, and meretricious ornament was never so much in vogue as at present; it disgraces every branch of our art and manufactures, and the correction of it should be an earnest consideration with every person who desires to see the real principles of art restored.

I will now briefly notice the exquisite productions of the ancient gold and silversmiths. As reformers and puritans have left us nothing but the mere name of the glorious shrines and ornaments which formerly enriched our cathedral and other churches, and as revolutionary and heretical violence has been almost equally destructive on the continent, were it not for a few places which have preserved their ancient treasures, we should be unable to conceive half the art, half the talent, half the exquisite beauties of this class of ecclesiastical ornaments. In the sacristy of Aix-la-Chapelle is a treasury of inestimable value, consisting of shrines, reliquaries, crosses, crowns, ampuls, chalices, pyxes, books of the Holy Gospels, paxes, and enamelled images of silver, all executed during the finest periods of Christian art, the richness of their material being only surpassed by that of their design. To enumerate even a tenth part of these wonderful productions of the goldsmith's art would occupy far too much time for my present purpose; but I will make a few remarks respecting them to illustrate the purpose of my Lecture.

Their construction and execution is decidedly of a *metallic character*. The ornament is produced by *piercing, chasing, engraving, and enamel :* many of the parts were first formed in thin plates of metal, and then shaped by the pliers.   Engraving is a style of ornament peculiar to metal.   The old goldsmiths were undoubtedly the inventors of our present engraved plates for printing.   They increased the effect of the ornamental engravings, by hollowing out the ground in certain parts, and filling it in with coloured enamels.   The annexed engraving of an ancient pyx will show the style of

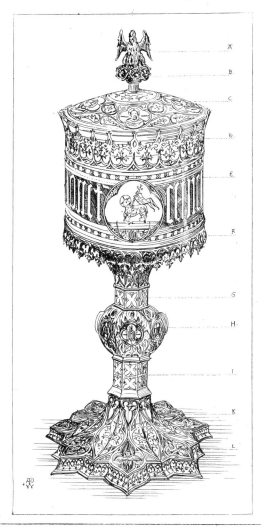

A   The Pelican, chased.

B   The nest, composed of twisted silver wire.

C   Engraved and enamelled.

D   Pierced and engraved.

E   Engraved, and the centre enamelled.

F   Pierced and engraved.

G   Quatrefoils enamelled.

H   Knop beat up with enamelled quatrefoils.

I   Quatrefoils enamelled.

K   Foot hammered up, then engraved and enamelled.

L   Engraved.

working silver, as practised during the middle ages. There are some exquisite examples of chalice feet enamelled with sacred subjects in the sacristy of Mayence Cathedral, and a circular reliquary at Aix, which Dr. Rock considers to have been used as a pax, which is a transcendant specimen of the art of enamel. The covers of the great books of the Holy Gospels were enriched with chasing, enamels, and even jewels ; the crucifixion of our Lord in the centre, and the emblems of the Evangelists at the corners of an elaborate border. Precious stones of every description were studded on these ornaments, which presented a wonderful combination of richness and beauty, produced by gold enamel of various hues and sparkling gems, arranged with the purest design and most harmonious effect. As it would occupy a whole work to illustrate these objects separately, I have endeavoured to convey some idea of their beauty by the annexed engraving of a reliquary chamber. Plate V.*

These treasures, which Aix now alone possesses, were by no means superior to many of those splendid ecclesiastical ornaments formerly to be found in all the large churches of this land, but which fell a prey to the rapacious tyrant Henry and his abettors, in the general wreck of faith and art at the period of his lamentable schism.

Silversmiths are no longer artists ; they manufacture fiddle-headed spoons, punchy racing cups, cumbersome tureens and wine-coolers ; their vulgar salvers are covered with sprawling rococo, edged with a confused pattern of such universal use that it may be called with propriety the *Sheffield eternal.* Cruet-stand, tea-pot, candlestick, butter-boat, tray, waiter, tea-urn, are all bordered with this in and out shell-and-leaf pattern, which, being struck in a die, does not even possess the merit

* REFERENCES TO PLATE V.—I. Ferettum or portable shrine. II., II. Books of the Holy Gospels. III. Relics in a silver bust. IV. Reliquaries. V. Relic of the holy cross. VI. Paxes for the kiss of peace during the mass. VII. Morse for fastening a cope. VIII. Head of a processional cross. IX. Precious mitres. X. Pastoral staff. XI. Cantor's staff. XII. Images of silver gilt.

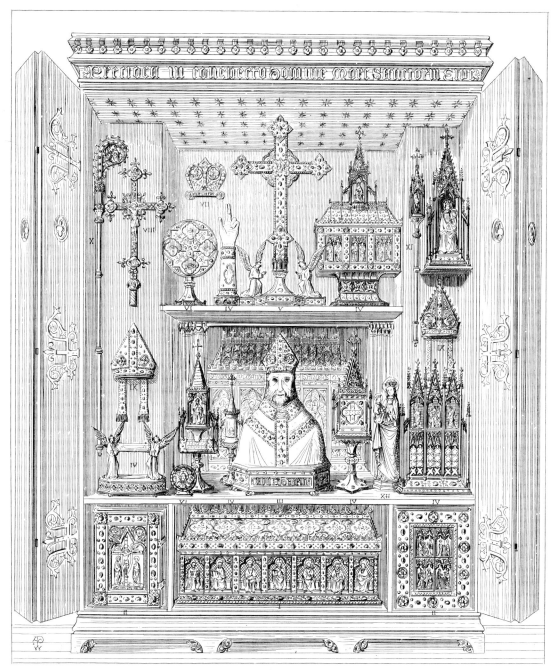

ALMERY IN A RELIQVARY CHAMBER

Plate V.

London Published by John Weale 59, High Holborn. 1841.

of relief. Like every thing else, silver-work has sunk to a mere trade, and art is rigidly excluded from its arrangements.

Iron-smiths were artists formerly, and great artists too; Quentin Matys, for instance, whose beautiful well-top stands in front of Antwerp Cathedral, and whose splendid picture of the entombment of our Lord is the greatest ornament of the Musée of that city. Quentin Matys are not, however, of our generation; if you want some objects executed in iron rather different from what are in ordinary use, and go to a smith to whom you explain your wishes and intentions, the vacant stare of the miserable mechanic soon convinces you that the turning up of a horse-shoe is the extent of his knowledge in the mysteries of the smithy: you then address yourself to another, and one who is called a *capital hand;* and if he be sufficiently sober to comprehend your meaning, he will tell you that what you want is quite out of his line, that he only makes a particular sort of lock, and that he does not think there is a man in the trade who could undertake the job, which, after all, is perhaps a mere copy of a very ordinary piece of old iron-work; and this is a true picture of the majority of our artizans in the nineteenth century, the enlightened age of mechanics' institutes and scientific societies.

Mechanics' institutes are a mere device of the day to poison the minds of the operatives with infidel and radical doctrines; the Church is the true mechanics' institute, the oldest and the best. *She was the great and never failing school in which all the great artists of the days of faith were formed.* Under her guidance they directed the most wonderful efforts of her skill to the glory of God; and let our fervent prayer ever be, that the Church may again, as in days of old, cultivate the talents of her children to the advancement of religion and the welfare of their own souls;—for without such results talents are vain, and the greatest efforts of art sink to the level of an abomination.

LECTURE II.

WE will now proceed to consider decoration with regard to constructions in wood, which are founded on quite opposite principles to those of stone.   With timber you may attain a great height, or extend over a great breadth, by means of a single spar reared on its base or supported at the ends.   The strength of wood-work is attained by bracing the various pieces together on geometrical principles.   This is beautifully exemplified in ancient roofs, either of churches or domestic buildings: the construction of these, so far from being concealed, is turned into ornament.   The principal tie-beams, rafters, purloins, and braces, which in modern edifices are hidden at a vast expense by a flat plaster ceiling, are here rendered very ornamental features, and this essential portion of a building becomes its greatest beauty.   Plate VI. figs. 1 and 2.

The stupendous roof of Westminster Hall, decidedly the grandest in the world, illustrates this principle fully, and so do all the roofs in the collegiate halls of Oxford and Cambridge, as well as those of the palatial edifices at Eltham, Hampton Court, Croydon, and many others belonging to manorial residences.

Of wooden roofs over churches we have beautiful specimens in various parts of England, but especially in Lincolnshire, Norfolk, and Suffolk. The beams of these roofs are beautifully moulded and enriched with carvings.   Figs. 3, 4.

Nor were these carvings without a mystical and appropriate meaning; they usually represented angels, archangels, and various orders of the heavenly hierarchy, hovering over the congregated faithful, while the spaces between the rafters were painted azure and powdered with stars and other celestial emblems, a beautiful figure of the firmament.   Some of these angels held shields charged with the instruments of the passion, the holy name, and other emblems; others labels with devout scriptures. Every portion of these roofs was enriched with painting, and when in their glory must have formed splendid canopies to the temples of the

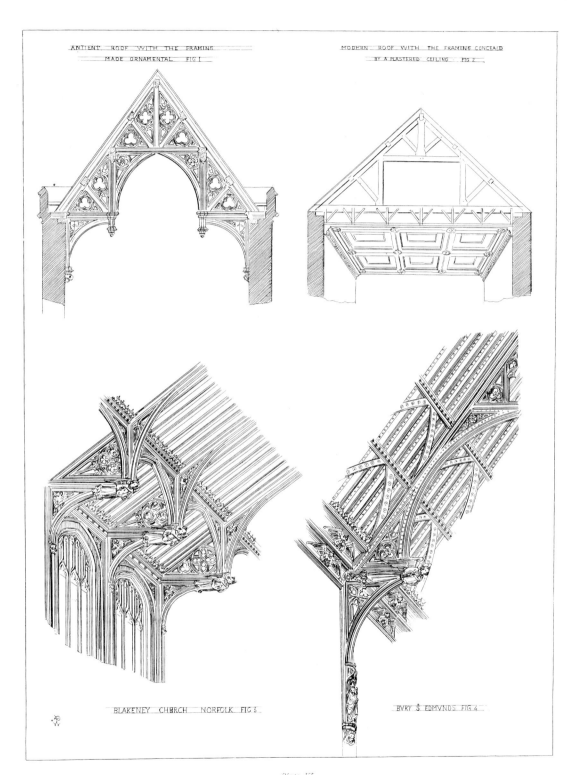

ANTIENT ROOF WITH THE FRAMING
MADE ORNAMENTAL FIG I

MODERN ROOF WITH THE FRAMING CONCEAL'D
BY A PLASTERED CEILING FIG 2

BLAKENEY CHURCH NORFOLK FIG 3

BVRY S EDMVNDS FIG 4

Plate VI.

London Published by John Weale, 59 High Holborn 1841.

living God; and what is peculiarly useful to illustrate my present purpose, these roofs were of an entirely different construction to coverings of stone. *Wooden groining* is decidedly bad, because it is employing a material *in the place and after the manner of stone, which requires an entirely different mode of construction.*

I am aware that ancient examples of wooden groining are to be found in the cloisters of Lincoln Cathedral, Selby Church, and some others; but in these cases, as well as any others in which it may be found, an inspection of the building will clearly show that they were originally intended to have been groined with stone, and that the springing ribs have been carried up some height in that material, but that owing to a real or supposed weakness in the side walls, which were not considered capable of resisting the lateral pressure of stone vaulting, the expedient of an imitation groining in wood was resorted to as a case of absolute necessity; and I am decidedly of opinion that had not the original intention been to have groined these churches in stone, their builders would have made an entirely different arrangement in their upper parts, suitable to an ornamental wooden roof.

At Bury St. Edmund's is a glorious roof, of which I have given a sketch. At every pair of principals are two angels as large as the human figure, bearing the sacred vessels and ornaments used in the celebration of the holy sacrifice; these angels are vested in chasubles and dalmaticks, tunicles and copes, of ancient and beautiful form; the candlesticks, thurible, chalice, books, cruets, &c., which they bear are most valuable authorities for the form and design of those used in our ancient churches. The roofs of St. Peter's and All Saints, in that truly catholic city of Norwich, are very fine; and in Lavenham and Long Melford churches, in Suffolk, are admirable specimens of carved timber roofs.[4]

But, alas! how many equally fine roofs have been demolished and burnt by the brutal ignorance of parish functionaries!—how many have

---

[4] In the last number of the British Critic is a most admirable article on open roofs, well worthy the perusal of all who are interested in the revival of ancient ecclesiastical architecture.

been daubed over by the remorseless whitewasher!—how many painted in vile imitation of marble, as at Yarmouth, (especially if the church-warden for the time being happened to be a *grainer!*)—how many of these fine roofs have been spoiled of their beautiful and appropriate decorations by the execrable fanaticism of the puritan faction, who actually have made entries in the parish accounts of the cost of their demolition!—how many concealed from view by lath and plaster ceilings of miserable design tacked up under them!—and although a somewhat better spirit has at length arisen, still how many of these beautiful memorials of the piety and skill of our ancestors are yet being mutilated or utterly destroyed under the pretext of reparation!—a plea which is not unfrequently urged by those in authority for selling the lead and massive oak beams, the solid

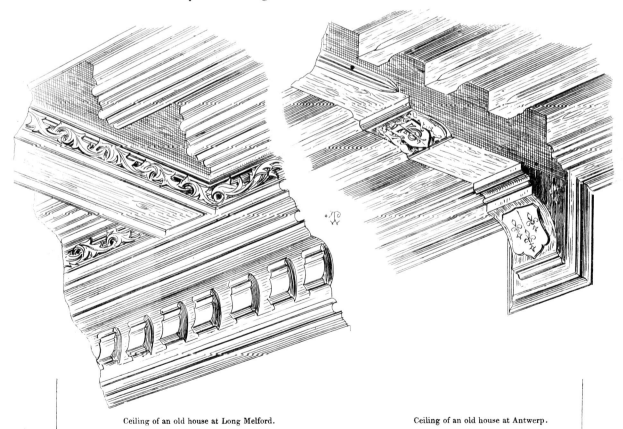

Ceiling of an old house at Long Melford.   Ceiling of an old house at Antwerp.

covering of antiquity, and substituting a plastered ceiling and meagre slates in their stead, which detestable practice is still in full force in many parts of England.

Not only do we find the construction of roofs ornamented, but there are numerous examples of common joist floors and the carrying beams which are rendered exceedingly beautiful by moulding and carving.

Ceiling of the Clopton Chauntry, Long Melford.*

In the ancient timbered houses of which such interesting examples yet remain in many of our old cities, especially at Coventry, York, and Gloucester, we do not *find a single feature introduced beyond the decoration of what was necessary for their substantial construction.* What can be stronger, and at the same time more ornamental, than the curvilineal bracing by which due advantage was taken of crooked pieces of timber!—

* The ground of this ceiling is azure; the stars are of lead, gilt; the inscription on the rafters is Ihu Mercy, and Gramercy; the arms on the shields are those belonging to different branches of the Clopton family, with their names inscribed beneath. The scripture on the large scroll is extracted from the Psalter, the whole richly painted.

The ancient French cities, Rouen, Beauvais, Abbeville, Lisieux, and others, were full of timber houses covered with carved beams and most varied ornaments ; but these are rapidly disappearing to make way for monotonous plaster buildings, which are constructed also of *wood ;* but as modern architects have not the skill to ornament that construction, the whole of the timbers are

Example of *ornamented construction* in an ancient timber house.

concealed by mock cornices and pilasters, so that the houses of modern

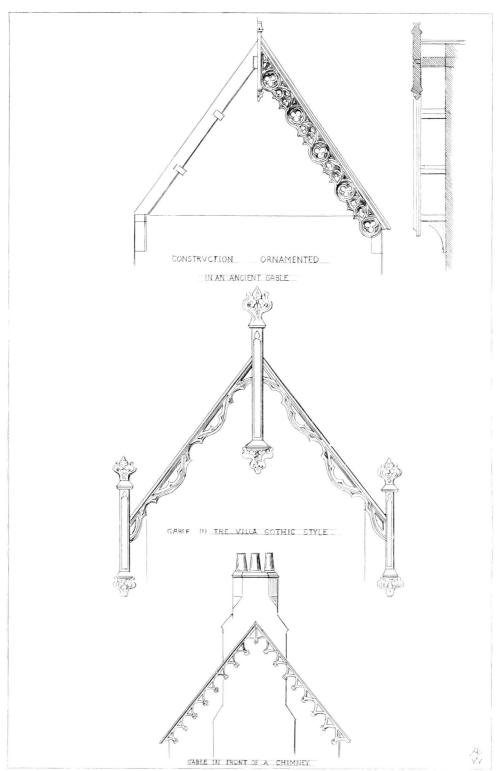

CONSTRVCTION ORNAMENTED

IN AN ANCIENT GABLE

GABLE IN THE VILLA GOTHIC STYLE

GABLE IN FRONT OF A CHIMNEY

Rouen have all the disadvantages of the old wooden buildings, without one particle of their beauty.

As gable-ends form most prominent features of the old buildings, and as they are continually attempted by modern Gothic builders, I will draw your attention to their real use, and then point out some of the egregious blunders frequently committed by modern architects when they attempt to introduce them.

The barge boards of gables are intended to cover and preserve the ends of the purloins which projected over to shelter the front of the building.

The hip knop which terminated the ancient gables was in reality a king post fixed at the junction of the barge boards, and into which they were tenanted. To the upper part of these was usually affixed a vane, and the bottom was finished off in the form of a pendant. Plate VII.

In modern gable ends the barge boards are generally so *slight and cut so open* that they become mere skeletons, and utterly useless for the purpose for which they should be fixed, that of covering the timber ends. Again, the knop really useful at the apex of the gable is repeated in modern gables at the extremities, hanging down to an extravagant depth, and loaded with bunchy finials and pendants. Pl. VII.

Of these we may say with Puff in the Critic, when he hears the three morning guns, " Give these fellows a good idea, and they will work it to death." A king post in the centre of the gable is good, because it is really useful, but at the lower extremities these excrescences cannot serve any purpose except to add useless weight and unnecessary expense.

It is a common practice, when a chimney shaft is carried up in the centre of a gable end, for the barge boards *to be fixed before it.* This is absurd; flues must necessarily stop the passage of timbers; consequently the barge boards, which are only coverings of those timbers, should stop also. Pl. VII.

If we examine the ancient wood-work which decorated rooms, we shall find that it consisted of mere panelling, more or less enriched by carving, with large spaces left for hangings and tapestry.   Plate VIII.

Were the real principles of Gothic architecture restored, the present objection of its extreme costliness would cease to exist.   In pointed decoration *too much* is generally attempted; every room in what is called a Gothic house must be fitted with niches, pinnacles, groining, tracery, and tabernacle work, after the manner of a chantry chapel.   Such fittings must be enormously expensive, and at the same time they are contrary to the true spirit of the style, which does not admit of the introduction of these features in any situation but that to which they properly belong.   The modern admirers of the pointed style have done much injury to its revival by the erroneous and costly system they have pursued: the interiors of their houses are one mass of elaborate work; there is no repose, no solidity, no space left for hangings or simple panels: the whole is covered with trifling details, enormously expensive, and at the same time subversive of good effect.   These observations apply equally to furniture;—upholsterers seem to think that nothing can be Gothic unless it is found in some church.   Hence your modern man designs a sofa or occasional table from details culled out of Britton's Cathedrals, and all the ordinary articles of furniture, which require to be simple and convenient, are made not only very expensive but very uneasy.   We find diminutive flying buttresses about an armchair; every thing is crocketed with angular projections, innumerable mitres, sharp ornaments, and turreted extremities.   A man who remains any length of time in a modern Gothic room, and escapes without being wounded by some of its minutiæ, may consider himself extremely fortunate.   There are often as many pinnacles and gablets about a pier-

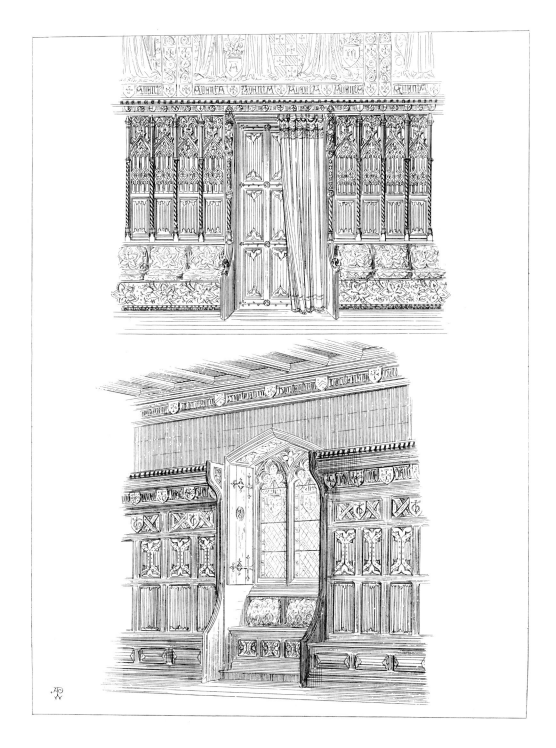

Plate VIII.

London. Published by John Weale, 59, High Holborn. 1841.

Illustration of the extravagant style of Modern Gothic Furniture and Decoration.

glass frame as are to be found in an ordinary church, and not unfrequently the whole canopy of a tomb has been transferred for the purpose, as at Strawberry Hill. I have perpetrated many of these enormities in the furniture I designed some years ago for Windsor Castle. At that time I had not the least idea of the principles I am now explaining; all my knowledge of Pointed Architecture was confined to a tolerably good notion of details in the abstract; but these I employed with so little judgment or propriety, that, although the parts were correct and exceedingly well executed, collectively they appeared a complete burlesque of pointed design.

I now come, in the last place, to consider decoration with reference to propriety; what I mean by propriety is this, *that the external and internal appearance of an edifice should be illustrative of, and in accordance with, the purpose for which it is destined.* There is a vast difference between a building raised to God and one for temporal purposes; again, in the first of these a great distinction necessarily exists between a cathedral and a parochial church, between a collegiate chapel and a private oratory; and in the second, between a royal residence and a manorial mansion,—between monuments raised for public or national purposes and erections for private convenience.

The scale of propriety in architecture must always be regulated by purpose, and to illustrate this more fully I will divide edifices under three heads,—Ecclesiastical, Collegiate, and Civil. The greatest privilege possessed by man is to be allowed, while on earth, to contribute to the glory of God: a man who builds a church draws down a blessing on himself both for this life and that of the world to come, and likewise imparts under God the means of every blessing to his fellow creatures; hence we cannot feel surprised at the vast number of religious buildings erected by our Catholic forefathers in the days of faith, or at their endeavours to render those structures, by their arrangement and decoration, as suitable as their means could accomplish for their holy and important destination. It must have been an edifying sight to have overlooked some ancient city raised when religion formed a leading impulse in the mind of man, and when the honour and worship of the Author of all good was considered of greater importance than the achievement of the most lucrative commercial speculation. There stood the mother church, the great cathedral, vast in height, rising above all the towers of the parochial churches which surrounded her; next in scale and grandeur might have been discerned the abbatial and collegiate churches with their vast and solemn buildings; each street had its temple raised for the true worship of God, *variously beautiful in design, but each a fine example of Christian art.* Even the bridges and approaches were not destitute of religious buildings, and many a beautiful chapel and oratory was corbelled out on massive piers over the stream that flowed beneath.

The great object I have in directing your attention to such a Catholic city is to illustrate the principle of decorative propriety in ecclesiastical buildings. We have here various edifices of various dimensions, various degrees of richness, various in arrangement, yet each bears on its very face the stamp of Catholic;—cathedral or abbey, church or oratory, they all show that they are dedicated to the one true faith, raised by men actuated by one great motive, the truly Catholic principle of dedicating the best they possessed to God. It would be both unjust and unreasonable to expect a few parishioners to erect as sumptuous an edifice to the Almighty as the clergy of a vast cathedral, and even if they could practically achieve such a result, it would be out of character for the use and intentions of a parish church; neither ought we to look to a private chapel or oratory erected by the unassisted piety of an individual for the extent or ornaments of a public church, unless, indeed, that individual was possessed of great wealth, and then, although not in dimensions, it should surpass in glory the usual decoration of such buildings. In a word, architectural propriety as regards ecclesiastical buildings requires that they should be as good, as spacious, as rich and beautiful, as the *means and numbers of those who are erecting them will permit.* The history of our present vast and magnificent churches fully exemplifies this principle; many of them in their origin were little better than thatched barns; it was the best that could be done at that early period: but when the wealth and influence of the Church increased, they were soon demolished to make way for more fitting structures; these in their turn were rebuilt with still greater magnificence. The ancient clergy were never satisfied, never content, never imagined that they had done enough; the scaffoldings were round the walls and the cranes on the towers of many of the English abbeys at the time of their suppression.

It is not incumbent on all men to raise vast and splendid churches; but it *is* incumbent on all men to render the buildings they raise for religious purposes *more vast and beautiful than those in which they dwell.* This is all I contend for; but this is a feeling nearly, if not altogether, extinct. Churches are now built without the least regard to tradition, to mystical reasons, or even common propriety. A room full of seats at the least possible cost is the present idea of a church; and if any ornament is indulged in, it is a mere screen to catch the eye of the passer-by, which is a most contemptible deception to hide the meanness of the real building. How often do we see a front gable carried up to a respectable pitch, and we might naturally infer that this is the termination, both as regards height and form, of the actual roof; but on turning the corner we soon perceive that it is a mere wall cramped to hold it in its position, and that it conceals a very meeting-house, with a flat roof and low thin walls, perforated by mean apertures, and without a single feature or detail to carry out the appearance it assumed towards the street. Now the

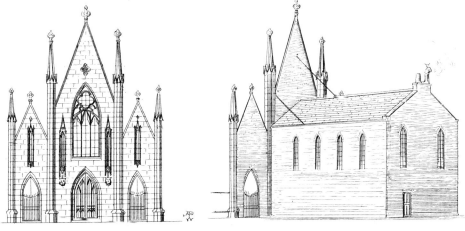

Street Elevation.   Side Perspective.

severity of Christian architecture is opposed to all deception. We should never make a building erected to God appear better than it really is by artificial means. These are showy worldly expedients, adapted only for those who live by splendid deception, such as theatricals, mountebanks, quacks, and the like. Nothing can be more execrable than making a church appear rich and beautiful in the eyes of men, but full of trick and falsehood, which cannot escape the all-searching eye of God, to whom churches should be built, and not to man. Even under the Mosaic dispensation, the Holy of Holies, *entered only by the high priest*, was overlaid with gold; and how much more ought the interiors of our tabernacles to be lined with precious material, which are ten times more holy and deserving of it than the figurative tabernacle of the old law!—and yet in these times all that does not *catch the eye is neglected.* A rich looking antipendium often conceals rough materials, a depository for candle ends, and an accumulation of dirt, which are allowed to remain simply because they are out of sight. All plaster, cast-iron, and composition ornaments, painted like stone or oak, are mere impositions, and, although very suitable to a tea-garden, are utterly unworthy of a sacred edifice. " Omne secundum ordinem et honeste fiat." Let every man build to God according to his means, but not practise showy deceptions; better is it to do a little substantially and consistently with truth, than to produce a great but fictitious effect. Hence the rubble wall and oaken rafter of antiquity yet impress the mind with feelings of reverent awe, which never could be produced by the cement and plaster imitations of elaborate tracery and florid designs which in these times are stuck about mimic churches in disgusting profusion.

It is likewise essential to ecclesiastical propriety that the ornaments introduced about churches should be appropriate and significant, and not consist of *Pagan* emblems and attributes for buildings professedly erected for Christian worship. If the admirers of classic decoration were consistent, on the very principles which induced the ancients to set up their divinities, they should now employ other and more appropriate ornaments; as all those found in the temples and other buildings of the Pagans were in strict accordance with their mythology and customs: *they never intro-*

duced any emblem without a mystical signification being attached to it. Now, great as may be their enormities, I think it would be unjust to charge the advocates of revived Pagan decoration with an actual belief in the mythology of which they are such jealous admirers; hence they are guilty of the greater inconsistency, as the original heathens proceeded from conviction. They would not have placed urns on the tombs, had they not practised burning instead of burying the dead; of which former custom the urn was a fitting emblem, as being the depository for the ashes. Neither would they have decorated the friezes with the heads of sheep and oxen, had they not sacrificed those animals to their supposed gods, or placed inverted torches on the mausoleums, had they believed in the glories of the Resurrection. But what have we, as *Christians*, to do with all those things illustrative *only of former error?* Is our wisdom set forth by the owl of Minerva, or our strength by the club of Hercules? What have we (who have been redeemed by the sacrifice of our Lord himself) to do with the carcasses of bulls and goats? And how can we

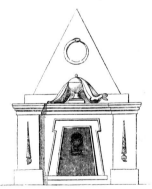

(who surround the biers of our departed brethren with blazing tapers, denoting our hope and faith in the glorious light of the Resurrection,) carve the *inverted torch of Pagan despair* on the very tomb to which we conduct their remains with such sparkling light? Let us away with such gross inconsistencies, and restore the Christian ideas of our Catholic ancestors, for they alone are proper for our imitation. But not only are the

Modern Tomb in the revived Pagan style. details of modern churches borrowed from Pagan instead of Christian antiquity, but the very plan and arrangement of the buildings themselves are now fashioned after a heathen temple; for which unsightly and inappropriate form modern churchmen and architects have abandoned those which are not only illustrative of the great mysteries of the Christian faith, but whose use has been sanctioned by the custom of more than twelve centuries.

I will now give the following distinct reasons why the architecture of the Greek temples cannot be introduced or imitated with propriety by Christians.

1. These temples were erected for an idolatrous worship, and were suited only for the idolatrous rites which were performed in them. 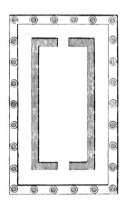 The interior, entered only by the priests, was comparatively small, and either dark or open at top, while the peristyle and porticoes were spacious, for the people who assisted without. There is not the slightest similarity between our worship and the idolatrous worship of the Greeks. We require that the people should be *within* the church, not outside. If, therefore, you adopt a perfect Greek temple, your interior will be confined and ill-suited for the intended purpose, while your exterior will occasion an enormous outlay without any utility. If, on the other hand, you strip a Greek temple of its external peristyle, and build your external walls in the place of the pillars, you entirely destroy the most beautiful feature of the architecture, and the building becomes a miserable departure from the style it professes to imitate.

2. The Greeks did not introduce windows in their temples ; they are essentially necessary with us. Perforate the walls with windows, and you again destroy the simplicity and unity of Greek architecture, which its admirers extol as one of its greatest beauties.

3. Christian churches require bells, by the sound of which the faithful may be called to their devotions. The bells, to be distinctly heard, must be suspended in a tower or belfry, and these are features utterly unknown in Greek architecture. A tower composed of a number of small porticoes, set over one another, and placed in front of a mock

temple, is a most glaring absurdity; nor is a tower of this description, starting out of nothing at the top of a portico, any better.   Figs. 1 and 2.

Figure 1.   Figure 2.

4. Our northern climate requires an acute pitch of roof to prevent the accumulation of snow and to resist weather.[5] The Greeks, whose climate is the reverse of ours, had their roofs and pediments exceedingly flat; nor could they be raised to our proper pitch without violating the character of their architecture. Fig. 3.

Fig. 3.

In short, Greek temples are utterly inapplicable to

[5] It is to be remarked that flat-pitched roofs were not introduced into English pointed churches till after the decline of that style, and the marks of the old high gabled roofs are generally to be seen in the towers of those churches where the present roofs are flat, proving them to have been altered subsequent to the original erection of the buildings.

the purpose of Christian churches;[6] and the attempt is little short of madness when our country is literally covered with beautiful models of ecclesiastical structures of every dimension, *the architecture and arrangement of which have originated in their wants and purpose.* An old English parish church, as originally used for the ancient worship, was one of the most beautiful and appropriate buildings that the mind of man could conceive; every portion of it answered both a useful and mystical purpose. There stood the tower, not formed of *detached and misapplied* portions of architectural detail stuck over one another to make up a height, but solid buttresses and walls rising from a massive base, and gradually diminishing and enriching as they rise, till they were terminated in a heaven-pointing spire surrounded by clusters of pinnacles, and forming a beautiful and instructive emblem of a Christian's brightest hopes. These towers served a double purpose, for in them hung the solemn sounding bells to summon the people to the offices of the church, and by their lofty elevation they served as beacons to direct their footsteps to the sacred spot. Then the southern porch, destined

[6] Neither are they better adapted for domestic purposes; for it is still more absurd to see two or three tiers of windows introduced in the shell of a Greek temple, the roof of which is broken by numerous stacks of vainly disguised chimneys. Yet notwithstanding the palpable impracticability of adapting the Greek temples to our climate, habits, and religion, we see the attempt and failure continually made and repeated: post-office, theatre, church, bath, reading-room, hotel, methodist chapel, and turnpike-gate, all present the eternal sameness of a Grecian temple outraged in all its proportions and character.

for the performance of many rites,—the spacious nave and aisles for the
faithful,—the oaken canopy carved with images of the heavenly host, and
painted with quaint and appropriate devices,—the impressive doom or
judgment pictured over the great chancel arch,—the fretted screen and
rood loft,—the mystical separation between the sacrifice and the people,
with the emblem of redemption carried on high and surrounded with
glory,—the great altar, rich in hangings, placed far from irreverent gaze,
and with the brilliant eastern window terminating this long perspective;
while the chantry and guild chapels, pious foundations of families and
confraternities, contributed greatly to increase the solemnity of the

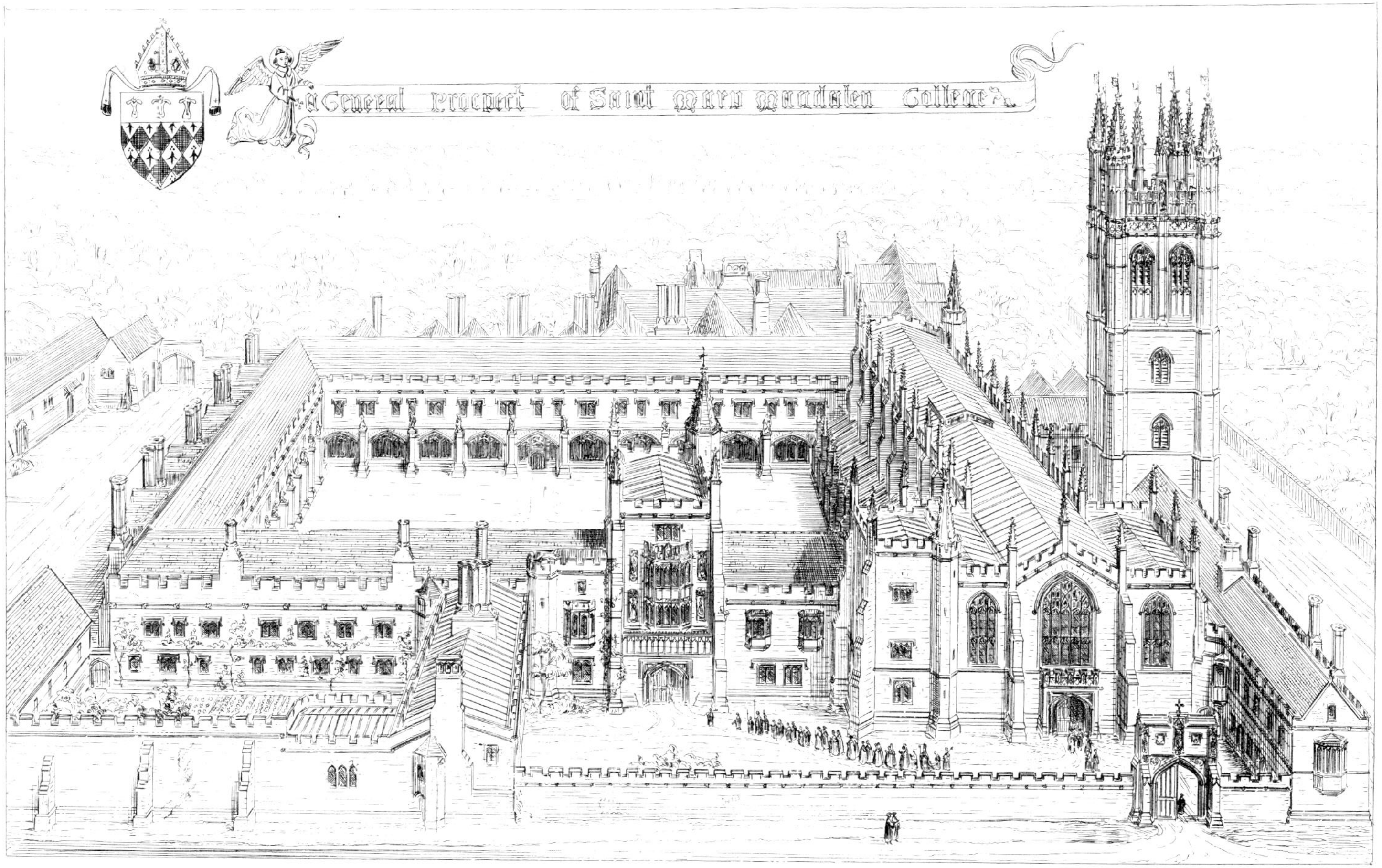

A General Prospect of Saint Mary Magdalen College.

Plate IX.

London Published by John Wade Holroyd anno 1840.

glorious pile. Such is but a faint outline of the national edifices which have been abandoned for pewed and galleried assembly rooms, decorated only with gas fittings and stoves, and without so much as one holy or soul-stirring emblem about them.

We will now examine architectural propriety with reference to collegiate architecture. Our old English Catholic colleges (Plate IX.) will illustrate most beautifully the principle I wish to demonstrate. The main feature of these buildings was the chapel: to our Catholic forefathers the celebration of the divine office with becoming solemnity and splendour formed a primary consideration, and ample was the provision made for this purpose in all the old collegiate foundations. The place set apart for this holy purpose generally towered over the surrounding buildings. The chapels of King's College and Eton can be distinctly seen many miles before the subordinate buildings can be discerned. Oxford, at a distance, presents a complete grove of towers, spires, and pinnacled turrets, rising from the collegiate churches. After this principal feature, every portion of these edifices had its distinguishing character and elevation: in order to give due effect to the gate-house, refectory, and other important parts of the building, the chambers never exceeded the height of one story above the ground floor.[7] A very characteristic feature of the old collegiate buildings is the position of the chimneys, which are made to project from the front walls of the buildings. This, I am well aware, has been considered a defect by ignorant modern artists, but will be found on examination, like all other practices of the ancient architects, to be based on excellent practical reasons.

The advantages of this arrangement are as follow: 1. All the internal

[7] In those ancient colleges where these chambers have been raised in modern times, the effect of the original design has been completely ruined, and the new collegiate buildings at St. John's, Cambridge, from their height, have all the appearance of a Gothic warehouse or factory. This is another instance of the folly of using pointed details without following the spirit of the ancient buildings.

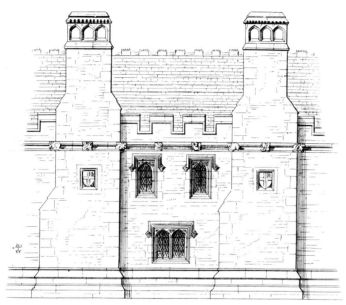

space usually occupied by chimney stacks, and which is very considerable, is gained to the apartments.— 2. The stacks of chimneys thus placed act as buttresses to the wall.—3. The danger of fire consequent on chimney flues passing through the wood-work of the roofs is entirely avoided.—4. A great variety of light and shadow, and a succession of bold features, are gained in the building. It is impossible to conceive any buildings better adapted for collegiate purposes, either as regards arrangement or design, than the two establishments founded by that great and good man, William of Wykeham, at Winchester and Oxford. He had two classes to consider in his foundation at Winchester, the clergy and the students. For the former he provided beautiful cloisters retired from the rest of the edifice, suited for contemplation and devotion; while for the latter he assigned ample space for healthy recreation in bad weather, and level meadows for summer sports. The whole character of these buildings is at once severe, elegant, and scholastic; it is precisely what it should be, as the will of Henry the Sixth specifies of the domestic portion of his college at Cambridge, that it should be built *without too great superfluity of detail or busie moulding;*[8] and on this principle Wykeham designed

---

[8] Notwithstanding the directions contained in this will, where the founder's intentions regarding his collegiate buildings are fully and distinctly expressed, the architect (when the glorious opportunity offered a few years since of fulfilling them to the letter, and erecting a

his building. The external ornaments are few, but admirably selected: an image of our blessed Ladye with our Lord is placed over each gateway, in reference to the college being dedicated to God, under the invocation of his blessed mother, towards whom the good bishop entertained an extraordinary devotion, even from his tender years. The other images on either side of the centre niche are those of the angel Gabriel, and Wykeham himself in a kneeling position.

The interior of the chapel (now wofully disfigured) as left by the founder, must have been glorious in the extreme; it consisted of a choir and ante-chapel, by the side of which rose the bell tower, simple, but elegant and lofty.

The members of the society were buried in the cloisters, and also in the ante-chapel, as their memorials of beautifully engraved brass testify. The intention of these was, doubtless, both to incite the surviving community to pray for their souls' repose, and to remind them continually of the similar fate that would inevitably befall them. How Catholic wisdom and Catholic piety stand conspicuous in all the arrangements of these noble buildings! how great the master mind who planned and executed them, and yet how few are there in these days able to understand or willing to imitate them! Can we conceive a more atrocious scheme to destroy the solemn grandeur of Wykeham's church than to allow such a man as Sir Joshua Reynolds to design a transparency for the western end, and appoint *James Wyatt the destructive* to overturn the ancient features and arrangements, setting up the subsellæ of the stalls as brackets for book-desks, and covering the walls with meagre decorations and Bernasconi Gothic!

Modern collegiate buildings,[9] especially on the continent, are the reverse

---

truly fine building) was allowed to depart entirely from them, and raise a florid structure, arranged in direct opposition to all old collegiate traditions, and the very decorations of which were misapplied details taken from the original chapel, which had been elaborately enriched by the ancient builders for the purpose of distinguishing its sacred destination from the surrounding erections.

[9] It is impossible to conceive a more uncollegiate looking building than what is called the

of all that I have been describing. In them we look in vain for the solemn quadrangle, the studious cloister, the turreted gate-house, the noble refectory with its oak-beamed roof, the mullioned windows and pinnacled parapet, and lofty tower of the church : not a ghost of these venerable characteristics of a college is to be seen, but generally one uniform mass, unbroken either· in outline or in face, undistinguishable from other large buildings which surround it.   As to its purpose, it might

be taken for a barrack hospital or asylum.   How is it possible to expect that the race of men who proceed from these factories of learning will possess the same feelings as those who anciently went forth from the Catholic structures of Oxford and Winchester !   We cannot sufficiently admire our English universities ; there is nothing like them existing on the continent, notwithstanding the miserable additions and modernizations which have so greatly disfigured the ancient buildings. There is more Catholic scholastic architecture to be found united at Oxford than in any place I have ever visited.   Let us hope and pray that its glories may not exist in vain, but that learned and thinking men may be led to draw a parallel in their minds between the faith of those good souls who founded these noble institutions, and our present degraded and half-infidel condition, by which consideration they may be led back to Catholic unity and faith, in which great works can be alone accomplished, or blessings derived from them.

In the third and last place, we will consider architectural propriety with reference to domestic and civil architecture.   Most of the mansions erected at the present day in the Italian or pointed architecture, are either bur-

London University, with its useless dome and portico.   It may, however, be urged in its defence that any thing *ecclesiastical or Christian* would be very inappropriate, and that the *Pagan* exterior is much more in character with the intentions and principles of the institution.

lesques or false applications of both these styles. In the first place, what does an Italian house do in England? Is there any similarity between our climate and that of Italy? Not the least. Now I will maintain and prove that climate has always had a large share in the formation of domestic architecture, and the Italian is a good illustration of the truth of this remark. The apertures are small; long colonnades for shade, and the whole building calculated for retreat, and protection from heat; the roofs are flat in pitch, from the absence of heavy snow; and plan and outline are both suited to the climate to which the architecture belongs. But we demand in England the very reverse of all this for comfort. We cannot fortunately import the climate of a country with its architecture, or else we should have the strangest possible combination of temperature and weather; and, within the narrow compass of the Regent's Park, the burning heat of Hindoostan, the freezing temperature of a Swiss mountain, the intolerable warmth of an Italian summer, with occasional spots

of our native temperature. I wonder if these ideas ever occur to those who design Italian gardens on the moorlands of England. Truly it will not be a matter of surprise if some searcher after novelty try to cultivate a jungle for imitation tiger-hunting on some old English estate.

Another objection to Italian architecture is this,—we are not Italians, we are Englishmen. God in his wisdom has implanted a love of nation and country in every man, and we should always cultivate this feeling ;—we ought to view the habits and manners of other nations without prejudice, derive improvement from all we observe admirable, but we should never forget our own land. Such is, indeed, the extraordinary amalgamation of architecture, style, and manners now in progress, that were it not for the works of nature which cannot be destroyed, and the glorious works of Christian antiquity which have *not yet* been destroyed, Europe would soon present such sameness as to cease to be interesting. Already a sort of bastard Greek, a nondescript modern style, has ravaged many of the most interesting cities of Europe ; replacing the original national buildings with unmeaning lines of plaster fronts, without form, without colour, without interest. How many glorious churches have been destroyed within the last few years (*pour faire une place*) for the occasional exercise of the national guard ! where a few stunted trees and a puddle of water in a stone basin, which spouts up occasionally some few feet in height, is all we have to see in exchange for some of the most interesting memorials of ancient piety.

England is rapidly losing its venerable garb ; all places are becoming alike ; every good old gabled inn is turned into an ugly hotel with a stuccoed portico, and a vulgar coffee-room lined with staring paper, with imitation scagliola columns, composition glass frames, an obsequious cheat of a waiter, and twenty per cent. added to the bill on the score of the modern and elegant arrangements. Our good old St. Martin's, St. John's, St. Peter's, and St. Mary's streets, are becoming Belle-vue Places, Adelaide Rows, Apollo Terraces, Regent Squares, and Royal Circuses. Factory chimneys disfigure our most beautiful vales ; Government preaching-houses, called churches, start up at the cost of a few hundreds each, by the side of Zion chapels, Bethel Meetings, New Connexions, and Socialist Halls. Timbered fronts of curious and ingenious design are swept away before the resistless torrent of Roman-cement men, who buy their ornaments by

the yard, and their capitals by the ton.   Every linen-draper's shop apes to

be something after the palace of the Cæsars; the mock stone columns are fixed over a front of plate glass to exhibit the astonishing bargains; while low-ticketed goods are hung out over the trophies of war.   But this is not all; every paltry town has a cigar divan, with something stuck out to look Turkish, and not unfrequently a back parlour travestied into a vile burlesque of eastern architecture.   In short, national feelings and national architecture are at so low an ebb, that it becomes an absolute duty in every Englishman to attempt their revival.   Our ancient architecture can alone fur-

nish us with the means of doing this successfully; but, unfortunately, those who profess to admire pointed architecture, and who strive to imitate it, produce more ridiculous results than those who fly to foreign aid. What can be more absurd than houses built in what is termed the castellated style? Castellated architecture originated in the wants consequent on a certain state of society: of course the necessity of great strength, and the means of defence suited to the military tactics of the day, dictated to the builders of ancient castles the most appropriate

Modern Castellated Mansion.

style for their construction. Viewed as historical monuments, they are of surprising interest, but as models for our imitation they are worse than useless. What absurdities, what anomalies, what utter contradictions do not the builders of modern castles perpetrate! How many portcullises which will not lower down, and drawbridges which will not draw up!—how many loop-holes in turrets so small that the most diminutive sweep could not ascend them!—On one side of the house machicolated parapets, embrasures, bastions, and all the show of strong defence, and round the corner of the building a conservatory leading to the principal rooms, through which a whole company of horsemen might penetrate at one smash into the very heart of the mansion!—for who would hammer against nailed portals when he could kick his way through the green-house? In buildings of this sort, so far from the turrets being erected for any particular purpose, it is difficult to assign any destination to them after they are erected, and those which are not made into *chimneys* seldom get other occupants than the rooks. But the exterior is not the least inconsistent portion of the edifices, for we find guard-rooms without either weapons or guards; sally-ports, out of which nobody passes but the servants, and where a military man never did go out; donjon keeps, which are nothing but drawing-rooms, boudoirs, and elegant apartments; watch-towers, where the housemaids sleep, and a bastion in which the butler cleans his plate: all is a mere mask, and the whole building an ill-conceived lie.

We will now turn to those mansions erected in what is termed the Abbey style, which are not more consistent than the buildings I have just described. To this class Fonthill belonged, now a heap of ruins, and modern ruins, too, of mere brick and plaster. In such a house something of an ecclesiastical exterior had been obtained at an enormous expense, and a casual passer-by might have supposed from some distance that the place really belonged to some religious community; but on a nearer approach the illusion is soon dissipated, and the building, which had been raised somewhat in the guise of the solemn architecture of religion and antiquity, discovers itself to be a mere toy, built to suit the caprice of a wealthy individual, and devoted to luxury. The seemingly abbey-gate turns out a modern hall, with liveried footmen in lieu of a con-ventual porter; the apparent church nave is only a vestibule; the tower, a lantern staircase; the transepts are drawing-rooms; the cloisters, a furnished passage; the oratory, a lady's boudoir; the chapter-house, a dining-room; *the kitchens alone* are real; every thing else is a deception. Articles of fashionable luxury, glasses in profusion, couches and ottomans, fill the chambers of the mock convent, from whence a prayer never ascends or into which a religious man never enters;—all, in fine, is a mockery and thing of fashion, transient and perishable as the life of its possessor; and if the structure be substantial enough to last his time, it soon after becomes the subject of some auctioneer's puff: its walls are covered with placards; brokers divide the moveables; the whole falls to decay, and is soon only mentioned as a splendid folly.

The old English Catholic mansions were the very reverse of those I have been describing; they were substantial appropriate edifices, suited by

Old English Mansion.

their scale and arrangement for the purposes of habitation. Each part of these buildings indicated its particular destination: the turreted gate-house and porter's lodging, the entrance porch, the high-crested roof and

Louvred hall, with its capacious chimney, the guest chambers, the vast kitchens and offices, all formed distinct and beautiful features, not *masked or concealed under one monotonous front*, but by their variety in form and outline increasing the effect of the building, and presenting a standing illustration of good old English hospitality ; while the venerable parish church in the immediate vicinity, with its grey spire and family chantry, showed that the care spiritual was not neglected by our ancestors in the erection of their temporal dwellings.

Every person should be lodged as becomes his station and dignity, for in this there is nothing contrary to, but in accordance with, the Catholic principle ; but the mansions erected by our ancestors were not the passing whim of a moment, or mere show places raised at such an extravagant cost as impoverished some generations of heirs to the estates, but solid, dignified, and Christian structures, built with due regard to the general prosperity of the family ; and the almost constant residence of the ancient gentry on their estates rendered it indispensable for them to have mansions where they might exercise the rights of hospitality to their fullest extent. They did not confine their guests, as at present, to a few fashionables who condescend to pass away a few days occasionally in a country house ; but under the oaken rafters of their capacious halls the lords of the manor used to assemble all their friends and tenants at those successive periods when the church bids all her children rejoice, while humbler guests partook of their share of bounty dealt to them by the hand of the almoner beneath the groined entrance of the gate-house. Catholic England was merry England, at least for the humbler classes ; and the architecture was in keeping with the faith and manners of the times,—at once strong and hospitable. There is a great reviving taste for ancient domestic architecture, but a vast many pretended admirers of old English beauties, instead of imitating the Tudor period, when domestic architecture was carried to a high state of perfection, stop short at the reign of Elizabeth, the very worst kind of English architecture ; and, strange to say, these unmeaning conglomerations of debased forms have been classed into a regular style, and called after the female tyrant during whose reign they were executed. . The only reason I can assign for the fashionable rage for this architecture (if so it may be called) is, that its character is so corrupt, mixed, and bad, that the anachronisms and anomalies so frequently perpetrated by modern architects are made to pass muster under the general term of Elizabethan; and certainly I cannot deny that the appellation is very appropriate when applied to corrupted design and decayed taste.

I must here mention two great defects very common in modern pointed buildings, both of which arise from the great fundamental principle of decorating utility not being understood.   In the first place, many architects apply the details and minor features of the pointed style to classic *masses and arrangements*; they adhere scrupulously to the regularity and symmetry of the latter, while they attempt to disguise it by the mouldings and accessories of the former.   They must have two of every thing, one on each side: no matter if all the required accommodation is contained in one half of the design, a shell of another half must be built to keep up uniformity.   What can be more absurd?   Because a man has a real door to enter his house by on one side, he must have a mock one through which he cannot get in on the other.   How inconsistent is it to make and glaze a window which is to be *walled up* ab initio! But to see the full absurdity of this system, let us only imagine the builders of the ancient colleges, after having finished a church and refectory on one side of a quadrangle, running up something to repeat them by way of a pendant on the other, so as to appear two churches and two dining-halls to one college.   In the second place, when modern architects avoid this defect of regularity, they frequently fall into one equally great with regard to irregularity; I mean when a building is *designed to be picturesque*, by sticking as many ins and outs, ups and downs, about it as possible. *The picturesque effect of the ancient buildings results from the ingenious methods by which the old builders overcame local and constructive difficulties.*   An edifice which is arranged with the principal view of looking picturesque is sure to resemble an artificial waterfall or a made-up rock, which are generally so *unnaturally natural* as to appear ridiculous.

An architect should exhibit his skill by turning the difficulties which occur in raising an elevation from *a convenient plan* into so many *picturesque beauties;* and this constitutes the great difference between the principles of classic and pointed domestic architecture. In the former *he would be compelled to devise expedients to conceal these irregularities;* in the latter *he has only to beautify them.* But I am quite assured that all the irregularities that are so beautiful in ancient architecture are the result of certain necessary difficulties, and were never purposely designed; for to make a building inconvenient for the sake of obtaining irregularity would be scarcely less ridiculous than preparing working drawings for a new ruin. But all these inconsistencies have arisen from this great error,—*the plans of buildings are designed to suit the elevation, instead of the elevation being made subservient to the plan.*

Under the head of architectural propriety we have also to consider the scale and proportions of buildings. Without vastness of dimensions it is impossible to produce a grand and imposing effect in architecture; still, unless these be regulated on true principles, they may destroy their effect by their very size; and here I wish to draw your attention to a point which will prove the great superiority of the Christian architecture of the middle ages over that of classic antiquity, or of the revived pagan style. In pointed architecture the different details of the edifice are *multiplied with the increased scale of the building:* in classic architecture they are *only magnified.*

To explain this more fully, if the pointed architects had a buttress and pinnacle to erect against some vast structure, such as the Cathedral of Cologne or Amiens, they did not merely increase its dimensions by gigantic water tables, enormous crockets, and a ponderous finial. No! they subdivided it into a *cluster* of piers and pinnacles; they panelled the front, enriched it by subordinate divisions, and by these means the pinnacles of Cologne appear five times as large as those of an ordinary church,[10] which could never have been the case had they only *enlarged the scale instead of multiplying the parts.* But the very reverse of this is the case in classic architecture; a column or cornice is the same, *great or small,* whether they are employed in front of an ordinary house or of a vast temple; no distinction except that of size is ever made;

[10] A pillar in classic architecture is a mere cylinder, of large or small diameter. In the pointed style a pillar is subdivided into shafts, which increase in number with its size, and form beautiful clusters.

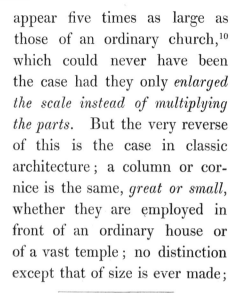

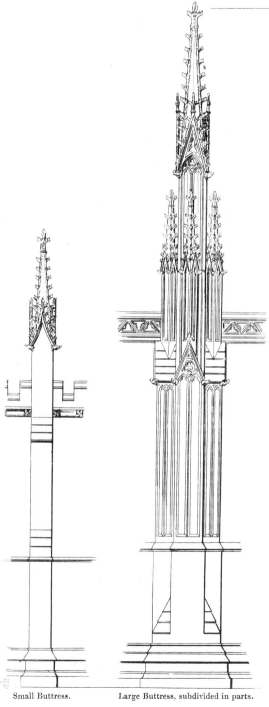

Small Buttress.   Large Buttress, subdivided in parts.

there are the *same number of diameters*, the *same number of mouldings*, the *same relative projections*;—it is merely a *magnifying power* applied to architecture. What is the result? Till you actually stand under these buildings, and find that your chin does not come up to the plinth of the base, you do not perceive the scale. This is perfectly exemplified at St. Peter's. The effect on all who first enter it is that of disappointment; it does not appear any thing like so large as they anticipated. Some of its admirers have tried to pass this off as a great beauty, and have attributed it to its beautiful proportion. This reasoning will not, however, stand the test of close examination; it is essentially false. One of the great arts of architecture is to render a building more vast and lofty in appearance than it is in reality. The contrary effect produced by St. Peter's is not the least among its many defects, and it is purely owing to the *magnifying* instead of the *multiplying principle* having been followed. The great size of its various parts and mouldings required the introduction of colossal figures, which are certain to reduce the appearance of size in any buildings where they are used.

The human figure is a general standard for scale. We are accustomed to assimilate the idea of about five feet nine inches with the height of a man. Hence, be a drawing ever so small, by inserting a diminutive human figure it will immediately convey an idea of the intended size; and on the contrary, if the figures in a drawing be over large, the apparent space represented is immediately reduced in appearance. So is it in architecture: a figure of eighteen feet high will reduce one hundred feet to less than forty in appearance; and the mystery of the disappointing effect of scale in St. Peter's is satisfactorily accounted for. It is all very well for guides and valets de place to astonish travellers by stating that three persons may sit on the great toe of a statue, or that if a figure were laid on its back five men might straddle across the nose; *so much the worse for the effect of the building where such a figure is placed.*

In pointed architecture we seldom find any images larger than the human size, and generally much less. Hence the surprising effect of height and scale conveyed by many old Catholic buildings, which are not in reality half the size of some of their more modern and semi-pagan rivals at Rome.

Illustration of the different effects of scale produced by large or small statues in the same space.

In general our English churches are deficient in internal height; not that our national style of Christian art does not possess some fine specimens of this important feature, as in the glorious church of St. Peter, Westminster; but I think the internal vastness of Amiens, Beauvais, Chartres, and others of the French churches, should serve as useful examples to us in this respect in the revival of Pointed and Christian architecture in England. Nothing can be conceived more majestic than those successions of arches divided by light and elegant clusters of shafts running up to an amazing height, and then branching over into beautiful intersected ribs, suspending a canopy of stone at the enormous height of not unfrequently one hundred and fifty feet. Internal altitude is a feature which would add greatly to the effect of many of our fine English churches, and I shall ever advocate its introduction, as it is a characteristic of foreign pointed architecture of which we can avail ourselves without violating the principles of our own peculiar style of English Christian architecture, from which I would not depart in this country on any account. I once stood on the very edge of a precipice in this respect, from which I was rescued by the advice and arguments of my respected and revered friend Dr. Rock, to whose learned researches and observations on Christian antiquities I am highly indebted, and to whom I feel it a bounden duty to make this public acknowledgment of the great benefit I have received from his advice. Captivated by the beauties of foreign pointed architecture, I was on the verge of departing from the severity of our English style, and engrafting portions of foreign detail and arrangement. This I feel convinced would have been a failure; for although the great principles of Christian architecture were every where the same, each country had some peculiar manner of developing them, and we should continue working in the same parallel lines, all contributing to the grand whole of Catholic art, but by the very variety increasing its beauties and its interest.

In conclusion, Christian verity compels me to acknowledge that there are hardly any defects which I have pointed out to you in the course of this Lecture which could not with propriety be illustrated by my own productions at some period of my professional career. Truth is only gradually developed in the mind, and is the result of long experience and deep investigation. Having, as I conceive, discovered the true principles of pointed architecture, I am anxious to explain to others the errors and misconceptions into which I have fallen, that they, profiting by my experience, may henceforward strive to revive the glorious works of Christian art in all the ancient and *consistent* principles. Let then the Beautiful and the True be our watchword for future exertions in the overthrow of modern paltry taste and paganism, and the revival of Catholic art and dignity.

Laus Deo!

IOHAN WEALE